AUTHORS SERIES · VOLUME I

THE NORWEGIAN-AMERICAN HISTORICAL ASSOCIATION

LIONEL G. THORSNESS, *President*

Board of Publications:

THEODORE C. BLEGEN, *Honorary Member*

C. A. CLAUSEN

EINAR HAUGEN

PETER A. MUNCH

CARLTON C. QUALEY

KENNETH O. BJORK, *Editor*

AUTHORS SERIES · VOLUME I

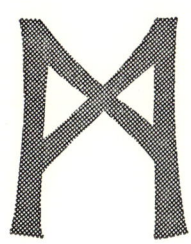Hjalmar Hjorth Boyesen

by CLARENCE A. GLASRUD

1963
The Norwegian-American Historical Association
NORTHFIELD · MINNESOTA

COPYRIGHT 1963 BY THE NORWEGIAN-AMERICAN HISTORICAL ASSOCIATION
PRINTED IN THE UNITED STATES OF AMERICA AT THE
LUND PRESS, MINNEAPOLIS, MINNESOTA

THE figure that appears on the cover and title page of this book is one of twenty-four letters in the older Germanic runic alphabet used in the Scandinavian countries from about 200 to 800 A.D. In addition to representing the sound "m," approximately as in modern English, it also has a name, meaning "man" or "mankind." It thus serves here as a symbol for the humanities.

Foreword

WITH this volume the association introduces its *Authors Series*, with the hope that eventually it will include the American writings of such Norwegian authors as Bjørnstjerne Bjørnson, Kristofer Janson, and Knut Hamsun, besides interpretations of their activities — individually and as a group — in the New World.

More important, the series invites scholarly contributions about Norwegian Americans whose works have become, or should be, an integral part of our culture. Included in the future, we are confident, will be studies of creative writers of the stature of O. E. Rølvaag, Marcus Thrane, Waldemar Ager, Simon Johnson, Julius Baumann, Johannes B. Wist, and Jon Norstog, as well as of such journalists as Svein Nilsson, Rasmus B. Anderson, Knud Langeland, and Kristian Prestgard.

It might seem strange that a volume about Hjalmar Hjorth Boyesen, whose career barely skirted the boundaries of Norwegian-American life and whose fiction reveals little understanding of his fellow countrymen in the New World, should be the first book in this series. But as Professor Glasrud points out, Boyesen has been an "undeservedly neglected figure," and an interpretation of his role as a champion of realism in American literature has been "long overdue." This mature and competent study, originally a Harvard doctoral dissertation and now thoroughly revised, makes it clear that Boyesen's Norwegian background accounted in large part for his popularity during his lifetime, his incurable romanticism, and his defense of European writers unacceptable to American editors and critics. Thus his career as an author, which Mr. Glasrud examines "in the

Hjalmar Hjorth Boyesen

light of his life and times," and his fiction, a forerunner of the kind that "eventually replaced the idealistic, romantic, and genteel," comes within the purview of the association's interest.

It may well be, as Professor Glasrud suggests, that a study of Boyesen "should have been written thirty-five years ago." But it is true, also, that for over a half century his books have been all but forgotten, and that only now is this period of neglect apparently ending — at least among scholars, who are beginning to link the immigrant author with a victorious "trend toward realism." Whatever the ultimate appraisal may be, Mr. Glasrud's scholarly work should be invaluable in getting at the brilliant, impressionable, and, in some respects, tragic figure of Boyesen the man.

Again we are indebted to Miss Jane McCarthy, production manager of the University of Minnesota Press, for assistance in choosing binding cloth, stamping, and type, for her imaginative design of the backbone and the symbol used on the cover and title page, and for her layout of preliminary, chapter, and text pages. To her and to Helen Thane Katz, who performed the detailed work of editing and indexing, go our many thanks.

KENNETH O. BJORK

St. Olaf College
Northfield, Minnesota

Acknowledgments

MY INTEREST in Hjalmar Hjorth Boyesen dates back to 1946, when Professor Howard Mumford Jones of Harvard University suggested that Boyesen was an undeservedly neglected figure and that an investigation of his role as a pioneer realist and liaison man between European and American literature was long overdue. A preliminary study in 1946 led to a doctoral dissertation, and I am much indebted to Professor Jones for his advice and encouragement in the preparation of the manuscript, completed and submitted in 1952. I owe thanks, too, to Professor Perry Miller for his help with the writing.

Three members of the Norwegian-American Historical Association's board of publications have given generous assistance over the years since I first began working on Boyesen. Dean Theodore C. Blegen encouraged me to complete the study and recommended that it be submitted for publication. Professor Carlton C. Qualey edited my essay, "H. H. Boyesen and the Norwegian Immigration," which was included in volume 19 of *Norwegian-American Studies and Records*. And Professor Kenneth O. Bjork has struggled with me for more than a year to trim, shape, and improve the present study. To him and to Helen Thane Katz, who has done the word-by-word editing, checked my information, and prepared the copy for the printer, I owe a very great debt indeed.

I am grateful to Hjalmar Hjorth Boyesen III of Leicester, England, grandson of the writer, for allowing me free use of the Boyesen Papers and giving me permission to quote from them. Other members of the family have been helpful: the late Austa Boyesen, sister of the novelist;

his niece, Louise Tompkins; and Stephen Rowan, a nephew of Mrs. H. H. Boyesen II.

In recent years I have been encouraged by the work of two scholars. Mr. Marc Ratner of Amherst, Massachusetts, completed a doctoral dissertation on Boyesen at New York University in 1959 and during the past two years has published sections of Boyesen's correspondence. Mr. Per Seyersted of Oslo, who began his investigation of Boyesen more recently, very generously extended his help in the late stages of my present study.

For aid in collecting materials I am indebted to the curators, archivists, and librarians of the several libraries, especially those of the Columbiana Collection, at Columbia University; the libraries of Harvard University; the Howard-Tilton Memorial Library, Tulane University; the archives division, University of Illinois Library; the Cornell University Library; the Moorhead (Minnesota) State College Library; the Concordia College (Moorhead) Library; the Vineland (New Jersey) Historical and Antiquarian Society; and the libraries of the *Detroit News*, the *Indianapolis News*, and the *St. Paul Dispatch Pioneer Press*.

For assistance in various ways I owe thanks to my colleagues Dennis Flood, Duane Scribner, and Kenneth Smemo; to Mrs. Richard B. Hobart of Cambridge, Massachusetts, Mrs. T. Catesby Jones of New York City, and the late Mildred Howells; to Charles Olmsted of South Hadley, Massachusetts, and Professor Stuart Atkins of Cambridge; and to a pair of accomplished and patient typists, Elmer Jackson and Lavonne Leach. To my wife, Barbara Crawford Glasrud, typist, editor, and constant adviser, I owe much more than I can acknowledge or express. And finally, I wish to express my gratitude to my parents by dedicating this volume to them.

CLARENCE A. GLASRUD

Moorhead State College
Moorhead, Minnesota

Contents

1	BOYHOOD IN NORWAY	3
2	A NEW AMERICAN WRITER	20
3	THE CORNELL YEARS	36
4	*GUNNAR* TO *FALCONBERG*	54
5	A LITERARY LIAISON MAN	77
6	THE MOVE TO NEW YORK CITY	93
7	A BOLDER CHAMPION	109
8	THE UNEVEN ROAD TO REALISM	127
9	EXIT POET, ENTER CRITIC	150
10	THE BEST AND LAST FIGHT	162
11	*MAMMON* AND ITS AFTERMATH	184
12	THE FINAL SALVO	196
13	BOYESEN IN THE TWENTIETH CENTURY	217
	BIBLIOGRAPHY	229
	INDEX	238

Illustrations following page 102

HJALMAR HJORTH BOYESEN

1

Boyhood in Norway

BECAUSE Hjalmar Hjorth Boyesen's name is so unmistakably Scandinavian, he is often spoken of as "a Norwegian writer." The label is misleading. Although he was born in Norway, Boyesen became a citizen of the United States, married an American girl, lived his entire adult life in this country, and wrote all of his twenty-four books in English. He had every right to call himself an American, and did so proudly.

The matter of identification is closely related to Boyesen's importance as a literary figure. He tried to put aside his European heritage, which was idealistic, poetic, and romantic, and to write realistic American fiction. He made some noteworthy attempts in this direction, but on the whole he failed. When, only a few years after his death, the battle for realism was won, Boyesen's name had been forgotten and his books were no longer being read. His failure as a realist, despite his convictions and determination, can be charged to his Scandinavian background as well as to his career in America.

His formative years in Norway were idyllic and happy; he was sheltered from the harsher realities of life. Information about this period has been largely supplied by Boyesen himself. For newspaper reviewers he recalled high lights of his boyhood; he included a few biographical episodes in his magazine articles; and he used his own youthful experiences in some of his fiction — an "autobiographical" novel, short stories about Norwegian Americans, and tales for boys, all with settings in the old country. Unfortunately, these sources throw little light on a situation that

Hjalmar Hjorth Boyesen

must have affected his life vitally. His father, Captain Sarolf Fredrik Boyesen, and his maternal grandfather, Judge Georg Martin Hjorth (with whom he spent most of his youth), apparently were incompatible. They differed on every important issue of the day. Yet there is no evidence of an open break or any resulting bitterness in the family relationships. Hjalmar shared his father's belief in progress, democracy, and America; but emotionally he was closer to Judge Hjorth, who put his faith in tradition and the established order. Because Hjalmar was an idealist like his father, he made a sentimental compromise, and this compromise shaped his entire literary career.[1]

In later years, when he recalled his youth, Boyesen spoke of the "guileless pair of blue eyes" that looked out upon "a rarely beautiful world." He was not exaggerating, for he spent his childhood in one of Norway's most magnificent fjord regions, that of Middle Sogn. The grandparents who reared him were the gentlefolk of their rural district, and young Hjalmar was the petted and privileged heir to the estate. He grew up convinced that the world was fair and that he had a special place in it. The idyllic beauty of this boyhood home and the happiness of these early years are clearly reflected in Boyesen's writings, and in the character of their author.[2]

Quite naturally, this boy's first ambition was to be a rural landlord like his grandfather. His second, which he retained for the rest of his life, was to be a writer. At twelve he gloried in the dream that he was a poet, and he filled his copybook with rhymes. So strong was this urge, said Boyesen, that until his twenty-fifth year he was accustomed to viewing life through literature. Needless to say, the medium through which he peered had a distinctly rose-colored, romantic tinge.[3]

---

[1] Georg Martin Hjorth (1796–1877) was *sorenskriver* (district judge) in Outer Sogn, 1850–64. He later held official positions in Bergen and Christiansand. In 1838 he married Christine Sophie Smith Petersen (1792–1875). Information furnished by Erling Grønland of the University of Oslo Library.

[2] Hjalmar H. Boyesen, "Norwegian Hospitality," in *Lippincott's Magazine*, 53:267 (February, 1894); W. H. Rideing, *The Boyhood of Living Authors*, 163–169 (New York, 1887). Rideing says in his preface, "The sketches in this little volume have been prepared with the consent, and in most instances with the assistance, of the authors represented." Boyesen gave such assistance; see his letter to Rideing, May 23, 1887; a copy is in the Boyesen Papers, Columbiana Collection, Columbia University Library. The Columbia Library has microfilm copies of the Boyesen Papers. Rideing was editor of the *Youth's Companion*, which published stories and articles by Boyesen.

[3] Boyesen, "Writing My First Book," in *Philadelphia Inquirer*, October 1, 1893. The same article appeared as "Boyesen's First Book," in *Indianapolis News*, Sep-

Boyhood in Norway

Hjalmar Boyesen's father, Captain Sarolf Boyesen, was born September 1, 1817, on a thousand-acre estate, Hovind, near Christiania (now Oslo). The Boyesen family had been landed proprietors for generations. Peter Boyesen, owner of Hovind at the beginning of the nineteenth century, married Helga Tullberg, daughter of a Christiania merchant. Their son Sarolf was deeply stirred by the social and political unrest of the post-Napoleonic period. After a youthful revolt against parental authority and the constrictions of his class, he settled down at the age of thirty, married, and began raising a family.

The girl for whose sake Captain Boyesen resolved to conform was Helga Helene Tveten. Eleven years younger than her husband, she was born in 1828 at Sandefjord, where her father was an organist; but she was adopted by Judge Georg Hjorth of Systrand, a relative of the Tveten family, and brought up as his daughter. Because Judge Hjorth had no children, the first son born to Sarolf and Helga Boyesen was named for him and was his intended heir.[4]

Hjalmar Hjorth Boyesen was born September 23, 1848, at Fredriksværn, in southern Norway. This little town of fifteen hundred people, situated near the point where Larvik Fjord empties into the Skagerrak, was an important naval station a hundred years ago, and the seat of the Norwegian naval academy. Captain Boyesen was a mathematics instructor at this academy in 1848, though he held an army commission. Three years after Hjalmar was born, the captain was transferred to Kongsberg, site of the royal mint and of the national arms and munitions works.

While Captain Boyesen was stationed at Kongsberg, 1851 to 1854, his fortunes changed drastically. He and his family abandoned the Lutheran faith to become members of the Swedenborgian Church of the New Jerusalem.[5] With this step Captain Boyesen ended his military ca-

tember 30, 1893. See also Boyesen to Rideing, May 23, 1887; Boyesen, "A Visit to Tourguéneff," in *Galaxy* (New York), 17:456 (April, 1874).
[4] Most of these facts are taken from Laurence M. Larson, *The Changing West and Other Essays*, 82–115 (Northfield, 1937). Larson's information came from Austa Boyesen, a sister of Hjalmar. Her letters to Larson, in the University of Illinois Library, yield some material not included in Larson's essay. See also Arthur Stedman, "Boyesen's Boyhood," in *Detroit Sunday News-Tribune*, April 8, 1894.
[5] Followers of the Swedish philosopher-mystic Emanuel Swedenborg or Swedberg (1688–1772) founded religious societies based on his teachings in England and America and, with less success, in countries on the Continent. A century after Swedenborg's death, the General Convention of the New Jerusalem (or New Church) had a hundred member societies. Their missionary and educational activities are described by Marguerite Beck Block in *The New Church in the New World* (New York, 1932).

Hjalmar Hjorth Boyesen

reer; servants of the state, military or civil, were expected to be members of the state church, even though an act passed by the Norwegian Storting in 1845 had given dissenters moderate protection. Sarolf Boyesen was a nonconformist in other ways, too. Dissatisfaction over the union with Sweden had fostered a rebellious, increasingly democratic spirit in Norway, but most army officers and state officials sided with the Swedish crown. Captain Boyesen, on the other hand, was an ardent republican. He was restless and ambitious, impatient with the slow, conservative ways of mid-nineteenth-century Norway; and the evidence suggests that he was also impractical. Hjalmar admired his father and was strongly influenced by his opinions, and never openly criticized his decisions; the son's reticence about him is explained by a younger sister: "He [*Hjalmar*] was quiet about family affairs, I suppose, because he had been brought up in comfort and plenty, and when Father refused to subscribe to the State Religion and gave up, thereby, part of his income and also lost his inheritance, the family was obliged to practice 'primitive simplicity.' This condition seemed humiliating to him." [6]

Captain Boyesen left Norway in 1854 and remained abroad for nearly two years. He spent some time in America, perhaps as much as a year, and was greatly impressed by the new nation. Yet, though "he liked this country better than his own," Hjalmar's father returned to Norway. Apparently he decided that it was too late to change his nationality, and that he could find new opportunities in the homeland. There was one positive result of this American visit, however: Thirteen years later Sarolf Boyesen sent his sons to visit the New World before they committed themselves to pursuing careers in Norway.[7]

While Captain Boyesen was abroad, his wife and children lived at Systrand. No doubt Judge and Mrs. Hjorth were happy to have Mrs. Boyesen and her small children with them. The white manor house facing the fjord was a spacious one, and life on the rural estate must have been lonely for the childless, aging couple. The estate, or farm, had a full complement of peasant retainers, but families with whom the Hjorths mixed socially were a day's journey distant.[8]

[6] Larson, *The Changing West*, 82; Rideing, *Living Authors*, 163–169; Austa Boyesen to Laurence M. Larson, December 6, 1936.

[7] Frank E. Heath, "Hjalmar Hjorth Boyesen," in *Scribner's Monthly*, 14:776–782 (October, 1877). This was the first published biographical sketch of Boyesen. See also Rideing, *Living Authors*, 163–169; Larson, *The Changing West*, 86; Stedman, in *Detroit Sunday News-Tribune*, April 8, 1894.

[8] John D. Barry, "A Talk with Professor Boyesen," in *New York Illustrated*

Boyhood in Norway

Captain Boyesen returned to Norway in 1856 and re-established a home for his family. Three years later, in 1859, when the sixth child was still a baby, Helga died. Hjalmar Boyesen, in an article written in 1895, paid a tribute to his mother and described the family circle. "When I look back," he wrote, "through the long gallery of noble Scandinavian women whose portraits my memory retains, the embarrassment of riches makes me loath to choose. One, however . . . I may, without invidious comparisons, select as fairly representative, and the man of whose home she was the bright and shining focus would have been the first to claim for her every ideal perfection. It has always been a marvel to me how this mother of six children . . . could yet preside with a calm and gentle dignity at the great dinners which her husband's position compelled him to give, superintend a large household . . . and yet preserve, amid innumerable harassments, which would have driven a man to distraction, a benign, unruffled amiability, and an unfailing helpfulness which ever gave and gave, without thought of demanding anything in return. . . . Though she left no record behind her, except in the hearts of her sons and daughters, who mourned her early loss, I cannot conceive of a nobler life than hers, nor one dispensing a richer blessing." [9]

After Helga Boyesen's death, Hjalmar and perhaps some of the other children made their home with Judge and Mrs. Hjorth at Systrand. Judge Hjorth's opinion of his son-in-law can be surmised, for the old magistrate's conservatism was as ingrained as was the impatience of the young man with traditional authority. With the death of the one who provided the tie between them, an open break might have been expected. Although Sarolf Boyesen soon remarried and reared a second family, he did not lose contact with the children living with the Hjorths. Surprisingly, he retained some authority over them, for he influenced his sons to make decisions that were opposed by their grandfather.[10]

American, 17:178 (February 9, 1895). This was the last biographical interview with Boyesen.

[9] Boyesen, "The Scandinavian Wife," in *North American Review*, 161:435–437 (October, 1895). Captain Boyesen died at Vineland, New Jersey, in 1894, the year before the article was written.

[10] Boyesen to George Washington Cable, January 20, 1878, included in Arlin Turner, "A Novelist Discovers a Novelist: The Correspondence of H. H. Boyesen and George W. Cable," in *Western Humanities Review* (Salt Lake City), 5:353 (Autumn, 1951). Boyesen's letters to Cable are in the Tulane University Library. Most of the quotations from them used here, however, are in the Turner article. Cable (1844–1925) was the author of *Old Creole Days* (1879) and other realistic interpretations of Southern life.

Hjalmar Hjorth Boyesen

Boyesen's autobiographical novel, *A Norseman's Pilgrimage*, presents a romanticized version of the Judge Hjorth-Captain Boyesen relationship. The "Judge Varberg" of the novel is Judge Hjorth, with an only son instead of a son-in-law. This son has most of Captain Boyesen's traits. He marries, and attempts to conform and settle down in accordance with his father's wishes. But when his young wife dies, he rebels again, goes to America, and dies at Gettysburg. Just before the battle, he writes to his son in Norway, urging him to come to America after he has finished college. A sum of money put in trust for the son can be claimed upon his arrival in the United States. The boy carries this letter next to his heart and, when he comes of age, migrates to the New World.[11]

Other versions of this dramatic and colorful relationship appear in a number of Boyesen's short stories. In every instance the two antagonists are reconciled sentimentally, but with no resolution of the ideological differences that separate them. The younger man is always shown to be in the right, and his faith in democracy, progress, and America is vindicated. Emotionally, however, the author is invariably committed to the other side, and the old gentlemen patterned on Judge Hjorth win the reader's sympathy.[12]

Apparently Hjalmar Boyesen had a choice of two paths. He could remain at Systrand as heir to Judge Hjorth's estate, or he could seek his fortune in America, which Captain Boyesen insisted was the land of the future. That Hjalmar's first ambition was "to be a dignified landlord like his grandfather" is understandable. But before long he was won over by an even stronger aspiration — to be a writer. It was this that decided him to migrate.[13]

Life at Systrand made a profound impression on the six-year-old boy who went to live with his grandparents in 1854. Especially memorable were trips on Sognefjord in the official boat, when Judge Hjorth took his grandson along on visits through his district. Boyesen wrote later: "I remember sitting in the prow of my grandfather's cabin boat, rowed by

---

[11] *A Norseman's Pilgrimage*, 15–37 (New York, 1875). Boyesen himself called this novel autobiographical, but it is highly romanticized autobiography. His father did not fight in the Civil War.

[12] "The Norse Emigrant," in *Galaxy*, 15:199–203 (February, 1873); "A Child of the Age," in *Century*, 31:177–192 (December, 1885); and "A Perilous Incognito," in *Scribner's Magazine*, 2:120–128, 222–228 (July, August, 1887) are the best examples.

[13] Larson, *The Changing West*, 86; Rideing, *Living Authors*, 173. The quotation is from Boyesen to Rideing, May 23, 1887.

twelve sturdy oarsmen, when we sailed forth in state, twice a year, to hold court in the various districts of his circuit. The colonel who lived a day's journey from our place always stood on his pier, with a telescope in his hand, watching for that cabin boat, and when it hove in sight he ran up his flag as an invitation to the judge and his retinue to spend the night under his hospitable roof. . . . There were speeches of welcome made. . . . I, being a very small boy, was passed down the long row of the colonel's daughters (he had seven), and, much to my disgust, kissed by each of them. The twelve oarsmen were sent to the servants' hall, where they were abundantly entertained. . . . And thus we continued from day to day and from week to week our triumphal progress from place to place, in one fjord and out another."[14]

Boyesen considered the wild scenery of Sognefjord to be the grandest in all Norway, an opinion many less biased judges of natural beauty share with him. From Systrand, a strip of land on the north side of the fjord in Middle Sogn, the boy could cruise up and down the reaches of the great estuary. "How often have I drifted through the spacious summer days in my sharp-keeled wherry, upon those light, glittering waters, while the seabirds surged in airy waves above me, and the white clouds with a bewildering distinctness pursued their tranquil paths far down in the deep below! It gave one a feeling of being suspended in the midst of the vast blue space, hovering between two infinities. . . . Ah! it is the perfection of pure and simple being, one of those moments when the mere fact of living seems a great and glorious thing."[15]

Later, in a drab Midwestern prairie town, Boyesen was to write his first book, which vividly recalled the beautiful Norwegian home he had left behind. Before this early romance was printed, it had to be cut drastically, for a large part of it was merely the author's rapturous evocation of a well-loved scene. As he gained more experience he avoided such excesses, but in all of his works there is a disproportionate emphasis on setting, on the beauty or ugliness of the physical scene. The young boy's sensitivity to the natural world seems to explain this marked tendency in Boyesen the writer.[16]

[14] Boyesen, in *Lippincott's Magazine*, 53:267; see also Stedman, in *Detroit Sunday News-Tribune*, April 8, 1894.
[15] Rideing, *Living Authors*, 165.
[16] Boyesen, in *Philadelphia Inquirer*, October 1, 1893; see also "H.H.B.," in *Book Buyer* (New York), 3:343 (October, 1886). The editor explained of the latter item: "When asked for a few facts the author [*Boyesen*] gave me the following notes, which are reproduced in his own words as far as possible."

Hjalmar Hjorth Boyesen

Boyesen's biography in Rideing's *The Boyhood of Living Authors* is specific about his activities at Systrand: "His most pronounced trait at this period was his love of animals: he had several hundred pigeons, and besides these a lot of rabbits, dogs, cows, and even horses." Many of Boyesen's stories for boys deal with hunting and fishing expeditions. The Rideing biography explains the source of these tales: "There was an old tenant on the Hjorth estate, named Gunnar, who took a great fancy to the boy, and initiated him into all the mysteries of wood-craft. . . . Sometimes the boy spent entire nights with him in the woods, sleeping in the mountain chalets or saeters. . . . As a result, his senses were as alert as those of an Indian, and he was a good shot and an expert fisherman." In another account of his life as a youthful sportsman, Boyesen mentions a younger companion: "My chief occupations were those of primitive man, fishing and setting traps for birds and beasts. There was a boy named Nils Kampen, a few years older than myself, who was my chief instructor in fishing and woodlore. He knew all the haunts of the otter, the ptarmigan, and the mountain cock. I sold the proceeds of our expeditions to my grandmother and gave him half the profits."[17]

Hjalmar's talk "was of fjords and glaciers, of firs and birches, of hulders and nixies, of housemen and gaardmen," said William Dean Howells of the young Norwegian he met in 1871. Boyesen found a ready market in American magazines for tales and poems woven out of such simple materials. He had an explanation for his knowledge of peasant superstitions, of Norse folklore and legends: "The servants' hall [at Systrand], which lay apart from the principal mansion, was to me [a] forbidden but enchanted realm. Much was said there that was not for ears polite, but for all that I was drawn thither by an irresistible fascination. After having kissed my grandparents good night and when supposed to be sleeping soundly, I often stole down on tiptoe to the servants' hall and listened spell-bound to the old ballads, fairy tales and traditions which were recounted there during the winter nights."[18]

Possibly Hjalmar's grandmother was trying to keep the imaginative boy from being frightened. The old people of the rural districts still believed in the nixies and trolls and *huldre* (enchantresses) that inhabited

---

[17] Rideing, *Living Authors*, 167; this book, of course, was aimed at youthful readers. See also Stedman, in *Detroit Sunday News-Tribune*, April 8, 1894.

[18] Howells, *Literary Friends and Acquaintance*, 263 (New York, 1900). See also Stedman, in *Detroit Sunday News-Tribune*, April 8, 1894; Rideing, *Living Authors*, 169.

the mountains and the waterfalls, the hillside springs, and the tall trees. These peasants could interpret the workings of the invisible world, and they told their weird tales vividly. The grandmother, however, may have been chiefly concerned about maintaining social distinctions. Hjalmar learned early to distinguish between the cultivated class, to which he belonged, and the country people who worked the estate or guided him on hunting or fishing trips. He displays this class consciousness most clearly in his juvenile stories involving boys' battles. The heroes of these tales are usually wellborn, the sons of army officers, judges, or other gentry. The farm boys who dare to pit their strength and toughness against these lads are invariably defeated. Breeding always tells.[19]

When Hjalmar was twelve years old, he was sent away to school, exchanging the carefree outdoor life at Systrand for the confinement of classrooms at the Drammen Latin School. The boy missed his indulgent grandparents and was homesick. He dreamed of the outdoors when he should have been at his books. Although his natural ability kept him near the middle of the class, he thoroughly disliked the Greek and Latin grammar he had to study. Eventually he was reconciled to learning, but not to city life.[20]

In one of his juvenile tales, Boyesen touches on the nationalistic spirit prevalent in Norway during his boyhood. The schoolboy hero of "The Sons of the Vikings," like young Boyesen, dislikes studies in general but loves "tales, poems, and histories of the Norsemen in ancient times." He always closes his prayers, "And I thank thee, God, most of all, because thou madest me a Norseman, and not a German or an Englishman or a Swede." The author explains this sentiment: "To be a Norseman appears to the Norse boy a claim to distinction. God has made so many millions of Englishmen and Russians and Germans, that there can be no particular honor in being one of so vast a herd; while of Norsemen He has made only a small and select number. . . . Thus he is taught to reason by his parents and instructors." The hero of this particular tale had, for a history teacher, a "Norse-Norseman" of a superpatriotic type who drew Boyesen's gibes in several other stories and articles. This teacher "had on one occasion, with more patriotic zeal than discretion, undertaken to

---

[19] Larson, *The Changing West*, 84. See "The Battle of the Rafts," "The Sons of the Vikings," and "Lady Clare: The Story of a Horse," in Boyesen, *Boyhood in Norway: Stories of Boy-Life in the Land of the Midnight Sun* (New York, 1892).
[20] Rideing, *Living Authors*, 170–172.

pick out those boys in his class who were of pure Norse descent; whose blood was untainted by any foreign admixture." Such nationalistic excesses repelled rather than attracted a youth whose very family name suggested Danish origin.[21]

From the Drammen Latin School young Boyesen went on to a Gymnasium in Christiania, and then to the Royal Fredrik University. Some accounts say that he also took courses at the University of Leipzig in the 1860's. There is no information about the time or duration of these university studies, only the statement that they revealed his "remarkable aptitude for literature and language."[22]

Boyesen once told an interviewer that the general cultural training he received in the secondary schools was more valuable than his advanced work, because the national university of Norway was old-fashioned, rigid, and provincial. But one university lecture series, that of Professor H. C. Christie on physics, impressed him and affected his life.[23] "I had gone into the classical course," he told the interviewer, "and I felt that I needed to study some science in order to keep myself from working in one channel only. It seems to me that interest in a science broadens a man greatly, gives him a new outlook on life; at any rate, I like to think that my work in physics did that for me."[24]

When Boyesen recalled the Norway of his youth, he preferred to dwell on the wonderful days at Systrand. Yet, scattered throughout his writings are descriptions of parts of Norway and of life there that were far from idyllic. Perhaps the bleakest spot was the fishing village of Vardø on an island within the Arctic Circle, where Boyesen spent part of one summer vacation. "I remember, as a boy of 14, visiting a relative of mine who was a clergyman in the north of Norway. Being greatly struck by the small number of graves in the cemetery, and those, as the headstones

---

[21] Boyesen, *Boyhood in Norway*, 96.

[22] See *Chautauquan* (Meadville, Pennsylvania), 22:229 (November, 1895), and *Critic* (New York), 27:237 (October 12, 1895). See also Heath, in *Scribner's Monthly*, 14:777; Larson, *The Changing West*, 85. It is doubtful that Boyesen studied at Leipzig before 1873: He would have mentioned it himself and used the experience in his writings. Probably this confusion arises from his return to Europe in 1873 to visit Norway and study at Leipzig.

[23] Hartvig Caspar Christie (1826–73) became a lecturer (*lektor*) at the national university in 1859 and a professor in 1866. His death at forty-six was a severe loss to the university and to Norway.

[24] Barry, in *New York Illustrated American*, 17:178. When Boyesen gave this interview, he may have been prejudiced: He was battling for the modern languages and the sciences in the college curriculum, as against the intrenched classical languages.

showed, nearly all of women and children, I asked my kinsman jocosely, if the men were immortal in his parish. . . . 'There,' he said pointing with his stick toward the ocean, 'there is their cemetery.' " [25]

The town of Vardø became the setting of Boyesen's short novel, *Against Heavy Odds*, written in the Horatio Alger tradition. The plot is trite but included are picturesque scenes of a poor cottage "which smelled of smoked salt fish and wet clothes." The author was aware that life in Vardø was grim business for the fisherfolk who lived in such hovels. He explained: "People up in that Arctic wilderness are usually wet, and a good deal of their time is taken up in the effort to get dry. They have to extract their scanty living from the vast, wild Polar Sea, and if generations of struggle and hardship had not toughened them, they would perish miserably in the course of one winter." [26]

During the summer vacation, Hjalmar customarily walked the long road to Sogn with a group of companions; and he wrote several firsthand accounts of these trips over the difficult but varied terrain between the capital and his home. When he reached Lærdalsøren at the head of Sognefjord, he continued to Systrand by boat, but a stopover in the bleak little town was usually necessary. "I remember in my student days," Boyesen writes, "there lived here a highly cultivated lawyer, whose charming family always brightened my enforced sojourns (on my way home from the university), and illuminated the gloomy valley with their genial hospitality. I remember, too, that this lawyer had a handsome, high-bred daughter, with a sweet melancholy in her face. . . . She told me once that she felt as if she were living in the bottom of an enchanted well, from which there was no escape, until her predestined prince came and released her." [27]

In 1867 Boyesen, not content with his regular two-hundred-mile walking stint, undertook, with three friends, a more extended trip which covered "the length and breadth of Norway." At sundown one day, he relates, they came upon a group of rural folk gathered to hear the reading of an America letter by the local schoolmaster. A family of five sons and three daughters was planning to emigrate. Their father had died recently. By dividing his ample farm among them, each could earn a bare

---

[25] Boyesen, "Village Life in Norway," in *Chautauquan*, 18:7 (October, 1893).
[26] *Against Heavy Odds: A Tale of Norse Heroism*, 21 (New York, 1890). Two shorter stories are also set in Vardø: "The Sunless World," and "Life for Life," in *Norseland Tales* (New York, 1894).
[27] "The Fjords of Norway," in *Cosmopolitan*, 17:152 (June, 1894).

living, but the family name would no longer stand for pre-eminence in the little valley. Rather than face loss of prestige, they had agreed to sell the holdings, take their stake to America, and buy sufficient land there for a proper farm for each.[28]

The kindred phenomena of the America letter, the "America fever," and the American emigrant agent were becoming increasingly prevalent in Norway during the years when Boyesen was growing up. To be sure, these influences usually affected the farmers and cotters as well as the impoverished *bourgeoisie*, not the cultured class; but Captain Boyesen's trip to America and his strong bias in favor of the new republic gave his son a keen interest in the westward migration. The curious young student observed the movement carefully, but his stories reveal that he knew much more about the Norwegian end of the ordeal than about the problems of pioneering in America.

The tears and heartbreak of parting, the drama and romance of the great adventure in the New World appear in Boyesen's early, romantic stories. Boasting letters written to the folks back in the old country, embellished to increase the writer's stature, amused Boyesen. He recognized the preposterous elements in the situation, and commented:

"If I had told my grandmother in Norway that two and two made five in America, I do not believe it would have surprised her. She had seen what was to her a much more startling phenomenon. A slovenly, barefooted milkmaid named Guro, who had been in her employ, had returned from the United States, after an absence of five years, with all the airs of a lady, and arrayed in silks and jewelry which in Norway represented a small fortune. My grandmother was convinced that Guro (who had never been a favorite with her) had crossed the ocean for the sole purpose of dazzling her, triumphing over her, and enjoying her discomfiture. For she had prophesied Guro a bad end, and she bore a lasting grudge against the country which had brought her prophecy to naught."[29]

In "The Norse Emigrant" the Civil War veteran visiting his home valley tells a tale that is his own true story. Between thirty and forty people accompany him when he returns to America; and though there is much weeping at the leave-taking, this is healthy pathos and not real sorrow. The old folks look on such visits from the New World with apprehension, of course, because they know the consequences to themselves. In

[28] "The Modern Migration of Nations," in *Chautauquan*, 9:281 (February, 1889).
[29] *Literary and Social Silhouettes*, 118 (New York, 1894).

Boyhood in Norway

another early tale Boyesen describes a champion of the conservative viewpoint: "Bjarne Blakstad, like the sturdy old patriot that he was, had always fiercely denounced the America rage. . . . He had stayed behind to remind the restless ones among the youth of their duty toward their land, or to frighten some bold emigration agent who might have been too loud in his declamations." [30]

There is little likelihood that young Boyesen had much sympathy with conservatism, despite his love for Judge Hjorth. But if the forces that attempted to stem the tide of emigration seemed stubborn and unenlightened, the young student recognized that the emigrant agent could be a sinister figure, the tool of railroad and land companies whose motives were far from disinterested. In "A Born Chieftain," a story for boys, the opening scene pictures a rural churchyard after the service is over and the pastor has returned to his parsonage:

"A man had climbed up on the stone fence and was making a speech. All the people flocked together about him and listened. He was a tall, pale-complexioned fellow, with a shrewd, vulgar face. He was dressed in broadcloth, and wore a lot of cheap imitation jewelry. 'Friends,' he said, 'I reckon you don't know me, though I know you. It isn't so very many years since I ran barefooted among you and as ragged as a scarecrow. Look at me now, lads; I don't want to brag, but I ask you to look at me. I don't look much like what I used to, do I? You remember little James Forest — or Jens Skoug, I mean — as frowsy and dirty a little ragamuffin as ever you clapped eyes on. You remember him? Yes, I see you do. Well, lads, you can all dress in fine store clothes and carry a gold watch and chain (here the emigration agent dangled his elegant gilt brass chain), and be as well off as I am if you only want to. You have heard of California, I reckon. Well, you would scarcely believe me, but I have picked up gold nuggets there as big as my fist, and worth thousands of dollars. In one hour you may gain more money there than here you would by toiling and slaving for a lifetime. I reckon you will take it that I am lying when I tell you there is no winter there, so that you can raise two and sometimes three crops off the same piece of ground in one year.'" [31]

The Judas in this sensational tale sells four hundred of his emigrant

---

[30] *Tales from Two Hemispheres*, 102 (Boston, 1876); Boyesen, in *Galaxy*, 15:199–203.

[31] *Norseland Tales*, 131.

Hjalmar Hjorth Boyesen

countrymen into slavery in Mexico, and the young hero rescues them. Rather curiously, Jens Skoug or James Forrest (two "r's" this time, and wearing a tall, shiny hat) is the villain of another story; his fast talk lures "Fiddle John's" family to equally fantastic, though smaller-scaled, adventures in the New World.[32]

These accounts of life in Norway were written many years after Boyesen made his observations at first hand, but they are not the product of hazy and inaccurate recollections. The young man had looked at these phenomena from a writer's viewpoint, recording in notebooks the events that interested him. The extended walking tour that covered all of Norway was undertaken to provide the kind of knowledge a writer must have. It was part of his preparation for a literary career.[33]

Boyesen's urge to write came early. Perhaps a copy of Esaias Tegnér's *Fritiof's Saga*, a gift on his twelfth birthday, was the most potent stimulus. This romantic tale in verse, although written by a Swede, is a legend of ancient Norway, closely identified with the Sogn area. King Bele's tomb is a few steps from Judge Hjorth's Systrand home, and Fritiof had landed on the beach before the house, seeking a tryst with his beloved Ingeborg. A huge old birch tree growing on a grassy tomblike mound became Hjalmar's favorite haunt. Sitting under it, he identified himself with the saga and the place: "He felt sure that it was a scald who was buried here; for in the songs of the wind he had seemed to recognize the same strain that had rung in his ears so often while reading the scaldic lays in the old sagas. Then strange emotions would thrill through his breast; he felt that he was himself a scald, and that he was destined to revive the expiring song and the half-forgotten traditions of the great old time." Soon after reading *Fritiof's Saga*, he wrote a long poem of his own, "The Saga of the Scald." He remembered it as his first triumph: His grandmother cried over it for a whole day. Judge Hjorth, however, did not approve of the boy's literary efforts; to him, music was the only art that deserved a gentleman's attention.[34]

Even in Boyesen's later years, after he became a realist, he had a fanciful explanation for the urge to write that took possession of him when he was a boy:

"There was not a suspicion of literary atmosphere about my neigh-

---

[32] *Norseland Tales*, 131–170; *The Modern Vikings*, 211–274 (New York, 1887).
[33] Boyesen, in *Chautauquan*, 9:281.
[34] Rideing, *Living Authors*, 164; Barry, in *New York Illustrated American*, 17:179.

Boyhood in Norway

borhood, and I am therefore at a loss to account for the Delphic madness which seized me at the age of twelve. I have since come to regard it as a case of atavism. Some ancestor of mine, in remote antiquity, was, perhaps, a skald at the court of Harold, the Fair-haired, or Olaf the Saint; or some later progenitor, more directly responsible for my existence was smothered, like a tongueless nightingale, by his missing songs. For the latter I have been able to spot, and I have taken considerable satisfaction in the thought that (whatever the quality of the songs) I have afforded a sort of posthumous outlet for this inspiration." [35]

But at twelve Boyesen was not concerned about an explanation for his lyrical outburst. "I simply wrote on with a savage zest of ferocity, filling copybook after copybook . . . and revelled all the while in a sense of clandestine greatness, than which I know no more delightful sensation." The copybooks, originally intended for Latin exercises, served a more useful purpose as repositories for his rhymes. His grandmother's praise aroused his ambition to excel in other directions, and the urge to write transformed the unwilling student into a good scholar.[36]

He filled six notebooks with boyhood rhymes, poems on "Yearning," "Grandfather's Birthday," "Norway," and a long series of legendary heroes. At fifteen, after a few visits to the Christiania theater, he began writing bloodcurdling tragedies: "The ghost scene in 'Svend Dyring's House' (by the Danish poet Hertz) made a tremendous impression upon me, and I promptly produced an old Norse tragedy called 'Angantyr,' in which the hero is killed in the first act and is a ghost in the remaining four. This I thought so good that I took my grandmother into my confidence. I read 'Angantyr' aloud to her with much gusto and fierce declamation and was much encouraged by her tears, which flowed with gratifying copiousness in all the moving passages." [37]

The grandmother's continuing approval encouraged the boy to try his verses on his father. Captain Boyesen brought the young poet down to earth: "Most boys pass through a period when they fancy themselves

---

[35] Boyesen, in *Philadelphia Inquirer*, October 1, 1893.
[36] Boyesen, in *Philadelphia Inquirer*, October 1, 1893.
[37] Boyesen, in *Philadelphia Inquirer*, October 1, 1893; Rideing, *Living Authors*, 171. Boyesen wrote Rideing that his model for the play was *Hamlet*. Henrik Hertz (1798–1870) was a Danish poet and dramatist whose romantic, lyrical plays were highly popular in the Scandinavian countries and throughout Europe in the late nineteenth century. *Svend Dyring's House* (1837), a romantic drama, was a spectacular success.

17

to be poets, as they pass through the mumps and measles. Your verses are no better and no worse than those which I myself wrote at your age." [38]

Although Hjalmar was deflated by his father's words, he did not give up his versifying. Some years later, when Captain Boyesen asked if he was still writing poetry, the young man confessed that he was. This time his father gave him some hope and advice, saying:

"It is barely possible that you will some day have something to say which is worth listening to. But let me tell you this, my boy, there is nothing but misery in store for an author here in Norway. This is a very small corner of the world, horribly Philistine, intolerant and narrow-minded; and, moreover, there are scarcely over ten or twenty thousand people in the whole country that take an interest in anything beyond the daily struggle for bread and butter. I have seen more of the world than you have, and I beg of you not to think of settling down and striking root here before you have been in America, where there is a far greater future in store for a man with your education and talents. If, then, you prove yourself strong enough to conquer a new language, and make it so perfectly your own that you can mold and bend it to your will, then I shall believe in your literary aspirations, and not until then." [39]

Hjalmar decided to go to America because he thought that it offered him the best opportunity to become a successful writer. His father, on the other hand, was more concerned about migration itself than about the choice of a career. Captain Boyesen had a poor opinion of a young man's chances in Norway. Probably this, rather than optimism about America, prompted him to send his son to the United States. He felt that his own wings had been clipped because he committed himself too early to the narrow confines of Norwegian officialdom. There is no indication that Hjalmar Boyesen ever found fault with his father's advice to emigrate. One of his fictional characters, who, like the author, went back to visit Norway after some years in the United States, thus described the activities of his university classmates who had remained in Norway:

"They were all engaged or married, and could talk of nothing but matrimony, and their prospects of advancement in the Government service. One had an influential uncle who had been a chum of the present minister of finance; another based his hopes of future prosperity upon

[38] Boyesen, in *Philadelphia Inquirer*, October 1, 1893.
[39] Boyesen, in *Philadelphia Inquirer*, October 1, 1893.

the family connections of his betrothed, and a third was waiting with a patient perseverance, worthy of a better cause, for the death or resignation of an antiquated *chef-de-bureau*, which, according to the promise of some mighty man, would open a position for him in the Department of Justice." [40]

Judge Hjorth, who did not want his favorite grandson to become a writer or go to America, was persuaded to give his grudging consent after Hjalmar took his degree in 1868 at the Royal Fredrik University in Christiania. The old magistrate won some concessions, however. Hjalmar was to try the New World for one year; the way was thus left open for an honorable retreat to Norway if the United States did not come up to his expectations. And the trip was to be put off for a year, to enable Ingolf Boyesen, Hjalmar's younger brother, to finish his course of study and go along. Hjalmar spent the waiting period at the national university taking a graduate course in philology, his "bread study." [41]

[40] Boyesen, *Tales from Two Hemispheres*, 73; Heath, in *Scribner's Monthly*, 14: 777.

[41] Heath, in *Scribner's Monthly*, 14:777; "Hjalmar Hjorth Boyesen," in *Chautauquan*, 22:229 (November, 1895).

2

A New American Writer

WHEN Hjalmar and Ingolf Boyesen arrived in New York in the spring of 1869, they were carrying out a plan their father had made for them many years before. According to a statement Hjalmar made in later life, Captain Sarolf Boyesen intended his sons to become American citizens and had prepared them for it: "My father made the choice before me, having visited the United States as a young man, and brought me up in sympathy with American institutions, which he sincerely admired. I therefore found myself more at home here, when I arrived, than in the country of my birth." The Boyesens came on a "year's visit"; at the end of it they were to stay in America or return to Norway, as they wished. This may have been only a subterfuge to reconcile Judge Hjorth to the fact of their departure. By the time the first months of travel were over, there was little doubt that the two young men were going to remain, although Hjalmar had some second thoughts about his (or his father's) decision later.[1]

The brothers saw a good deal of the United States. They visited New England, spent some time in the South (including a week in New Or-

[1] The quotation is from an address delivered by Boyesen in Washington, December 7, 1887, sponsored by the American branch of the Evangelical Alliance, later known as the National Council of Churches of Christ. The address was published under the title "Immigration," in *National Perils and Opportunities*, 55–76 (New York, 1888). For the words quoted, see p. 73. The most reliable and unprejudiced account of Boyesen's reason for migrating is Heath, in *Scribner's Monthly*, 14:778. Hjalmar Boyesen took out his first citizenship papers November 12, 1870; his final papers are dated April 14, 1875; Boyesen Papers.

A New American Writer

leans), and toured "all the Western States east of the Mississippi." Hjalmar Boyesen took "particular pains to study the condition of the German and Scandinavian immigrants" on this early trip, he told an audience in 1887. "Everywhere contentment and hopefulness were the rule. Nearly all the people I talked with told me that this was a good country."[2]

When the tour was over, the Boyesens settled down, because of their religious affiliation, in Urbana, Ohio. Urbana was a Swedenborgian center in the West, the site of a struggling and largely subcollegiate institution known as Urbana University. According to an interview Boyesen gave in 1895, he carried letters of introduction to people at Urbana and had an uncle who was a professor there.[3] Hjalmar considered going into the ministry, or so intimated, but another professional opportunity took him away from Urbana early in 1870.

"In America," Captain Boyesen had told Hjalmar, "there is a far greater future in store for a man with your education and talents." The young man's first chance to display these talents came when he was hired as an associate editor of the Dano-Norwegian weekly, *Fremad*. When the paper moved from Milwaukee to Chicago on March 10, 1870, the publisher announced that two university graduates had joined his editorial staff: Hjalmar H. Boyesen of Christiania, and P. G. Müller of Copenhagen. Boyesen held his editorship for about a year, while his brother remained in Urbana. Speaking later of his newspaper experiences, he told of using his position to advocate the Americanization of his fellow immigrants. He recalled writing editorials urging Norwegian Americans to send their children to public schools instead of the Lutheran parochial schools. The issues he edited show that his role actually was more modest than he remembered.[4]

Although Chicago was the setting of some of his early stories, Boye-

[2] Boyesen, in *National Perils*, 65; Heath, in *Scribner's Monthly*, 14:777; Boyesen to Cable, February 18, 1877. When Boyesen spoke of "contentment and hopefulness," he was referring to the western German and Scandinavian settlements. He was trying to prove a point when he made this statement.
[3] Barry, in *New York Illustrated American*, 17:179. Barry, who probably misunderstood Boyesen, gives the only known reference to the uncle.
[4] Boyesen, in *Philadelphia Inquirer*, October 1, 1893. *Fremad* (Forward) was founded in Milwaukee in April, 1868. The first editor-publisher, a Danish Jew named Just M. Caen, sold the paper to Sophus Beder, who presumably also was Danish. See Larson, *The Changing West*, 88–90. Larson investigated Boyesen's connection with *Fremad* and found that his claims were slightly exaggerated: He did not serve as editor for the entire period that he mentioned, and his crusading role was largely imaginary. A partial file of *Fremad* is at Luther College, Decorah, Iowa.

sen said little in later years about his experiences there, and he mentioned only one person. He told an interviewer that he became acquainted with "Dr. Dyer, the noted abolitionist," a wealthy man who had a fine house on the North Side, and added, "He invited me to live with him and I spent six months with his family."[5] It is strange that Boyesen did not explain this relationship, because a casual acquaintance would hardly play host for six months. There is, however, one clue: When Captain Sarolf Boyesen was in the United States he deposited a sum of money "with a friend in Chicago," to be paid to any of his sons who went to America to claim it in person.[6] If Captain Boyesen, an idealistic democrat who certainly sympathized with the abolitionists, met some of their leaders on his 1856 visit to the United States, the Dyer-Boyesen friendship may be explained.

The ambition to become a writer was uppermost with Boyesen, and he realized that he must learn English so thoroughly that it would supplant his Norwegian. In Chicago he spent his evenings reading Shakespeare, Shelley, and Keats; the poetical tone of his newly acquired speech amused his friends. When he found that mastering English was more than a spare-time activity, he gave up his position on *Fremad*, and with it the obligation to use Norwegian in his daily work. He went to Boston, where he took twenty or more lessons from an elocutionist, working hard to eliminate the Norwegian intonation from his English speech. In September, 1870, he returned to Urbana, where he rejoined Ingolf and a younger brother, Alf, who had recently arrived from Norway. He then took a position as tutor in Latin and Greek at Urbana University.[7]

Nothing about Urbana, either the "university" or the town, held much appeal for Boyesen. He was not an ardent Swedenborgian.[8] The monot-

---

[5] The quotation is from Barry, in *New York Illustrated American*, 17:179. Dr. Charles Volney Dyer, a practicing physician prominently identified with the Anti-Slavery League, was appointed by President Lincoln in 1862 to be the United States member of the Anglo-American mixed court at Sierra Leone, Africa. See *National Cyclopedia of American Biography*, 22:190 (New York, 1932).

[6] Rideing, *Living Authors*, 173.

[7] Boyesen, in *Philadelphia Inquirer*, October 1, 1893. A friend wrote to Boyesen: "How rapidly your English improves. You use the language like a native." Lydia F. Dickinson to Boyesen, September 15, 1870; letters from Mrs. Dickinson cited in this study are in the Boyesen Papers.

[8] "Literature was Boyesen's religion more than the Swedenborgian philosophy in which we had both been spiritually nurtured," wrote Howells; *Literary Friends*, 257. See also Larson, *The Changing West*, 93. Nonetheless, Boyesen was undecided, or perhaps discreet, on the subject during his first months in the United States and apparently even discussed a career in the ministry with his Swedenborgian friends.

onous landscape, the mud, and the drabness of the community were hideous to a Norwegian who remembered his native mountains and fjords. He found the citizens dull and materialistic. Worst of all, he was not interested in the subjects he was hired to teach. As a student in Norway he had disliked the ancient languages as much as he liked the modern tongues; and later, on more than one occasion, he was to question the value of a classical education.[9]

Among Boyesen's papers is a revealing commentary on the people of Urbana; he never published it, although he apparently intended it for a formal lecture:

"The people in the community where I was then sojourning were mostly small, harsh, cramped village souls, made up of petty pretensions, appetites and vanities. There were exceptions, to be sure, but generally speaking this was the complexion of society. Men and women were rigidly circumscribed in their ideals and sympathies, and exhibited toward an alien nothing but thorny prejudice or offensive though well-intentioned condescension. To talk with them was like conversing with a stone wall. A torturing sense of mutual alienation made all free interchange of thought impossible."[10]

That a young man with literary aspirations should have turned to imaginative writing as a refuge and release is not surprising, but once again the statement Boyesen made subsequently must not be taken too literally. Because he was born with "strong communicative impulses," Boyesen explained, he invariably worked off his excess energies by writing: "My first book, 'Gunnar,' was merely an expression of this communicative need; it was written merely to express my homesickness and longing for my beautiful native land during the first and second years of my sojourn in the United States. Reproducing the memories in words — lingering fondly over them — was a relief, and every fresh touch that gave vividness to the same added to my pleasure. The book was written without the remotest thought of publication, and it was due to an accident that it ever saw the light of publicity."[11]

It may be true that loneliness turned him to writing and that homesickness was responsible for the kind of story he wrote, but it does not follow that the book "was written without the remotest thought of pub-

---

[9] Boyesen, in *Philadelphia Inquirer*, October 1, 1893.
[10] Manuscript notes for a lecture, Boyesen Papers.
[11] "H.H.B.," in *Book Buyer*, 3:343.

lication." In fact, Boyesen told interviewers that he went to Cambridge in the summer of 1871 in search of a publisher.[12] Whether or not this was the chief purpose of the trip, he was foresighted enough to take the manuscript of "Gunnar" with him. The familiar story of the chain of events which followed is best told in his own words:

"One day in July, 1871, I happened to be in the Harvard College Library, Cambridge. Professor Ezra Abbott, who was then assistant librarian, begged me to write my name in the visitor's book. He became interested in it, philologically. He asked about my nationality, and hearing that I was a Norseman, begged leave to make me acquainted with Professor Child, who just then was in need of a Norseman. Professor Child was sent for and arrived. He gave me Landstad's collection of Norwegian ballads, and begged me read and translate a number of passages which he had marked. He was then at work upon his great book on ballads, two volumes of which have now appeared. We spent the whole afternoon reading Norse ballads written in different dialects, which were all familiar to me.[13]

"When we parted, Prof. Child exclaimed, 'You have a lot of valuable material in your possession. Why don't you make use of it? It would make an interesting article.' I replied that I had written something. He begged me to bring the MS. to him, and a few days later I was invited to dine at his house. Howells was among the guests; he was then editor of the *Atlantic*. After dinner I was requested to read a portion of my MS.; and I selected the chapter on the 'Skee Race,' and, being asked for more, read the chapter entitled 'The Wedding of the Wild Duck.' Howells became greatly interested; begged me to spend a couple of days at his house as his guest and read the rest of the tale. This invitation was accepted, and likewise the MS. It was this incident which had the most decisive influence upon my life, as it was probably the cause of my remaining in this country. I then became acquainted with Mr. Longfellow, Mr. Lowell, Henry James, Jr., and others.[14] It changed the face of the

---

[12] Stedman, in *Detroit Sunday News-Tribune*, April 8, 1894; Barry, in *New York Illustrated American*, 17:179.

[13] Francis James Child (1825–96), professor of English literature at Harvard, edited a five-volume work on popular ballads that was published between 1883 and 1898. This collection, *The English and Scottish Popular Ballads*, was reissued in New York in 1956. Pastor M. B. Landstad published his 900-page *Norske folkeviser* (Ancient Norwegian Ballads) in 1852–53, with a supplement consisting of folk melodies collected by L. M. Lindeman.

[14] William Dean Howells (1837–1920), pre-eminent figure in American literature

A New American Writer

United States to me, and launched me fairly upon my career as a man of letters. The book, as you know, made a hit. I seemed — to my youthful fancy — on the high road to glory."[15]

When Howells recalled the two-o'clock dinner, followed by coffee in the study while "the odor of the professor's roses stole in at the open windows," he suspected that Child had conspired "to have both the novel and the novelist make their impression at once upon the youthful sub-editor." The scheme worked. "Boyesen walked home with me," said Howells, "and for a fortnight after I think we parted only to dream of the literature which we poured out upon each other in every waking moment. I had just learned to know Bjørnson's stories, and Boyesen told me of his poetry and of his drama, which in even measure embodied the great Norse literary movement, and filled me with the wonder and delight of that noble revolt against convention, that brave return to nature and the springs of poetry in the heart and the speech of the common people."[16]

Howells also remembered his young friend's appearance: "He looked the poetry he lived: his eyes were the blue of sunlit fjords; his brown silken hair was thick on the crown . . . his soft, red lips half hid a boyish pout in the youthful beard and mustache. He was short of stature, but of a stalwart breadth of frame, and his voice was of a peculiar and endearing quality, indescribably mellow and tender when he read his verse."[17]

The impact on Boyesen's career of this meeting with Howells and the warmth of the friendship that grew up between the two men can scarcely be exaggerated. Boyesen's remark that Howells was the first man in America to understand him seems an understatement. The report of "great rages of conversation" which were interrupted only by sleep was almost literally true. Years later, after Boyesen's death, Howells recalled this fortnight of literary talk: "He was constantly at my house, where in

after the Civil War, succeeded James T. Fields as editor-in-chief of the *Atlantic Monthly* in 1871. Both Henry James and Boyesen were beginning their careers at this time; both became close friends of Howells; and their careers run parallel in other ways, i.e., in their associations with Turgenev and other European writers and in their attempts to write realistic fiction.

[15] "H.H.B.," in *Book Buyer*, 3:343.

[16] "This newly awakened interest, even a love for folk literature, nature, folk life, and language," arose in Norway in the middle of the nineteenth century; Einar Haugen, trans. and ed., Harald Beyer, *A History of Norwegian Literature*, 141 (New York, 1956).

[17] Howells' remarks are quoted from *Literary Friends*, 256.

25

an absence of my family I was living [as a] bachelor, and where we sat indoors and talked, or sauntered outdoors and talked, with our heads in a cloud of fancies, not unmixed with the mosquitoes of Cambridge: if I could have back the fancies, I would be willing to have the mosquitoes with them." [18]

Boyesen said, "Howells Americanized me." Judging by the reminiscences of the two friends, it was a pleasant process. In recalling that first summer at Cambridge, Howells asked Boyesen, "Do you mind our sudden attacks of hunger, when we would start on a foraging expedition into the cellar, in the middle of the night, and return, you with a cheese and crackers, and I with a watermelon and a bottle of champagne?" The two men agreed that there had never been "a single jarring note . . . to mar the harmony of our relation." [19]

When Boyesen returned to Urbana for the school year 1871–72, he could take refuge in his writing with the assurance that he had a friendly and sympathetic editor. He first broke into print as an American author with an unsigned review of Hans Christian Andersen's *A Poet's Bazaar* in the October, 1871, *Atlantic Monthly*. His name appeared for the first time in the *Atlantic* in February, 1872, when Howells printed a poem, "A Norse Stev," from the "Gunnar" manuscript.

Gunnar, Boyesen's first novel, was revised extensively before it appeared as an *Atlantic* serial in July, 1873. Howells went over the manuscript with the author in 1871. Said Boyesen: "A good many suggestions were made, and I was urged to abbreviate certain lyrical portions which were, perhaps, unduly prominent and retarded the progress of the story. When I returned to Urbana in the autumn I took the MSS back with me, and rewrote several chapters, and abbreviated others. Half a dozen poems which were scattered through the book were also omitted, and only two or three were permitted to remain." The story was revised again in 1872, when Boyesen spent the entire summer in Cambridge. Howells wrote later: "The proofs went back and forth between us till the author had profited by every hint and suggestion of the editor. He was quick to profit by any hint, and he never made the same mistake twice. He lived

---

[18] See Boyesen's obituary in *Literary World* (Boston), 26:351 (October 19, 1895); Howells, *Literary Friends*, 264.

[19] Barry, in *New York Illustrated American*, 17:179; Boyesen, "Real Conversations: I., A Dialogue between William Dean Howells and Hjalmar Hjorth Boyesen," in *McClure's Magazine*, 1:3–9 (June, 1893). The conversation was "recorded" by Boyesen.

his English as fast as he learned it; the right word became part of him; and he put away the wrong word with instant and final rejection." [20]

Going back to Urbana after these summers in Cambridge was not easy — Boyesen made no pretense about that. Howells, who knew Ohio, tried to console him: "When I first knew him he was chafing with the impatience of youth and ambition at what he thought his exile in the West. There was, to be sure, a difference between Urbana, Ohio, and Cambridge, Massachusetts, and he realized the difference in the extreme and perhaps beyond it. I tried to make him believe that if a man had one or two friends anywhere who loved letters and sympathized with him in his literary attempts, it was incentive enough; but of course he wished to be in the centres of literature, as we all do; and he never was content until he had set his face and foot Eastward." [21]

Perhaps Urbana seemed worse than it was because Boyesen contrasted the community, the college, and the people with Cambridge, Harvard, and Howells' New England circle. Furthermore, this little Ohio town and its struggling Swedenborgian school represented the meanest, least sympathetic, most provincial milieu he had ever encountered. A letter to Howells of December 21, 1872, gives only the slightest glimpse of Urbana, but it portrays Boyesen vividly:

"I have just completed a chapter of my 'Legend of the Midnight Sun,' which appears to me at this moment simply magnificent. O how I do wish I could read it to you! I cannot but believe that you too would find something good in it; at least if I read it to you now — in this very hour — you could not find it in your heart to say that it was worthless. What a strange life I live. Yesterday lonesome, wretched, miserable — today full of great aspirations & dreams, which excite me & make me happy, & that although I know even in this moment that they will never find their realization. But they enable me to work at all events as long as they last & I hope that the present one may endure through the holidays. I don't know why I write to you today, unless it should be to wish you a merry Christmas & to unload my mind of the enthusiasm, which fills it to overflowing. I have written two short poems this week. I don't know whether they are good for anything, & I am afraid of showing them to anybody for fear they should tell me that they are poor. I have determined again & again,

---

[20] Boyesen, in *Philadelphia Inquirer*, October 1, 1893; Howells, *Literary Friends*, 258.
[21] Howells, *Literary Friends*, 262.

Hjalmar Hjorth Boyesen

in moments when I have been keenly conscious of my own imperfections, that I shall never write another poem as long as I live. And still somehow or other I find myself committing the same folly over & over again. There are two things I have discovered I cannot do. I cannot make a fool interesting & I cannot conceive the character of a rogue, however much I may puzzle my brain with it. I shall therefore let fools & villains alone for the future. I have made up my mind that 'Mr. Bruce's Vocation' as it stands, is a poor performance & I am convinced that you entertain a similar opinion of it, although you were kind enough to say that the plot in itself was good. Mr. Sewall cannot be persuaded to cut his copy of the Atlantic, until Christmas has fairly set in.[22] . . .

"It is a strange thing that I cannot induce the Newsdealer here to get a single extra copy of the 'Atlantic,' unless I agree to pay for it. Thinking, however, that my poem was there I sent for five copies of the Jan. number, & was half prepared to get them all on my hands. But they went off like 'hot cakes'; so I am encouraged to repeat the same speculation for next month, of course with the same selfish motive. For my poems always sell here in town."

During Boyesen's third year in Ohio his literary output increased, and other magazines besides the *Atlantic* accepted pieces. The *Galaxy* printed his poem, "Norway," and a short story, "The Norse Emigrant," in February, 1873; and *Lippincott's* published another poem, "The Glaciers of Paradise," in April, 1873. To the *North American Review* Boyesen contributed twenty- and thirty-page articles on Kristofer Janson and Bjørnstjerne Bjørnson.[23]

---

[22] "Mr. Sewall" was President Frank Sewall of Urbana University. Mrs. Lydia Dickinson recommended Sewall as the man who could help Boyesen most: "He will not irritate you with any cold, politic, merely conventional ways. He has no axe to grind for himself. . . . He is a true man working disinterestedly for the truth *as he sees it*. . . . I want you to take lessons of him in self control morning noon and night"; Mrs. Dickinson to Boyesen, September 15, 1870. Boyesen's letters to Howells are in the Houghton Library, Harvard University. "Legend of the Midnight Sun" and "Mr. Bruce's Vocation" were never published; if they were, they appeared under other titles.

[23] The *Galaxy* (1866–78), a monthly literary magazine founded in New York, was intended to counteract the supposed provincialism of the *Atlantic Monthly*. It later sold its subscription lists to the *Atlantic*. *Lippincott's Magazine* (1868–1916) was a Philadelphia literary monthly, more national in scope than the *Atlantic*. It merged with *Scribner's* in 1916. The *North American Review* (1815–1940) was founded in Boston, a scholarly quarterly patterned on English and Scottish models. It became a monthly, moved to New York (1878), and lost its Brahmin character. When, after World War I, its circulation dropped sharply, it became a quarterly again. Boyesen's "Kristofer Janson and the Reform of the Norwegian Language," and "Bjørnstjerne

A New American Writer

Recalling Urbana in later years, Boyesen spoke of his writing as an escape from the prosaic existence he found so hard to endure: "Half the night I sat in my dreary room in the college hall and wrote with a delight which took no account of the hours. A sort of joyous restlessness possessed me, and I begrudged the time I had to spend in the class room drumming Latin and Greek grammar into the heads of stupid boys." Despite his unwillingness and his preoccupation with his own literary projects, Boyesen was a good teacher, according to President Sewall of Urbana University: "During his entire connection with the college, by his diligent and scholarly service, he rendered more than an equivalent for the meager compensation he received." [24]

The meager compensation was what kept Hjalmar Boyesen in Urbana. Some years later, he spoke of the obligations that tied him to his position and hindered his literary plans: "I have two younger brothers who came with me to this country.... I had to work for them, to educate them.... I yearned all the while with heart & soul to devote myself to the one calling I had loved from the time I was old enough to define my aspirations." [25]

At times when impatience got the better of him, he threatened to give up his position and return to Norway. Howells repeatedly urged him to hold on, to be forbearing for a while longer: "Don't, my friend, give up your place for another year yet, at any rate.... Perfect yourself. Get more reputation, and then go it if you wish. But I doubt if you can put yourself, for years, on so good a base as you now hold." Howells also came to Boyesen's aid when he was depressed: "You ought never to be really downcast about your future. That is assured.... There is no doubt of your power—your genius, as you know I may call it without attempting to flatter you." [26]

Escape from Urbana came sooner than Howells had expected. On

Bjørnson as a Dramatist," appeared in *North American Review*, 115:379–401, 116: 109–138 (October, 1872, January, 1873).

[24] Boyesen, in *Philadelphia Inquirer*, October 1, 1893; Frank Sewall to the *New York Daily Tribune*, July 1, 1878. Sewall wrote to refute a charge that Boyesen was an ingrate who had maligned his friends and benefactors in the short story, "Swart among the Buckeyes," in *Scribner's Monthly*, 14:547–559 (August, 1877).

[25] Boyesen to Cable, January 20, 1878. Boyesen was irked by teaching itself, as well as by having to live in provincial towns. At Cornell, as well as at Urbana, he yearned for the company of literary men and for freedom to write. He spoke constantly of this in his letters to Cable and Howells.

[26] Howells to Boyesen, September 6, 1872, March 27, 1873. Howells' letters to Boyesen are in the Boyesen Papers.

Hjalmar Hjorth Boyesen

April 25, 1873, President Andrew D. White of Cornell University wrote Boyesen offering him a position as "Assistant Professor of North European Languages . . . at a salary of one thousand dollars *per annum*." He accepted at once and his spirits soared. "It was a great step for him from the Swedenborgian school at Urbana to the young university at Ithaca; and I remember his exultation in making it," Howells wrote later. Boyesen wasted no time in leaving Urbana. He went immediately to Ithaca, and was given leave to go to Europe before assuming his new position. On June 18, 1873, he sailed from New York on the "Columbia" of the Anchor Line.[27]

Boyesen first went to Norway. His primary object was to visit his family, but the high light of this return to his native land was a meeting with Bjørnstjerne Bjørnson, described graphically in a letter to Howells. Boyesen remained in Norway for two months. It was to be his last visit for eighteen years.

His official purpose in making the European trip was to study at the University of Leipzig. On his way to Germany from Norway, he spent a week in Denmark, where he interviewed Hans Christian Andersen and met the literary men of Copenhagen. He reached Leipzig September 10. Although he worked out an ambitious program of study and attended a few lectures, his sojourn ended shortly after the university term began, and early in December he started home by way of Paris. He sailed from Liverpool on December 20, arriving in New York on January 2, 1874.[28]

A letter to Howells from Leipzig, September 27, 1873, reveals Boyesen's state of mind, and reports on the important events of the first three months of his trip:

"I have talked Norwegian & German so long, now, that, as you may perceive, my English is getting rather stiff.—Have you as yet spoken to Osgood of having 'Gunnar' published in book-form? The fate of my favorite hero engages my thoughts by night & day, & I shall not feel perfectly happy, until I know definitely what will become of him. Among the American-Norwegians, whose number is 800,000 (that is strictly speaking 600,000 Norsemen & 200,000 Danes who speak the same language) it is bound to sell, & from all the numerous letters I have received from the West, I am justified in thinking, that they are anxiously looking

---

[27] Howells, *Literary Friends*, 262; Boyesen to Willard Fiske, June 17, 1873. Boyesen's trip can be traced through his letters to Fiske; they are in the Fiske Collection, Cornell University. White's letters to Boyesen are in the Boyesen Papers.

[28] Boyesen to Fiske, September 21, 26, November 30, 1873.

forward to the publication of the book & that it will find a ready sale among them. And among Americans it will probably also find an audience. — At all events the publisher will run no risk of loss in bringing the book out, & if you will kindly interest yourself in its fate, I shall deem it a great favor. You have perhaps yourself once known the sufferings of incipient authorship, & will sympathize with me; but I know that publishers are unsentimental, & that it is naturally the mere financial side of the question which interests them. Therefore I have also tried to set aside my own feelings & to look upon the matter from a mere business point of view. How far I have succeeded I don't know.—But now, suppose Osgood should be unwilling to publish my story, what would you then advise me to do? For the book must come out, even if I should myself set the type.[29]

"In Norway I became very intimately acquainted with Bjørnson, who, as you may know is a great Republican, & a warm admirer of America. He invited me to make a journey with him to Gudbrandsdal, where there was a grand party made for him at Boe, the largest & richest estate in 'seven parishes round.' It was an experience never to be forgotten — regular Viking fashion—& in a literary point of view it was invaluable. There Bjørnson proposed the 'Dus Skaal' (thee and thou toast) with me & we made a kind of covenant of life long friendship. It may sound a little sentimental to Am. ears, but Bjørnson's personality excludes the thought of sentimentality; for something more fresh, healthy & Norse than him can hardly be imagined. He knew & had long followed my doings in America, having been informed by Ole Bull.

"One compliment which he paid me, I cannot help repeating — for it made me happier than I can tell. When we parted, he said: 'Hjalmar Hjorth B. I must now tell you, what has been on my lips ever since we first met. You are the first translator or critic who has ever rendered & understood the spirit of my writings. Therefore, if you will receive the monopoly of translating into English what I may hereafter write, you will find my heart even closer to you. I shall send you all in advanced proof sheets, so that you can anticipate all others. And still one thing more.

---

[29] James Ripley Osgood (1836–92) established (with James T. Fields) the Boston firm of Fields, Osgood, and Company in 1868; eventually it became Houghton, Mifflin, and Company. These firms published the *Atlantic Monthly*. Boyesen's estimate of a potential audience was a generous one. According to the best available information, the figure should be cut to less than 200,000. See Carlton C. Qualey, *Norwegian Settlement in the United States*, 217–250 (Northfield, 1938).

Hjalmar Hjorth Boyesen

Believe me I am in earnest when I say it. I never speak empty words. When you marry, or rather when you shall be betrothed, then ask your beloved, if she will come & stay with me & my family for half a year or as long as she may wish. I want the privilege of giving her the great impression of our Norse life. It does not matter where I am; I shall ever be ready. Give me your hand. You promise?' You can yourself imagine about what I answered to this; but I was very happy.[30]

"There is something so grand & so overpowering in the whole man,— he is a living Saga — a character like Harald Fairhair or Olaf Trygveson, & his speech is now soft & fragrant like a summer daydream, now wild like hurricane, now deep & stimmungsvoll (as a German would say) as the Northland forests. Now think of what significance such an acquaintance & the daily intercourse with such a man must have been to me. He has promised to come to America in 1875 to unveil the Leif Erickson's monument which the Norwegians are to erect in Madison Wis. (the same idea which Appleton once had in 'The Flowering of a Nation'). He will then visit me at Cornell & will also come to Boston.[31]

"At Bjørnson's house I met the Danish poet *Goldschmidt*, who immediately on my arrival in Copenhagen gave a grand dinner for me & invited several of the famous *literati* of the city. . . . Goldschmidt intends for the future to make himself the interpreter in the Scandinavian countries of American Literature & has given me many commissions to attend to on my return. My meeting with Hans Chr. Andersen is itself worthy of being made a book about; but I should never be ready, if I should attempt to describe it; it occupied twenty pages in my journal. Bergsøe, old Christian Winther, Ploug, the leader of the Scandinavian party & others were among my Copenhagen acquaintances. It was a most memorable week; &, as I hope, is to bear good fruit in the future.[32]

---

[30] Ole Bull, the Norwegian violinist (1810–80), first toured the United States in 1843. Boyesen mentioned one of Bull's tours in the short story "Anastasia"; *Century*, 25:839–852 (April, 1883). Boyesen continued to write enthusiastic articles about Bjørnson but apparently did not translate any of his works. Translations were made by Professor Rasmus B. Anderson, who also managed Bjørnson's speaking tour of 1881. Boe was the name of the Bjørnson estate.

[31] The Appleton mentioned by Boyesen was probably Thomas Gold Appleton (1812–84), poet, artist, essayist, and Longfellow's brother-in-law. The Leif Erickson monument was erected, not in Madison in 1875, but in Boston in 1887.

[32] Meïr Aron Goldschmidt (1819–87) was "the most significant forerunner of modern realism" in Denmark. As the youthful, brilliant, satirical editor of *Corsaren* (The Corsair), a critical weekly, he played a crucial role in Søren Kierkegaard's life; as a short-story writer and novelist, he influenced Henrik Ibsen and other Norwegian writers. His most famous work, a novel that is almost a memoir, is *En jøde* (A Jew —

A New American Writer

"Your sister Annie is indeed a most delightful correspondent; her letter, which arrived about simultaneously with yours, has begun to reconcile me to the disagreeable sides of German life. . . . The German ladies are not to talk with; they are only good to look at & to dance with. I have some idea of making a short trip to Italy in November."[33]

From Leipzig Boyesen also wrote to Willard Fiske, dean of the special faculty of North European languages at Cornell. He reported on the German and Scandinavian books Fiske had commissioned him to buy, inquired about his teaching assignments at Cornell, and asked permission to remain in Europe until the beginning of the winter semester. On November 30, just before he left Leipzig, he described for Fiske the ambitious and impressive program of studies he was pursuing:

"I have made a deep plunge into the Mittelhochdeutsch [*Middle High German*], & have come to the conclusion, that it has been an unpardonable assumption on my part to profess to understand our own Saga literature, as long as I was ignorant of the connection with the German Medieval classics. I have now read the greater part of Gudrun (partly privately, partly at Prof. Hildebrand's lectures) & have made a somewhat superficial study of the Nibelungenlied. The great Nibelungen scholar Fr. Zarnoke I have the pleasure of hearing every day. . . . Once a week he has a class (2 hours) in Njals Saga. I am, of course a member; & every Friday evening I spend two or three hours with him in 'Deutsche Seminar.' . . . So you see I have been making good use of my time."[34]

In the letters to Fiske the significant statement recurs: "So you see I am making good use of my time." The last report from Leipzig summed

---

Copenhagen, 1845), published under the pseudonym Adolph Meyer. See P. M. Mitchell, *A History of Danish Literature*, 166 (New York, 1957). Vilhelm Bergsøe (1835–1911) is best known for his novel, *Fra Piazza del Popolo* (1867), which describes the Scandinavian colony in Rome. Christian Winther (1796–1876) was a romantic poet whose major work was *Hjortens flugt* (The Flight of the Hart — 1855). Carl Ploug (1813–94) was a politician, journalist, and writer of popular patriotic verse.

[33] Boyesen probably first knew Annie Howells while she was visiting her brother in Cambridge; but they may have met at her parents' home in Jefferson, Ohio, while Boyesen was at Urbana.

[34] Boyesen to Fiske, September 21, 26, November 30, 1873. "Gudrun" is one of the poems, in the *Elder or Poetic Edda*, collected in the thirteenth century but composed earlier. Like the *Njals Saga*, a prose narrative of a little later date, the *Poetic Edda* is Icelandic in origin and was written in Old Norse. The subject matter of "Gudrun," and of most of the other poems in the *Poetic Edda*, is Germanic, the same legendary material as that of the Nibelungenlied.

up Boyesen's progress: "I feel that I have accomplished a great deal here, & consequently am well satisfied with the results of my journey." There is no reason to doubt his sincerity, even though the philological studies in Leipzig lasted only a few weeks. As his career shows, Boyesen was never primarily interested in philology, either classical or Germanic, and the German courses he taught were concentrated as much as possible on literature rather than language. His real enthusiasm was reserved for contemporary writing and for any experiences which might further his own literary career. Thus, as he reported it later, the most momentous event of his stay in Leipzig was not the Germanic philology lectures but a conversation with Dr. Julian Schmidt, the German critic and literary historian. Showing Boyesen a picture of Turgenev, Schmidt said, "And this is, in my opinion, perhaps the greatest author now living." [35]

Howells had introduced Boyesen to Turgenev's works in 1872, and the two men had read *Smoke* together. "I shall never forget what an eye-opener that book was to me as to the true art of novel-writing," Boyesen wrote later. He recalled Howells' comments on the book: "Each character is so convincing, so marvellously authentic. You feel that there is no obscuring literary medium between the novelist and the world which he depicts." [36] Since then Boyesen's admiration for Turgenev had steadily increased, and he was ready to agree heartily with Schmidt's appraisal.

Armed with a letter of introduction from Schmidt, Boyesen sought out Turgenev in Paris, in December, 1873. The Russian was won over by his ardor and enthusiasm just as Howells and Bjørnson had been. Turgenev had been in the depths of despair, suffering from what he called "Asiatic melancholy," when the young Norwegian American first went to see him. Boyesen's youthful admiration for his work cheered him and helped to drive away his depression. When they parted, Turgenev kissed him on both cheeks, saying, "You were my David; you played to me and the evil spirits departed." [37]

Boyesen's trip became a literary pilgrimage, but it is not clear just

---

[35] Boyesen to Fiske, September 21, 26, November 30, 1873. Dr. Julian Schmidt (1818–86) was a distinguished literary critic. He was coeditor (with the novelist Gustav Freytag) of the weekly review *Die Grenzboten: Zeitschrift für Politik, Literatur, und Kunst* (Leipzig). Schmidt's remark is in Boyesen's article in *Galaxy*, 17:456.

[36] Boyesen, in *Philadelphia Inquirer*, October 1, 1893.

[37] Boyesen, in *Galaxy*, 17:457; Barry, in *New York Illustrated American*, 17:179.

what his intention had been in making the journey. A visit to his family and friends in Norway — the triumphal return of a young man who was becoming a successful writer in his adopted country — may have been his chief motive.[38] The usual accounts of the trip stress the period of study in Leipzig, and Boyesen himself later encouraged the impression that he had gone to Europe "in order to study Germanic philology under the great masters Zarnoke and Hildebrand." Biographical sketches written during his lifetime speak of the year he spent at Leipzig; one interviewer made it a two-year stay! Yet Boyesen spent less than three months in Germany, and the University of Leipzig was in session during only one of those months. Although the projected visit to Italy did not materialize, he took time from his Leipzig studies to make an excursion to the Goethe and Schiller shrines at Weimar, and to spend a week or two of November in Dresden, where he visited Henrik Ibsen; and he left Leipzig early enough to allow time for stops in Strasbourg, Paris, and London before he embarked for America. After Boyesen's meeting with Turgenev, other events of the European tour faded into the background.[39]

---

[38] Boyesen's grandparents still had hopes of keeping him in Europe. A letter from his grandmother in the Boyesen Papers, dated November 27, 1873, bewails the news of his imminent return to the United States.

[39] Obituary in the student magazine, *Columbia Spectator* (New York), October 23, 1895; Barry, in *New York Illustrated American*, 17:179; Boyesen to Fiske, November 30, 1873; Boyesen, in *Galaxy*, 17:456.

3

The Cornell Years

WHEN Boyesen returned to the United States, he was more concerned about his literary projects than in getting off to a good start at Cornell. Before leaving Leipzig he had written to Dean Willard Fiske: "Hope then to reach New York about Jan 2nd, & shall be obliged to hasten on to Boston where I have some business matters (in regard to my book) to settle with Mr. Howells and Mr. Osgood. I shall do what I can to be at Ithaca in time for the opening of the term, & shall at all events not be more than one or two days late." Despite Boyesen's eagerness, Osgood did not hurry the publication of *Gunnar*. The book finally appeared in September, 1874, with a dedication "To Ivan S. Tourguéneff, with the love, gratitude, and reverence of the author." Boyesen later quoted his friend's acknowledgment: "I have just finished the poetical little book you have had the kindness to dedicate to me. I have found the first chapter a little allegorical to my taste, but the more I read the more I relished your tale. 'Gunnar' is certainly a good beginning; it is full of freshness and originality."[1]

The spell of Turgenev hung over Boyesen during the first months at Cornell. In his college study an autographed picture of his great new friend was prominently displayed, together with French and German translations of Turgenev's works, gifts of the author. Boyesen's first magazine contribution after his return was "A Visit to Tourguéneff,"

[1] Boyesen to Fiske, November 30, 1873; Boyesen, in *Philadelphia Inquirer*, October 1, 1893.

published in the *Galaxy* of April, 1874. As the title implies, the article is the report of a literary pilgrimage, an informal enthusiastic account of Turgenev's personality, ideas, and literary creed.

Boyesen did not let his valuable friendships grow cold. When it was impossible to make personal contacts, letters filled the gap. Writing to Howells from Ithaca on June 1, 1874, he reported on Turgenev's most recent letter. Another young American who was impressed by Turgenev was writing articles about him for American magazines. "He [*Turgenev*] says he was very much amused at all the aristocratic attributes with which H. James had honored him in the N[orth] Am[erican] R[eview] article." Boyesen added that he was forwarding to Turgenev, according to a promise, "the most remarkable productions of late American literature." Boyesen had designated Howells and Thomas Bailey Aldrich as "representatives of this new literary era." [2]

Boyesen wrote to Howells in the same letter, "One month more & I shall see you. The novel is progressing satisfactorily." Doubtless this novel was *A Norseman's Pilgrimage*. It was finished during the next few months, but Howells did not publish it in the *Atlantic*; the first installment appeared in the *Galaxy* in December, 1874.

Boyesen's reasons for bringing out the novel in the *Atlantic's* rival can be surmised. Osgood and Company did not publish *Gunnar* until eight months after its run in the *Atlantic* was completed, but the Sheldon Company, publishers of the *Galaxy*, brought out *A Norseman's Pilgrimage* in July, only two months after the last serial installment. Perhaps their dual offer of magazine and prompt book publication tempted Boyesen, whose eagerness to see his work in print can be observed in the letter to Howells from Leipzig. On the other hand, Howells was not eager to put out the new novel. Although *Gunnar* was an undoubted success, both as a serial and as a book, *A Norseman's Pilgrimage* was a much more hurried effort, and Howells would not have printed it without some reworking. It could not have been written until after the European trip, yet it began to run in the *Galaxy* less than a year after Boyesen's return. New duties at Cornell must have occupied most of his time

---

[2] Theodore Stanton, "Professor Boyesen at Cornell University," in *Open Court* (Chicago), 10:4813 (February 13, 1896); Boyesen to Howells, June 1, 1874. Royal A. Gettmann, in "Turgenev in England and America," *Illinois Studies in Language and Literature*, 27:80, 103 (Urbana, 1941), is impressed by James's articles, not at all by Boyesen's. Thomas Bailey Aldrich (1836–1907), poet, essayist, and novelist, succeeded Howells as editor of the *Atlantic Monthly*.

during the school year, leaving only the summer months for concentrated work on the novel. *A Norseman's Pilgrimage* shows haste, even to the extent of careless proofreading.³

In spite of the demands of Boyesen's new teaching position and the pressure of work on his novel, he found time for other writing. His magazine output from 1874 to 1876 was varied and considerable. Three essays on the German romantic movement came out in the *Atlantic*, and seven of his reviews appeared unsigned in the *Atlantic* and in the *North American Review*. The *Galaxy* used two poems, the Turgenev article and the serialized *A Norseman's Pilgrimage;* and three more appeared in the *Atlantic* and in *Scribner's Monthly*. *Scribner's* became Boyesen's chief outlet, using five of his short stories during this period. These, with a sixth story which had come out in the *Atlantic*, were collected into *Tales from Two Hemispheres*, published by Osgood late in 1876; and when the Osgood firm failed, Charles Scribner's Sons took over Boyesen's copyrights and brought out new editions of *Gunnar* and *Tales from Two Hemispheres*.⁴

Boyesen later described his friendship with Dr. J. G. Holland, editor of *Scribner's Monthly* from its beginning in 1870 until his death in 1881: "He . . . welcomed me to the pages of his magazine with a kindness and courtesy which I shall never forget. I spent a summer with him at Bar Harbor in 1876. We took long walks together, discussed literary plans and he showed an interest in my work all out of proportion to its merits." But Holland was primarily a moralist, not an artist, and Boyesen did not agree with his opinions. In 1877 he wrote, "Dr. Holland is a good friend of mine in spite of the disparity in years, but unfortunately in our literary tastes we are greatly at variance." Boyesen put more value on the criticism of *Scribner's* associate editor, Richard Watson Gilder, who performed most of the editorial functions of the magazine, and added, "He and his charming, intelligent wife completed the work of identifying me with American life."⁵

---

³ Financial necessity, plus an eagerness to get this novel into print, may have impelled Boyesen to sell *A Norseman's Pilgrimage* to the first publisher who would take it as it was. There is some evidence that Boyesen started it before his European trip.

⁴ See the bibliography at the end of this volume for a chronological listing of Boyesen's magazine contributions during these years.

⁵ Stedman, in *Detroit Sunday News-Tribune*, April 8, 1894; Boyesen to Cable, March 17, 1877. Josiah Gilbert Holland (1819–81), poet, novelist, editor, and moralist, was associated with Samuel Bowles on the *Springfield* (Massachusetts) *Repub-*

The Cornell Years

Boyesen's regard for Scribner's as a publishing firm is shown in his recommendation to George Washington Cable in 1879: "The Scribner's are in my opinion the best & fairest firm in the U.S. & their semi-annual statements are absolutely reliable. You know an author has no way of controlling his publisher & if he falls into the hands of sharpers (of which there are several in the publishing business) he is completely at their mercy. It is therefore of the utmost importance to select a reliable firm (or to be selected by one) at the outset whereby a thousand inconveniences will be spared one. I can assure you that the Scribner's are such a firm."[6]

Boyesen's position at Cornell led to a friendship with an illustrious American literary figure, Bayard Taylor, who was a nonresident lecturer on the special faculty of North European languages. Taylor had been in Leipzig in 1873, examining the Hirzel Goethe collection; but Boyesen, who failed to gain the same privilege, had not dared to approach him. They finally met in the autumn of 1874, and when Taylor went to Cornell to give his 1874–75 lectures they became fast friends. The young professor was impressed by Taylor's ability to recite poetry by the hour, in many languages. When Boyesen forgot his lines while quoting Tegnér's *Fritiof's Saga* in Swedish, Taylor finished the passage for him. Boyesen was also impressed by Taylor's translation of *Faust* in the original meters. In a general evaluation made in later years he rated it the best translation of Goethe into English.[7]

When Taylor returned to Cornell the next year to deliver his lecture series, he found Boyesen at work on his first scholarly book, *Goethe and Schiller*. Boyesen, who knew that Taylor was writing a biography of Goethe, modestly insisted that he was not to be considered a rival; but Taylor urged him to have confidence in himself, and offered his help. From then on they corresponded frequently about Goethe.[8]

---

lican until he became editor of *Scribner's Monthly*. Richard Watson Gilder (1844–1909) was an assistant editor of *Scribner's Monthly* from 1870–81, when it was succeeded by the *Century*. As editor of the new magazine, he was an acknowledged aesthetic and social leader, and the *Century* was probably the best "family" magazine during the great age of American periodicals.

[6] Boyesen to Cable, August 26, 1879.

[7] Boyesen, "Reminiscences of Bayard Taylor," in *Lippincott's Magazine*, 24:209–216 (August, 1879), and *Essays on German Literature*, 119 (New York, 1892).

[8] Boyesen, in *Lippincott's Magazine*, 24:211. Taylor's *Studies in German Literature* appeared in New York in 1879, the year after his death, but he did not write a biography of Goethe. Boyesen's *Goethe and Schiller: Their Lives and Works, Including a Commentary on Goethe's Faust* was published in New York in 1879.

Hjalmar Hjorth Boyesen

To Howells, Bjørnson, Turgenev, and Bayard Taylor, Boyesen was the ambitious young author honored by the friendship of famous men of letters. But when he wrote George Washington Cable February 18, 1877, it was Boyesen who was the established author offering to help a new and comparatively unknown writer. He had admired Cable's early magazine stories in *Scribner's*, and when Richard W. Gilder told him that Cable was working on a novel, Boyesen offered his assistance. Cable sent him a sketch of his plot, and Boyesen replied enthusiastically: "The magnificence of the material for your novel quite dazzled me. . . . You have such a superb grip on reality . . . & still you are so far removed from being a mere dry, materialistic photographer of actual events." In November Boyesen announced that he had talked to Dr. Holland, who hoped that Cable's book would be sent to him as soon as it was finished. When this novel, *The Grandissimes*, appeared two years later, Boyesen reviewed it in *Scribner's*.[9]

Boyesen had performed his service to Cable as a friend rather than as a literary critic. Remembering his own struggles, he gave Cable the sympathy, admiration, and encouragement he needed. Like Boyesen, Cable desperately wanted to see his stories in book form, but Scribner's declined to take the risk of publishing a volume by a little-known writer. Only after Boyesen, as an established Scribner's author, guaranteed the publishers against loss did they agree to bring out *Old Creole Days* in 1879. Cable did not learn of his friend's generosity until two years later.[10]

Cornell University was only seven years old when Boyesen went there in 1874, and the new professor looked at the institution with a critical eye. Although his lecture room in South Building offered a fine view over Lake Cayuga, Boyesen recalled (in 1889) a less lovely impression: "The writer can well remember the time, not so very remote, when the campus was an ungraded, rough-looking hilltop, surmounted by three ugly barracks of gray sandstone." In the spring "the clayey roads were rivers of mud," and it was not uncommon for a professor to arrive at his classroom thoroughly bespattered.[11]

---

[9] Boyesen to Cable, February 18, March 17, November 24, 1877. Boyesen's review appeared in *Scribner's Monthly*, 21:159–161 (November, 1880). On Cable, see chapter 1, footnote 10.

[10] Boyesen to Cable, January 8, 1878, August 26, 1879.

[11] Boyesen, "Cornell University," in *Cosmopolitan* (New York), 8:60–66 (November, 1889).

The Cornell Years

The new university drew a strange collection of students and professors during its first years, Boyesen thought, including "not a few of the all-pervasive species, the American crank." Such odd specimens were gradually eliminated, though when it came to turning away students there was always opposition from old Ezra Cornell. The founder felt strongly that anyone, whatever his preparation, could profit by a college education and should have an opportunity at Ithaca. Boyesen was dubious about another matter: A student who spent half a day plowing, and attended classes the other half, was likely to fall asleep over his books. The idiosyncrasies of both university and founder are sharply satirized in *The Mammon of Unrighteousness*, although, in a magazine article published two years earlier, Boyesen treats Ezra Cornell with kindness and respect.[12]

One kind of educational pioneering—the scientific courses offered at Ithaca—appealed to Boyesen. He had begun his own study of science at the Norwegian national university, and he was pleased to discover that Cornell had some outstanding teachers in the field, including an authority on Darwin. When his own duties permitted, he attended lectures in the science department. Boyesen's admiration for Darwin had irritated Hans Christian Andersen when they met in 1873: "He [*Andersen*] had heard of Darwin and took him to be a very absurd and insignificant crank who believed that he was descended from a monkey." The patronizing tone is understandable; when Boyesen wrote an article on Hans Christian Andersen, he was careful to identify himself as a realist: "My intimate acquaintance with Bjørnson and Tourguéneff has greatly influenced my views of life; but still more the course of scientific study I took up while I was Professor of German Literature at Cornell. I dare say I am, without being a scientific specialist, fairly abreast of the scientific thought of the day, because I believe that no man can ignore it without a very great detriment to his intellectual life."[13]

The department of North European languages included German, and all of Boyesen's teaching was in that field: advanced courses in literature and in *Faust*, and some freshman and sophomore classes. Cornell also offered Swedish and Icelandic, as well as Gothic and Old and Mid-

---

[12] Boyesen, *The Mammon of Unrighteousness*, 5–51 (New York, 1891); Boyesen, in *Cosmopolitan*, 8:60–66.

[13] Boyesen, "An Acquaintance with Hans Christian Andersen," in *Century*, 43:787 (March, 1892); "H.H.B.," in *Book Buyer*, 3:343.

Hjalmar Hjorth Boyesen

dle High German, but these were taught by Dean Fiske or other members of the department.[14]

A student impression of Boyesen was recorded by Theodore Stanton, who attended the university from 1872 to 1877. Stanton wrote his sketch in 1874, when he was a sophomore, and published it twenty years later, almost exactly as it had been set down: "'H.H.' [*Helen Hunt Jackson*] once expressed surprise that the author of 'Gunnar' could find the atmosphere of Cornell University congenial.[15] But like many others, who form their opinion concerning this institution without visiting it, the gifted poetess does not know that there is that about the young, free University on Cayuga Lake which exactly chimes in with the fresh liberal soul of Boyesen. The grand scenery about Ithaca, the many-sided sermons at Sage Chapel, the equality of scientific and literary studies, the union in one faculty of men of letters and men of science, the mingling in the college world of a body of intelligent and cultivated women, a close association of students and professors, and everywhere a general spirit of freedom and independence,— all this produces an atmosphere not to be found perhaps in any other university center in America, an atmosphere just suited to the intellectual lungs of the Norse novelist."

"Boyesen the professor does not differ materially from Boyesen the author," said Stanton. "An aesthetic nature, enthusiasm, refined humor and great breadth of mind crop out in his lectures as well as in his romances." He was one of the few teachers who could "make grammar secondary to the poetry of speech. . . . He is all life and his enthusiasm is contagious." The student's hero-worshipping effusion made Boyesen a professorial paragon: "Professor Boyesen's liberalism also displays itself in the lecture-room, but never in a way to offend the most conservative of his hearers. Though a zealous republican in politics, he is not a Jingo; though a reformer, he is not a fanatic; though an independent thinker in religion, he is not an atheist; and in literature and art, while a worshipper of the beautiful, he is not a defender of artistic immorality. Broad-minded but not extreme in any of his views, his lecture room is pervaded by an air that strengthens, enlarges, and elevates the mental and moral nature." Finally, Stanton spoke of Boye-

---

[14] Boyesen to Fiske, November 8, 1879, May 2, 1880. See also Larson, *The Changing West*, 92; Cornell University catalogues, 1874–80.

[15] Helen Hunt Jackson (1831–85) is best known for her romance about the California Indians, *Ramona* (1884). Mrs. Jackson published many poems in the *Atlantic Monthly* and other periodicals during the 1870's.

The Cornell Years

sen's "artistic faculty," which involved "not only an innate love of the beautiful, but also a technical acquaintance with the fine arts." This "critical knowledge" he had acquired from friends in Norway and in European galleries. Boyesen once considered becoming an art critic, said Stanton.[16]

In Boyesen's letters, references to fellow faculty members reveal close friendships and strong antipathies. He liked men with broad interests. He was particularly close to Dean Willard Fiske, and this relationship continued after both men severed connections with Cornell. His admiration for President Andrew D. White was evidently reciprocated, and their relations were not strained by Boyesen's dissatisfaction with Ithaca and with his position at the college. Other friends were Hiram Corson and Charles C. Shackford, who taught English literature and rhetoric, Thomas F. Crane, professor of Italian and Spanish, and Burt G. Wilder, professor of comparative anatomy and zoology.

Boyesen's friendships reveal his strong preference for modern languages, modern literature, and all branches of science, and an antipathy toward classical studies and philology, especially in their narrower, more traditional aspects. He considered the other members of his own department to be mere pedants. More than two years after he had left Cornell, when faculty rivalry could not have influenced him, he offered his opinion of one member, W. H. Hewett: "His mind is peculiarly unelastic, unprogressive, incapable of taking large views of anything. He is certainly in no sense a talented man."[17]

Boyesen's financial burdens were lightened in June, 1874, when his brother Ingolf graduated from Northwestern University and found a good position in Chicago. Shortly thereafter, the younger brother, Alf, also became self-supporting.[18] By 1876 Hjalmar Boyesen felt he was at last free to give his time exclusively to writing. Then a new financial burden descended on his shoulders. His father announced that he could no longer endure the climate of Norway (supporting this with medical

---

[16] Stanton's remarks are taken from his article in *Open Court*, 10:4812–4814. In the Boyesen Papers there are notes for a series of lectures on European painters.

[17] Professor Hewett was chairman of the department of North European languages, 1883–1910. The quotation is from Boyesen to Fiske, November 26, 1882. See also Boyesen to Fiske, August 21, 1878–November 26, 1882; Andrew D. White's letters to Boyesen, Boyesen Papers.

[18] Ingolf Boyesen was a prominent lawyer in Chicago for many years; Alf Boyesen practiced law in Fargo, North Dakota, 1880–87, and later in St. Paul, Minnesota. See O. N. Nelson, *History of the Scandinavians in the United States*, 1:348 (Minneapolis, 1893).

Hjalmar Hjorth Boyesen

opinion) and said that he wanted to emigrate. "His life was virtually laid in my hand," his son wrote Cable. After Hjalmar's mother died, Captain Boyesen had married a young girl and now had a second family of eight small children. The entire ménage became Hjalmar's responsibility, and he was forced to borrow money to bring them all to America.

The transfer of the Sarolf Boyesen family to the United States was difficult for everyone concerned. "I went to Virginia & bought some land," Boyesen wrote to Cable, "intending to build & renting in the meanwhile a vacant house. The family arrived, but found that the climate did not agree with them. They were all taken very ill except father, & two of the children died. Again an appeal was made to me & I was obliged to provide another home for them. I then bought a property near Vineland, New Jersey, and have been struggling hard and long to pay for it. Of course I had to run into debt, but next month [*February, 1878*] I shall have the satisfaction of paying off the last cent. Thus vanished my long cherished dream of independence & a purely literary life — I have almost to support the whole family; father has, as a retired officer of the Norwegian army, a small pension ($400); but for so large a household it is of course entirely insufficient." [19]

Boyesen shared this concern with his friends, as his correspondence shows. The physical strain undermined his robust health, and the financial pinch became obvious to his associates. Many years later, one of his half sisters said that her brother gained an undeserved reputation for being "stingy and close" because of his extreme self-sacrifice during these years: "He assumed responsibilities which other members of the family refused to assume. He bought a farm and home for the family and contributed what he could to maintain it. He was a dutiful son and kind brother. He was interested in the education of his younger sisters and brothers and he did all he could to contribute to their welfare." [20]

Boyesen became professor of German literature in 1877, retaining his assistant professorship in North European languages. The new title, which more accurately described the services he performed, indicated that his talents were recognized, for he now outranked two assistant professors who had been in the department longer than he. But he told Cable that he received the full professorship and a raise in salary to $1,500 a year only because he threatened to resign. Even with the ad-

[19] Boyesen to Cable, January 20, 1878.
[20] Austa Boyesen to Laurence M. Larson, December 6, 1936.

The Cornell Years

vancement, he was not satisfied for very long, though he knew that the whole faculty was underpaid, their salaries being geared to the inadequate income of the university. Every year, Cornell University graduated students who were soon earning more than their former instructors, he complained. "If the university expects to have its professors feel any loyalty for the institution, it must once and for all abandon this stepsisterly treatment, & learn to think less of brick and mortar & more of brains," he complained to Willard Fiske. But his protests were also prompted by confidence in himself. He was convinced, in the seventies, that he was destined for a more important role than that of teacher, although he rated himself a superior scholar and lecturer. He told Cable that he had accepted his professorship as a "temporary expedient." His resentment of Cornell was doubtless increased by the feeling that his services were neither fully appreciated nor properly compensated.[21]

In 1877 Boyesen thought he saw an opportunity to move to Harvard. That he had faith in his own abilities and in the scholarly book he was writing on Goethe and Schiller is made clear in a letter to Howells of October 30:

"I am informed that Dr. Hedge has resigned his professorship at Harvard & write to you to ask if you will allow me to refer to you as one who has known me long & intimately & would be willing to second my efforts as a candidate for the place left vacant by his resignation. I have already written to Mr. [Henry Wadsworth] Longfellow in regard to this matter & have obtained from him a very favorable answer. I have, as yet, had no communication with President [Charles W.] Eliot & hardly know whether it would be proper for me to send in an application to him, before knowing that he would be disposed to look favorably upon my candidacy. . . . I have during the two past years been slowly accumulating material for a volume on Goethe, Schiller & Lessing (containing also a commentary of Faust) & have now about half finished it. This is the reason for my long silence in the magazines. Osgood & Co. will publish the book in March or April uniformly with Stedman's 'Victorian Poets.' I have no hesitation in saying that it will be a thorough &, as I think, creditable piece of work, upon which I hope to found my reputation for scholarship in my special department.[22]

---

[21] Boyesen to Cable, January 20, 1878; Boyesen to Fiske, November 8, 1879. See also Larson, *The Changing West*, 92–94.

[22] Frederic Henry Hedge (1805–90) was a Unitarian clergyman, and professor in the Harvard Divinity School. He is credited with introducing the New England

Hjalmar Hjorth Boyesen

"For the last six years I have been devoting myself to the study of Germanic philology and literature & should be more than willing to enter into a competitive examination with any other candidate who would be disposed to enter the lists against me. That system, however, is not yet inaugurated, so, of course, it is out of the question. The prospect (vague as it is) of living near you & being able to discuss my literary plans with you & profit by your maturer judgment fills me with delight whenever I think of it. It is a matter of such vital importance to me, that it seems as if everything depended upon its success. I hope you will have no scruples in recommending me. . . . I am aware that I am writing you a very egotistical sort of letter; but you see the occasion calls for it."

This appeal was answered promptly. Although Howells was in no position to judge or recommend his friend as a scholar, he was willing to testify that Boyesen was a man "of philological genius," who had adopted a foreign language and made it his own, a phenomenon that occurs only once or twice in a generation. "Your English," Howells continued, "I consider to be little short of inspiration & I think your scholarship ought to be largely judged by the beauty & strength of your English style. . . . But if these college presidents ask me about your German I can only say that a man who can write Mr. Boyesen's English must know all the German there is. At this point the testimony of Prof. Fiske ought to be your all sufficient support." Howells closed with the observation that Boyesen's reputation "would do honor to any university" and the hope that Harvard would "see her interest" in securing him.[23]

The day after Boyesen appealed to Howells, he wrote Bayard Taylor to enlist his aid in securing the Harvard appointment. Subsequently Boyesen expressed his thanks and explained the urgency of the cause: "I have so long been yearning for a wider sphere of labor & for the privilege of living in a more civilized community. If this fails I shall go to New York & turn Bohemian. Fiske is the only redeeming virtue of this place." The Harvard campaign failed, but not through any fault of Boyesen's friends. "I am very sorry to say there is no vacancy," Longfellow wrote on November 23, after calling on President Eliot. "I found

---

transcendentalists to German idealistic philosophy: the Transcendental Club was sometimes called the Hedge Club. Edmund Clarence Stedman (1833–1908), poet, essayist, and critic, is best known as an editor and anthologist. He was also a Wall Street broker. Boyesen's *Goethe and Schiller* was published in 1879.

[23] Howells to Boyesen, November 2, 1877.

the President well-informed about you; so that there is no fear of your being overlooked in case of any change." The old poet offered the same advice Howells had given when Boyesen was at Urbana five years before: "Meanwhile you must be patient, and 'embellish your Sparta,' or rather your Ithaca. . . . Your present position is so good that you would be very unwise to change, unless for some very decided advantage."[24]

Nevertheless, Boyesen was determined to leave Cornell; writing to Cable on January 20, 1878, he gave as the reason, besides dissatisfaction with Ithaca, his impaired health. In December, 1877, he began to be troubled by sleeplessness. The doctors told him he must give up evening work, which meant he would have to abandon his writing. "This," said Boyesen, "I cannot and will not do." He chose the alternative: resigning his professorship. "I am happy to think I shall be forced to cut loose at last," he wrote Cable.[25]

Howells was disappointed with this decision and even more disturbed at Boyesen's announcement that he was going to New York to make his living entirely by his writing: "Why the desertion of Ithaca the fair? And why New York? I can understand your wanting to leave Ithaca, but not your wanting to go to New York."[26]

Boyesen's plan was to travel in Europe for a year before establishing himself in New York as a free-lance writer. He would be out of debt and free of pressing obligations by February, 1878, he had told Cable. He did not foresee any other complications: "You have a wife, a home & children of your own to work for; I have not & probably never shall have." Boyesen expected to finance the trip with the Goethe and Schiller volume, which was nearing completion, and with a new novel, *Falconberg*, which was ready for serialization in *Scribner's*. Furthermore, the European journey would yield material for magazine articles, even though the goal was rest and recuperation:

"I am obliged on account of my health to take a year of comparative leisure & have thought the best thing I could do would be to go to Europe. Here there is ambition in the air; a thousand plots and projects

---

[24] Boyesen to Taylor, October 31, November 11, 1877, Cornell University Library. Longfellow's letter is in the Boyesen Papers.

[25] Presumably Hjalmar Boyesen felt that his father could support himself and his second family on the farm near Vineland, New Jersey, where Captain Boyesen lived after his arrival in America.

[26] Howells to Boyesen, February 1, 1878. Howells later had a change of heart; he himself moved to New York in 1882.

would be ever haunting me & I should be at work as hard as ever. There idleness is not only respectable but highly honorable; a dignified ancestral laziness is transmitted from generation to generation with a sort of perceptible *crescendo*. Once at an aristocratic ball in Germany I actually felt ashamed of my industrious habits; I felt that intellect on the whole was disreputable. This is the feeling I am going in search of again; if I could once more attain to it, it would be a great boon to me — temporarily. I want to come back, a fine animal, to apply the animal vigor I shall have stored up to the tasks I shall now leave unfinished. — The most exasperating thing with me is that I still look as healthy as a bull & when I hint that I am unable to sleep, my friends are apt to laugh at me right to my face." [27]

But once again, just as Boyesen felt that he had cleared away the obstacles in his path, a complication arose to change his course. He broke the momentous news to Howells on March 10, 1878:

"I am engaged to a very beautiful young lady in New York, whose name is Elizabeth M. Keen. I shall not undertake to describe her to you in writing — it would require all the richness & glow of diction & all the splendor of epithet of which my pen is capable to do her justice. However, I should have small respect for that man's opinion, even if he were my most valued friend, who did not concede that she is divinely beautiful. She has all the grace and perfection of taste which distinguishes the real New Yorkeress (Pardon the violation of Webster); & is otherwise a sweet, unaffected & true-hearted girl. Has seen a good deal of fashionable society, but has not at all been spoiled by it. She is now twenty-two years old. I expect to be married, if nothing prevents, some time during the summer (probably in July) & our present intention, which may, however have to be revised, is to start immediately for Europe. I need not tell you that I have set my heart on having you present at the wedding. I cannot consent to listen to a refusal. You know I owe you so much already & this would be the crowning deed of your long series of friendly acts toward me. You are in part responsible for me, as I am, — I mean in my literary capacity; & I hope in time to prove myself worthy of your literary paternity. At all events you will never have occasion to be ashamed of me.

"I feel, at present, as if I could move mountains; & not by faith either, but by sheer force of muscle. . . . I have just finished that part of my

---

[27] Boyesen to Cable, January 20, 1878.

The Cornell Years

new book which relates to Goethe & commenced to struggle with Schiller. I am in much better condition for imaginative writing at present; but am obliged to finish this work before the vacation. The publication has been postponed until September or October. I should be very grateful if you could find time to write me a real letter, as you used to do in my literary infancy while I was groping about in the Egyptian darkness of Urbana. I have been re-reading some of those delightful epistles of late, & I cannot describe to you the pleasure they gave me."

Boyesen had been fascinated by the young ladies he met in the social circles of New York and Boston, Bar Harbor, and Newport. Their vivacity and independence set them far above the demure European girls he had known. He himself must have been an attractive escort. His appearance, with his curly red-blond hair and beard and blue eyes, his European manners, and his growing fame as a writer, made him a dashing and perhaps a romantic figure. There were at least two other girls who interested him before he met Elizabeth Keen. One was William Dean Howells' sister Annie, whom he met in Cambridge and may have visited later in Jefferson, Ohio; but Annie Howells married in 1877. The other is a more mysterious figure. There is a story in the Boyesen family that Hjalmar was engaged to a Longfellow girl who died, and that his "Elegy on A.G.L.," dated December 15, 1876, is a tribute to her.[28]

When Boyesen met Elizabeth Keen can only be guessed, but he had known her for at least a year before they married. The wistful reference, in his January 20, 1878, letter, to Cable's wife, home, and children may mean that Boyesen was discouraged about the success of his own suit; or possibly he felt that he had to discharge his own family obligations before he could propose marriage. Two months later, when he was free of debt, he announced his engagement.

Elizabeth Morris Keen came of an old Philadelphia family. Her parents had moved to Chicago, where her father, William Keen, owned the city's first large bookstore. In the seventies her parents were divorced, and Mrs. Keen took the two daughters to the East to give them the "advantage of New York society." They scorned "the stock-yards aristocracy of Chicago." Lillie Keen had been brought up as "a millionaire's

---

[28] See Austa Boyesen to Laurence M. Larson, April 19, May 3, June 24, 1936, on this story. The poem was published in *Scribner's Monthly*, 13:666 (March, 1877), and reprinted in Boyesen, *Idyls of Norway*, 8–10 (New York, 1882). The authorship of unsigned pieces by Boyesen has been determined by evidence found in his correspondence.

Hjalmar Hjorth Boyesen

daughter." She was accustomed to wealth and "good society," but, as Boyesen's letter to Howells showed, he believed that a girl with such a background could still be "sweet and unaffected." To him Lillie Keen must have embodied all the brilliant qualities that he so admired in the American girl. Her graces were to be reflected in dozens of Boyesen heroines to come, heroines unfailingly beautiful and intelligent but, sadly, sometimes spoiled and willful.[29]

A month after Boyesen broke the news to Howells, he wrote exuberantly to Cable, inviting him to the wedding: "You are very intimately identified with the progress of our love. I used to read your stories aloud to her last year & I doubt if they were ever read with a greater intensity of meaning. Now this marvelous girl . . . feels very grateful to you & wishes to be most kindly remembered to you." [30]

The date was set for June 27, and it was to be "a fine & select affair, no crowd, but almost all men of letters & personal friends: W. D. Howells, Chas. D. Warner, Gilder, G. P. Lathrop, etc." The trip abroad, planned as one of recuperation, was converted into a wedding journey. "I am going to start for Europe with my beautiful bride July 13," Boyesen told Cable.[31] He did not resign his Cornell post, but took a year's leave of absence.

The Goethe and Schiller volume was in the hands of the printers before the Boyesens sailed from New York. The preface is dated "Ithaca, June 16, 1878." The honeymooning couple made Berlin their "unpicturesque first stopping place" in Europe so that Bayard Taylor, now minister to Germany, could look over the proofs of the new book. The Boyesens met him in August. German burghers living on "the unfashionable street" where the newly married couple had their "Bohemian headquarters" were tremendously impressed, Boyesen reported, when a splendid (though rented) carriage drove up and the imposing American minister handed Mrs. Boyesen into the vehicle. Taylor insisted on reading the proofs of *Goethe and Schiller*, although he was seriously ill

---

[29] The quotations are from Austa Boyesen to Larson, December 6, 1936.
[30] Boyesen to Cable, April 16, 1878.
[31] Boyesen to Cable, May 29, 1878. Charles Dudley Warner (1829–1900) is best known for his collaboration with Mark Twain on the novel *The Gilded Age* (1873) and as editor of the *American Men of Letters Series*. George Parsons Lathrop (1851–98) was associate editor of the *Atlantic Monthly* (1875–77) and of other publications; he wrote fifteen travel books and novels. He edited his father-in-law's writings, *The Complete Works of Nathaniel Hawthorne, with Introductory Notes* (Boston, 1883).

when the Boyesens took their leave of him at the American legation in Berlin on October 13, 1878.[32]

During the last two weeks of October the Boyesens were at Leipzig, where the professor "investigated" the university. They spent most of November in Munich. Paul Heyse, the German novelist and poet, gave a large party for them, at which "all the literary men of Munich were present." Boyesen also reported a day spent at Gotha with Gustav Freytag, a brief stop at Weimar to see the Goethe and Schiller collection again, and a few days at Jena, where he gathered material for an article on German student life. Late in November they crossed the Brenner Pass into Italy, and stopped briefly at Verona, Venice, Bologna, and Florence. In Rome on December 1, 1878, Boyesen wrote the sonnet "To Bayard Taylor," which he used as the dedication of *Goethe and Schiller*. Three weeks later the news came that Taylor was dead.[33]

The couple remained in Rome until March, when they went to Naples for two weeks. From the middle of March until June they were in Paris. Boyesen did some writing — articles, short stories, and at least one review for *Scribner's* — but the European trip doubtless gave him the rest he needed. The fiction he wrote during the next ten years shows that he was also accumulating background material for a number of short stories and novels with settings in Paris, Rome, or one of the German cities.[34]

In Paris Boyesen renewed his acquaintance with Turgenev, and through him met Daudet, the De Goncourts, Renan, Zola, and Victor Hugo. He presented some of his American friends to Turgenev. Among them was Samuel Clemens, who made a strong impression on the Russian: "Now, there," he said, "is a real American — the first American who has had the kindness to conform to my idea of what an American ought to be. He has the flavor of the soil. Your other friends, Mr. A.

---

[32] Boyesen, in *Lippincott's Magazine*, 24:212–216.

[33] Boyesen to Fiske, December 4, 1878; Boyesen, in *Lippincott's Magazine*, 24:216. Paul Heyse (1830–1914) is best known for his highly polished short stories, published in a series of *Novellen* (Tales), and for his novel, *Kinder der Welt* (1873). His "children of the world" are troubled about nineteenth-century materialism and social change. Gustav Freytag (1816–95) made his reputation with *Soll und Haben* (Debit and Credit — 1855), a novel of business success that was achieved through German diligence and hard work. See Boyesen, *Essays on German Literature*, 240–263 (New York, 1892). Boyesen became a special pleader in the United States for the German "sociological fiction" being written by Heyse, Freytag, Friedrich Spielhagen, Theodor Storm, Berthold Auerbach, and Gottfried Keller.

[34] Boyesen to Fiske, February 16, April 24, 1879.

and Mr. G., might as well be Europeans. They are excellent gentlemen, no doubt, but they are flavorless." [35]

The presence of Samuel and Mrs. Clemens in Paris at this particular time was welcomed for another reason. Lillie was pregnant, and her health, never robust, was a matter of grave concern to her husband. The expectant father was uneasy, as he wrote Fiske from Paris on April 24: "As the time approaches, my anxiety increases, & I shall not breathe freely until the grand event is well over, & all doubt as to the result removed. It is a great comfort to me that Mrs. Clemens will probably remain here until the latter part of July. She is a dear & trusted friend, & Lillie & she are very fond of each other. But, pardon me, I forget that I am writing to a bachelor who can have little sympathy with my present apprehensions. Mark Twain is an inexhaustible mine in that respect (I mean of sympathy), but I have pity on him & say nothing. I find him a capital fellow & see a good deal of him."

In Rome the doctors had advised Mrs. Boyesen to put off the Atlantic crossing as long as possible. It was June before the Boyesens arrived in the United States. Hjalmar Hjorth, Jr., was born in Ithaca on July 7.[36]

The anxiety Boyesen showed for his wife was justified. She had been ill often during her pregnancy, and she nearly died when the child was born. For weeks afterwards she remained in grave danger, and Boyesen was convinced that the baby would not live. Lillie recovered in time, although she was never entirely well again; but the child was soon lusty and strong.[37]

Boyesen had talked of leaving Cornell because he wished to give all his time to writing. He had been deterred by the uncertainties of an income derived solely from that source while he was supporting his broth-

---

[35] Alphonse Daudet (1840–97) was the most tender and charming of the French naturalists, and as a result was widely read in England and America in his day. Edmond (1822–96) and Jules (1830–70) de Goncourt, who were collaborators, are often called the "inventors" of the naturalistic novel, partly because their *Germinie Lecerteux* (1865) antedates Zola. Ernest Renan (1823–92), philologist, historian, and critic, is best known for his rationalistic *Life of Jesus* (1863). Émile Zola (1840–1902) was the chief French naturalist. In the twenty novels of his *Rougon-Macquart* series he undertook to trace the natural and social history of a French family. Victor Hugo (1802–85), poet, novelist, dramatist, and critic, was the foremost champion of romanticism in his day. Turgenev's remarks are quoted in Boyesen, "The Plague of Jocularity," in *North American Review*, 161:532 (November, 1895). "Mr. A." was probably Thomas Bailey Aldrich and "Mr. G.," Richard Watson Gilder.

[36] Boyesen to Fiske, July 27, 1879.

[37] Boyesen to Fiske, February 16, July 27, 1879; Boyesen to Howells, April 2, 1880.

The Cornell Years

ers and later his father. Now that he was married, the need for steady earnings was still greater, but at the same time the pressure to leave Cornell also increased. He felt almost compelled to make the move to New York and to gamble on a career as a free-lance writer.

His dissatisfaction with Ithaca was encouraged by his wife, who was strongly prejudiced against it even before she went there to live. She convinced her husband that the climate of Ithaca was injurious to her health. Furthermore, the Boyesens were unable to live on the salary of $1,500 paid by Cornell, and the professor complained, "I am working myself to death by writing in order to make what I need to support my family." Lillie wanted to live in New York ("All her family and friends are there"), and she urged her husband to give up a position which promised nothing better than "respectable poverty." [38]

Boyesen's own ties with the university had been greatly weakened. The men whom he had most admired and respected at Cornell were in Europe in 1879 and 1880. President White had succeeded Bayard Taylor as minister to Germany, and Dean Fiske was in Italy because of his health. Boyesen was not on good terms with the interim administration: He considered that he was the ranking member of the department of North European languages, but Vice-President Russel, whom he and many other faculty members disliked, would not recognize this. Even before the 1879–80 academic year began, Boyesen had informed Fiske that he did not propose to be superseded by anyone who was his junior in service or rank. This meant, in effect, that he would not willingly serve under anyone but Fiske. As he said later, "I dislike even the appearance of working under —— [*MacKoon*]." [39] He resigned his position in the spring of 1880.

[38] Boyesen to Fiske, November 8, 1879.

[39] Boyesen to Fiske, July 27, November 8, 1879, May 2, 1880. Bela P. MacKoon was acting chairman of the department. Boyesen maintained that his own appointment as full professor came two years before MacKoon's. William Channing Russel was vice-president of the university, associate professor of history, and professor of South European languages; information furnished by Dean Thomas W. Mackesey of Cornell.

4

Gunnar
to *Falconberg*

BOYESEN'S first book, *Gunnar*, was an immediate success. During its serialization in the *Atlantic Monthly*, July – December, 1873, the story was mentioned favorably by newspaper critics; Boyesen was obviously elated by the notices Howells sent him while he was in Leipzig during September, 1873. A year later, when James Osgood and Company published *Gunnar* in book form, it was equally well received by the magazine reviewers. Scribner's, which took over Boyesen's copyrights from Osgood, brought out a new edition in 1880. Other editions continued to appear, the seventh in 1888 and the tenth in 1903.[1]

This first novel is the least interesting and yet the most important of Boyesen's works. As an indication of the author's "natural" or "original" literary inclinations, *Gunnar* is significant; for it was written before he had met Howells or Turgenev, both of whom became his close friends and exerted a strong influence on his work. It could be argued that *Gunnar* was Boyesen's greatest success because it was the product of his particular genius, because he wrote it before he became self-conscious about the author's obligation to record contemporary life in its most typical aspects. Later he dissipated his early promise by attempting something that temperamentally he was unfitted for. He never tried to write another book like *Gunnar*. It is probable, moreover, that he could not have repeated the process after he became Americanized; besides,

---

[1] Charles Scribner's Sons became Boyesen's chief publisher after the Osgood firm failed.

he would not have betrayed his faith in realism by returning to a more popular romantic pattern.

But if *Gunnar* was merely a false start in the career of a determined realist, it was immensely important in shaping Boyesen's life. He said several times that the success of his first novel kept him in America, and it certainly gave impetus to his literary ambitions. The popularity of the book was unfortunate in some ways. With Boyesen's reputation made and a ready market for his work assured, he was encouraged to write too voluminously and too rapidly, to overvalue popular success, and to attach too much importance to the money that such success brought him.

In later years, when Boyesen spoke of *Gunnar*, he always stressed the conditions under which the book was written. It was the fruit of a young Norwegian's lonely first years in America and of a nostalgic love for his native land. *Gunnar* was unmistakably a product of the literary environment of his boyhood. One contemporary writer pointed out that its allegorical opening chapter showed the influence of Hans Christian Andersen. That the book owed much to Bjørnstjerne Bjørnson, Boyesen did not deny. His own nostalgia produced a softer, more romantic version of Norwegian peasant life than did Bjørnson's early country tales, such as *Synnøve Solbakken* (1857) or *Arne* (1859); but if Boyesen's picture was less authentic it was not less appealing to American readers. Yet the writing of this book and its subsequent success removed the peculiar conditions and state of mind which had produced it. Boyesen himself said that he could never again write anything that resembled *Gunnar*.[2]

This was perhaps Boyesen's most carefully written book. More than two years elapsed between the lonely first months at Urbana, when he prepared the preliminary draft of *Gunnar*, and the appearance of the serial version in the *Atlantic Monthly*. During the interval it was carefully revised under Howells' guidance. It is impossible to say just what the book owed to Howells; a certain maturation and polish conspicuously absent in later novels may be credited to the editor rather than to the author. After Boyesen's death, Howells singled out *Gunnar* and *The Mammon of Unrighteousness* (1891) as his friend's best works. It is significant that *Mammon* was the only other novel which Boyesen

---

[2] Boyesen, in *Philadelphia Inquirer*, October 1, 1893; "H.H.B.," in *Book Buyer*, 3:343; Heath, in *Scribner's Monthly*, 14:780 (October, 1877).

worked over for years instead of months, and that on this book, too, he sought and received Howells' aid and advice.[3]

Although *Gunnar* was well treated by all the reviewers, the *Atlantic Monthly's* critique, almost certainly written by Howells, was especially detailed and sympathetic. One argument betrayed Howells' bias: even though *Gunnar* was a romance, it emphasized character development, not plot complication. On some points the reviewers were in agreement. The book was a phenomenal achievement: "Mr. Boyesen's citizenship is as new as the last election." The style was simple, but graceful and poetic. The subject matter was fresh and original. So revealing was the *Atlantic* article, both as to the nature of Boyesen's story and the critical temper of the time, that the review should be examined at first hand:

"Among the works of fiction printed in the English language this year, there can hardly be any so remarkable in some aspects as the idyllic story which Mr. Boyesen tells us. It is not only remarkable for being a good story, which is distinction enough, but it ought to be known to everyone who takes it up as an achievement almost singular in letters. It is not a translation from the Norwegian, as one might guess, but is the English of a Norwegian, thinking and expressing himself in our tongue with a grace, simplicity, and force, and a sense of its colors and harmonies, which we should heartily praise in one native to it. Mr. Boyesen has proved his genius both for literature and for language. . . .

"We like his Gunnar because it is the work of a poet, and announces its origin in all characteristics. It is of that good school of which Bjørnstjerne Bjørnson is the head, and to which we have nothing answering, of English root. It is an idyllic sort of story which regards simple things naturally, but at the same time poetically. . . .

"Gunnar is not that sort of fiction in which the reader's interest is made to depend upon his uncertainty as to how it is all going to come out. It concerns itself with the development of an artistic mind as it gropes darkly upward through the narrow conditions of a peasant's life."[4]

The *Nation's* reviewer thought Boyesen had followed Bjørnson's *Arne* a little closely at one or two points, but a peasant boy's success story tended to follow a timeworn pattern and Boyesen did not seem to excel as a plot builder:

[3] Boyesen, in *Philadelphia Inquirer*, October 1, 1893; Howells, *Literary Friends*, 259.

[4] *Atlantic Monthly*, 34:624 (November, 1874).

"His string of a love-story is as artlessly planned as the rest of the work, and the reader is from the beginning justly inclined to accept it without making difficulties. For whenever a simple 'houseman's' son, who while yet a boy has formed an affection for a 'gardman's' (rich man's) daughter, is early found to have a talent for drawing on birch-bark, and to be unfit for executive power about the farm and barn-yard, it is as certain as anything that by-and-by the pastor will be pleased with his catechism lessons, will accidentally see some of his drawings, and will use his influence to have the youth sent to the capital, where he will soon carry off the Academy's first prize and come home an eligible suitor for Ragnhild or Eli."

The unusual thing about the review in the *Nation* was that it found a place for *Gunnar* in an American literary genre:

"Although kept by its subject-matter and by the author's Scandinavian birthright up to a good level, 'Gunnar' essentially resembles those New England tales and sketches of years ago in which on a slender twist of plot and narrative were strung accounts of cattlefairs, militia musters, election trainings, cornhuskings, 'evening meetings,' meetings of the Dorcas Society, turkey-shoots at Thanksgiving time, and numerous other scenes and humors of life Down East. Similar scenes, but Norwegian instead of American, are the staple of Mr. Boyesen's book."

The reviewer conceded that *Gunnar* was superior to such Yankee stories: "Mr. Boyesen brings to the execution of the work more spirit than our old-fashioned writers were accustomed to bring to their donation parties and town-meetings, and he has also the use of a vein of poetry which sometimes does him good service."[5]

Despite Boyesen's high hopes, expressed in a letter to Howells of September 27, 1873, Scandinavians in the Northwest were less enthusiastic about *Gunnar* than were literary critics of the East. Boyesen wrote to Professor Rasmus B. Anderson of the University of Wisconsin, March 28, 1874, "By the way, without reference to myself, why don't the Scand. papers devote some space to Literature. I mean reviews & notices; what they have at present is next to nothing." Anderson's reply must have been sympathetic, for on April 18 Boyesen wrote again: "Your remark about the Scandinavian papers leads me further to explain what I meant by what I said in my last letter, & I hope I dare confide this little grievance to you. It seemed to me somewhat strange that while

---

[5] *Nation*, 19:222 (October 1, 1874).

Hjalmar Hjorth Boyesen

The Nation, The N. Y. Tribune, The Boston Globe & in fact all the leading American papers comment favorably upon my writings & honor me with frequent reviews, the Scandinavian papers have so far entirely ignored my doings." [6]

Anderson offered to remedy the situation, and Boyesen wrote again on May 22: "I heartily thank you for your willingness to bring me before the Scandinavian public, & should unhesitatingly accept your proposition, if I were not afraid that it would look like an unwarrantable effort on my part. . . . 'Gunnar' I should hardly wish elaborately reviewed, until it appears in book form, which will be in a few months & if you will then introduce it to my countrymen, I shall feel under great obligation to you." By June 16, 1874, Anderson had contributed at least two articles about Boyesen and his work to *Skandinaven*, a Norwegian-American newspaper that came out of Chicago in daily, weekly, semi-weekly, and monthly editions.[7]

Some Norwegian-American reviewers dismissed the book as an imitation of Bjørnson, although Erik L. Petersen, the most competent critic among them, thought that the actual borrowings from him were slight. Boyesen's assertion that *Gunnar* was "bound to sell" among the 800,000 "American Norwegians" of the Northwest was ridiculous: In his enthusiasm he multiplied the number of Scandinavian immigrants in the United States. His remark also indicated how little he really knew about his fellow immigrants, with whom he had nothing in common. If these people wished to read about Norway, they preferred a book written in Norwegian. If sufficiently Americanized to read English easily, they looked to American subjects. And Norwegian immigrants, brought up on peasant idyls, were not impressed by the freshness and originality of the work.[8]

[6] Boyesen's letters to Anderson are in the State Historical Society of Wisconsin.
[7] See Gerald H. Thorson, "First Sagas in a New World: A Study of the Beginnings of Norwegian-American Literature," in *Norwegian-American Studies and Records*, 17:119–121 (1952).
[8] Petersen, who wrote for the Norwegian-language weekly *Budstikken* (Minneapolis), evaluated Boyesen's debt to Bjørnson in the issue dated December 21, 1880; cited in Larson, *The Changing West*, 99. Rasmus B. Anderson wrote of Boyesen in *Skandinaven*, June 16, 1874: "I would recommend his writings to all who can read English, but especially to those who disdain everything that is called 'Norwegian,' so that they could therefore learn that Norway has a saga, a literature, a song, and a nature that it is worth while to know and to love." Quoted by Thorson in *Studies and Records*, 17:121. On the number of Norwegians in the United States, see Qualey, *Norwegian Settlement*, 217–250.

Although Boyesen later turned away from this novel in theme and treatment, the continued popularity of this romance was a constant reminder of the prevailing taste in fiction. How much this factor retarded his progress toward more realistic writing cannot be determined, but *Gunnar's* success may explain why Boyesen's later work retained so many romantic elements while he was theoretically committed to realism. A paragraph in *Scribner's* "Culture and Progress" department, announcing a new edition of *Gunnar*, reveals the kind of influence it represented: "It was this delightful little idyl of Norse life and scenery which six years ago introduced Mr. Boyesen to American readers. If the author's range has since become so wide that this volume does not represent his maturest habit of thought, it may none the less very properly stand for the poetic and romantic qualities which have kept his fiction noticeably free from the objectionable influences allied to the so-called realistic school." [9]

A Norseman's Pilgrimage (1875) is admittedly and obviously an autobiographical novel. The hero, Olaf Varberg, is a young Norwegian studying at the University of Leipzig. Olaf has spent five years in America and has published a book. In Leipzig, while searching for a Margarete (he has been reading *Faust*), he discovers Ruth Copley from Boston. This earliest of Boyesen's American heroines is analyzed and discussed at great length by the author-hero. Olaf gives himself the same treatment and soon discovers that he is romantic and that Ruth is realistic, that he represents Europe and she, America:

"It was a peculiarity of his mind that it wandered off, on the slightest provocation, into all sorts of dreamy vagaries, and now it was this very maiden, whom his fancy had clothed with all the attributes of romance, who sternly rent the veil, and by her realistic talk forced him to accept her in her true character. She was evidently not deficient in fancy, but she was a true product of American soil, and she represented those very qualities which he especially disapproved of in Americans — their realistic humor and their utter irreverence for tradition." [10]

When Boyesen steps out of his autobiographic role, he observes that each of these young people is somewhat biased and that union cannot be effected easily. Ruth makes things difficult for her would-be lover by laughing at him, as she laughs at nearly everything:

[9] *Scribner's Monthly*, 20:155 (May, 1880).
[10] *A Norseman's Pilgrimage*, 49.

Hjalmar Hjorth Boyesen

"Varberg had enjoyed her merry sarcasms; he had laughed at the drollness of her criticisms, and he had even succeeded beyond his expectation in entering into her mood. Nevertheless this was not his way of looking upon life; she saw only the grotesque and ludicrous, while his chief pleasure was to note the quaint and the picturesque, to detect the fleeting shades and *nuances* of color, and to catch characteristic glimpses of the land and the people among whom he was living. Unhappily they were both a little exclusive, and their point of view one-sided. Had Olaf possessed her quick sense of humor, or had she been gifted with his keen sight for the picturesque, they would have been more ideal companions, and would perhaps have reaped greater profit from their German sojourn than they did. As it was, their views and purposes came into constant collision." [11]

Such passages suggest that, in writing *A Norseman's Pilgrimage*, Boyesen was debating the issue of romanticism versus realism, Europe versus America. Olaf's state of mind is that of the earlier Boyesen of Norwegian and German background, who wrote *Gunnar* under Bjørnson's influence; and Ruth Copley represents the beckoning world of America, with its realistic, materialistic, cold-blooded attitudes, its eyes toward the future. *Gunnar* was dedicated to Turgenev, but Boyesen had completed it before he met the great Russian realist. Only now, while *A Norseman's Pilgrimage* was being written, did Boyesen begin to test the new approach to life, art, and literature that Turgenev represented.

Boyesen's early tales and letters show that he read Nathaniel Hawthorne and was influenced by him. George P. Lathrop, who married Rose Hawthorne and edited her father's works, was a close personal friend. Perhaps at Lathrop's instigation Boyesen had read the passage from Hawthorne's notebooks which Henry James quoted later in his critical study of the writer: "No author, without a trial, can conceive of the difficulty of writing a romance about a country where there is no shadow, no antiquity, no mystery, no picturesque and gloomy wrong, nor anything but a commonplace prosperity, in broad and simple daylight, as is happily the case with my dear native land." [12]

The following dialogue from *A Norseman's Pilgrimage*, prompted by a particularly romantic German setting, suggests that Boyesen was con-

---

[11] *A Norseman's Pilgrimage*, 87.

[12] Henry James, Jr., *Hawthorne*, 41 (New York, 1879). Lathrop, associate editor of the *Atlantic*, 1875–77, was one of the "men of letters & personal friends" Boyesen elected to have at his wedding.

cerned about the twin problems of theme and treatment which a person's complete transfer from the Old World to the New entailed:

"'What untold tragedies, what idyls and romances have been enacted within those walls,' said Varberg, pointing to the ruin.

"'I wonder what house in New England that is twenty years old has not been the stage of similar tragedies and romances,' answered Miss Ruth.

"'Yes; if you would call a drunken shoemaker, who ruins his family, a romantic character, or a Wall Street speculator, who kills himself when he has lost his last stake.'

"'I can hardly comprehend,' retorted she, with some little show of patriotic zeal, 'why a drunken baron should be any more romantic than a drunken shoemaker; and you will no doubt admit that drunkenness was even more prevalent among your feudal heroes than among the Massachusetts shoemakers.'

"'I once knew a man out in Indiana,' remarked Miss Bailey, 'who killed himself drinking, and then killed all his family too.'

"'I am glad he was sensible enough to kill himself first,' said her cousin dryly."[13]

It should be noted that the code of realism Howells was about to adopt, and which he certainly discussed with Boyesen, ruled out all violence as romantic and melodramatic, whether it involved a German baron or an American shoemaker. From the first, Boyesen tried to avoid such episodes in his stories. A letter to George W. Cable shows how self-conscious he was about using a spectacular scene in his fiction, even though it was a product of his observation rather than of his imagination: "The story grew out of an incident which we happened to witness in Rome, & is my first venture in the sensational line, & may possibly be my last."[14] But if Boyesen was ready to rule out plot complication and sensational episodes from his novels and stories, he still felt that European poetry and romance deserved a place in American life and in realistic fiction.

He never deviated from his opinion that crass and crude America could be improved by a liberal infusion of European culture. As a fervent young apostle of the arts, he observed that most of his fellow immigrants were uneducated, more likely to lower than to raise the cultural

[13] *A Norseman's Pilgrimage*, 60.
[14] Boyesen to Cable, July 13, 1879.

level in America. When Ruth Copley facetiously asks if gnomes and nixies could not be induced to emigrate to Boston and Cambridge, "where the transcendental tea meetings are in danger of reducing us all into mere abstract nonentities," Varberg gravely replies, "We get so many less desirable elements from Europe. . . . It would be well if we could also import some of her noble poetry and romance." Boyesen then considered it his function in American letters to transmit European poetry and romance. This would justify the mood of *Gunnar* and of many of the early tales.

While Boyesen was planning to enrich New World life and literature with European cultural importations, he was aware that his own Americanization was taking place. If he still considered himself a romantic, his outlook was becoming more realistic, less theatrical. Olaf Varberg destroys his poems because of his growing love for Ruth Copley: "From out of the old verses his former self seemed to stare at him. . . . It appeared a perfect mystery to Varberg that he had ever been as those poems showed him to have been." When he tears up the "wretched stuff" and flings the small pieces out of his window, his old romantic self "wondered if one of them might not reach Ruth's window, and he was about to construct a little romance out of it."

Then the new American, prompted by his love for Miss Copley, is reminded that this is a very trite and threadbare sentiment. At first he fears that he and Ruth are too far apart: "She has no two things in common with me; she ridicules the things I love, and has no more appreciation of the romantic than a bat." Yet Ruth and Olaf both gradually yield a little and come to a mutual understanding. When he acknowledges his love for her, the act symbolizes the author's emancipation from romantic sentimentality and theatricality, while Ruth's acceptance of Olaf marks the enrichment of American culture by an alliance with European poetry and romance.[15]

A Norseman's Pilgrimage was less popular than *Gunnar*, though the *Atlantic Monthly's* reviewer called it "a substantial success," predicting that the book's broad scope would gain for Boyesen "a wider audience than his initial romance, popular as it is." The reviewer also put his finger on the weakness of *A Norseman's Pilgrimage*: "Varberg and Ruth Copley assume at once the relative position which is maintained by them

---

[15] Quotations in this and the preceding two paragraphs are from *A Norseman's Pilgrimage*, 47, 65, 99.

Gunnar to *Falconberg*

up to the final pages."[16] There is no change in the situations, motives, or emotions of the characters; only the scene is shifted. The book is too personal to be a philosophical novel and even for Boyesen its arguments were dated. In February, 1878, he wrote to Cable: "'A Norseman's Pilgrimage' I profess to have outgrown long ago, & still if someone else should abuse it, I suppose I should gird my armor & stand up in its defence." The book never went through a second printing. It is of interest now only from a biographical standpoint.

"My best work, as it appears to me, is to be found in my 'Tales from Two Hemispheres,'" Boyesen wrote in 1878.[17] This first collection of short stories was published by Osgood in the autumn of 1876 and was subsequently reprinted several times by Scribner's after that firm took over the copyright. All of the tales had been published in magazines, five of them in *Scribner's* from November, 1874, through October, 1876, and the sixth, "Asathor's Vengeance," in the March, 1875, *Atlantic*. His *Tales from Two Hemispheres* brought together all of Boyesen's stories from before 1877 except his earliest fictional effort, "The Norse Emigrant," printed in the February, 1873, *Galaxy*. This simple, four-page story presumably was considered unworthy of republication.

"The Man Who Lost His Name," the first and longest story in the collection, was the last written. It is the only tale with a New World setting. Two other stories involve people who migrate to America, but the episodes in this country are summarized and the action concentrated in Norway. Three tales are entirely Norwegian in locale. The *Atlantic's* review of *A Norseman's Pilgrimage* had noted that "Mr. Boyesen is as yet more harmonious in his pictures of Norway than in others."[18] Boyesen, always keenly conscious of the public reaction to his work, was reluctant to abandon Norwegian settings and the portrayal of Norwegian character, which he felt he could do well. Yet, as a convert to Turgenev's literary creed, he was eager to record the contemporary American scene, which he was observing so critically. He knew by 1875 that reviewers and the general reading public, while willing to accept his European tales, were very dubious when this "Norwegian writer" portrayed New World characters or commented on their ways. Twenty years later they still questioned Boyesen's right to interpret his adopted country.

[16] *Atlantic Monthly*, 36:363 (September, 1875).
[17] Boyesen to Cable, February 17, 1878.
[18] *Atlantic Monthly*, 36:364.

Hjalmar Hjorth Boyesen

Many of Boyesen's tales about immigrants (nearly a dozen in all, written over a twenty-year period) follow the general outline of his first short story, "The Norse Emigrant." A young man goes to America, makes a fortune (the circumstances are hazy, but both hard work and providential happenings are involved), goes back to Norway for a reconciliation and justification, and finally announces that he must return to the land of the future. But "The Norse Emigrant" is really the story of old Aslak Lian, who was left to mourn in Norway, rather than of his emigrant son:

"Every spring, when the mild winds from the Gulf Stream come gambolling with spring-like sport in through the narrow fjords and gloomy valleys of Norway, with swelling rivers and sprouting bushes everywhere following in their track, then people might look in vain for Aslak, for he was nowhere to be found; and there was not the man living who could say where he had gone. The saying was that he fled the fever; for that breeze from the Gulf is laden with fever — not small-pox or yellow fever indeed, but a fever which, sweeping through the scantily populated valleys of Norway, leaves a sadder desolation behind it than ever marked the footsteps of any earthly epidemic — the American fever. And, forsooth, Aslak Lian had reason to dread the American fever; the only son he ever had that fever had carried off." [19]

Although Boyesen had become Americanized and had acquired theories about realism, his stories continued for some years to emphasize Norway instead of America: the old people who remained rather than the young men who migrated. These immigrant tales reveal an interesting dichotomy. The author, in conformity with his own actions and convictions, justifies the young man who migrates. In the closing scene this character must turn his face toward the New World. But, after making this clear deposition in favor of youth, progress, and emigration, Boyesen feels free to engage the reader's sympathies on behalf of the old people who are left at home, and to focus his story on picturesque, romantic Norway. This suggests that Boyesen had a natural affinity for the colorful aspects of a story, whatever his literary or social convictions might have been.[20]

"The Story of an Outcast," first of the *Tales from Two Hemispheres*

[19] *Galaxy*, 15:199.

[20] It also suggests that intellectually Boyesen was on the side of his father but emotionally was much closer to Judge Hjorth. See chapter 1.

Gunnar to Falconberg

collection to appear in print, reinforces this conclusion. It begins with the Norwegian father rather than the outcast who fled to America. Like Aslak Lian, Bjarne Blakstad clung to the past, "wore his hair long, as his fathers had done, and dressed in the styles of two centuries ago. . . . He loved everything that was old, in dress as well as in manners, took no newspapers and regarded railroads and steamboats as inventions of the devil." In contrast to this conservative peasant, "Hedin Ullern was looked upon as an upstart. He could only count three generations back. . . . He had read a great deal, and was well informed on the politics of the day; his name had even been mentioned for *storthingsmand*, or member of parliament from the district, and it was the common opinion, that if Bjarne Blakstad had not so vigorously opposed him, he would have been elected, being the only 'cultivated' peasant in the valley." [21]

The pattern of this story is clear: the plot will grow out of the differences which make these two characters incompatible. The situation is also a real and typical one. Boyesen knew that the old picturesque rural life in Norway was threatened and perhaps doomed by the "America fever," modern inventions, and new social and political ideas. But instead of bringing these two protagonists into conflict over obvious issues, as his opening pages seem to promise, Boyesen plays a shabby trick on Bjarne, Hedin, and the reader. Bjarne's spirited daughter is inexplicably attracted to Hedin's half-witted son. When it becomes obvious that she is pregnant, the heartbroken but inflexible father drives his daughter out into the storm. She is befriended by a humble fisherman and makes her way to America. The episodes in this country are quickly disposed of: "Why should I speak of the ceaseless care, the suffering, and the hard toil, which made the first few months of Brita's life on this continent a mere continued struggle for existence? They are familiar to every emigrant who has come here with a brave heart and an empty purse. Suffice it to say that at the end of the second month, she succeeded in obtaining service as milkmaid with a family in the neighborhood of New York."

A few paragraphs later, her boy is twenty-two years old and wins a partnership in the firm that employs him. When his mother's health breaks down, this dutiful son takes her abroad, as the doctor prescribes. In Norway a reconciliation with old Bjarne follows. (The Ullerns have

[21] *Scribner's Monthly*, 9:36–48 (November, 1874); *Tales from two Hemispheres*, 84, 85. Quotations to follow will be from *Tales from Two Hemispheres*.

Hjalmar Hjorth Boyesen

been forgotten.) The outcast dies as she clasps the hands of her father and her son: "Close under the wall of the little red-painted church, they dug her grave; and a week later her father was laid to rest at his daughter's side." [22] The young man returns to America.

The plot of "A Good-for-Nothing" is nearly as trite and sentimental as that of "The Story of an Outcast." Ralph Grim flees to America because a particularly outrageous student escapade makes it impossible for him to remain in Christiania. (He sends letters of proposal to six women and is promptly accepted by all of them!) In America the young ne'er-do-well undergoes a change, but it should be observed that it is a lady's approval that gives him his chance to rise in the New World: While he is working as a gardener's assistant, his employer's daughter is struck by "his culture and refinement of manner." Soon Ralph Grim is a successful journalist. His position has special advantages: "Society had flung its doors open to him. . . . He enjoyed keenly the privilege of daily association with high-minded and refined women; their eager activity of intellect stimulated him, their exquisite ethereal grace and their delicately chiseled beauty satisfied his aesthetic cravings, and the responsive vivacity of their nature prepared him ever new surprises. He felt a strange fascination in the presence of these women, and the conviction grew upon him that their type of womanhood was superior to any he had hitherto known." [23]

Like all the Boyesen heroes who are successful in America, Ralph Grim goes back to Norway for a time, to do the right thing by the peasant girl whose staunch character had sustained him during his absence. Then Boyesen proves that he is honestly trying to be a realist. Ralph and his Bertha discover that they have grown so far apart in six years that they can have no life together. In the final paragraph, as Ralph Grim sits in an open boat being rowed down the fjord to the steamer, Boyesen points the moral of the tale: "And in that hour he looked fearlessly into the gulf which separates the New World from the Old. He had hoped to bridge it; but, alas! it cannot be bridged." [24]

Boyesen's three all-Norwegian tales are less interesting in themselves and have less significance for their author's subsequent career than the other stories in *Tales from Two Hemispheres*. In "A Scientific Vaga-

[22] *Tales from Two Hemispheres*, 110, 128.
[23] *Tales from Two Hemispheres*, 162, 163. This story appeared in *Scribner's Monthly*, 10:361–372 (July, 1875).
[24] *Tales from Two Hemispheres*, 177.

Gunnar to *Falconberg*

bond" two noble but eccentric young people, an ornithologist and a woman reformer, are finally brought together in spite of their unworldly, intellectual predilections. Although there is no melodrama and the story is shaped by the foibles of the two main characters, neither their personalities nor their activities are convincing. "Truls, the Nameless" is pure melodrama. As the heroine is about to be married to the wrong man, she is killed by the explosion of the cannon fired to celebrate her wedding, and Truls gathers up her lifeless body and leaps into the waters of the fjord. "Asathor's Vengeance, or the Mountain-taken Maid" is a tale of the supernatural provided with alternate rational explanations. The pagan god Thor, long since supplanted by the White Christ, gains his vengeance on the Kvaerk family by luring away the strange maiden, Aasa, who hears the voices of nature. Although "Asathor's Vengeance" revealed a literary vein which Boyesen might have followed with some success, artistic as well as popular, he did not write any more stories like it. The inference is clear: Despite the popularity of such legendary Norse tales and his own natural affinity for romantic material, Boyesen was determined to portray life in its typical aspects, as it really was, and to concentrate on the American scene, which he felt was becoming increasingly familiar to him.[25]

By far the most significant story in *Tales from Two Hemispheres* is "The Man Who Lost His Name," the favorite of author and critics alike. Typically, a summary of the plot reveals the worst aspects of a Boyesen story. Halfdan Bjerk is a dilettante whose admiration for the ancient Greek republics leads to a corresponding enthusiasm for the United States. In New York City he is robbed, arrested for vagrancy, and reduced to a state of helplessness and hopelessness: "The Grand Republic, what did it care for such as he? A pair of brawny arms fit to wield the pick-axe and to steer the plow it received with an eager welcome; for a child-like, loving heart and a generously fantastic brain, it had but the stern greeting of the law."[26]

Bjerk is rescued by his plebeian countryman, Gustav Olson, who is on his way to a junior partnership. Olson introduces his dilettante friend to the Van Kirks, and Halfdan Bjerk becomes the music teacher Daniel Birch. He is a great success as a teacher and performer; but, more im-

[25] *Scribner's Monthly*, 9:731–736, 11:229–239 (April, December, 1875); *Atlantic Monthly*, 35:345–356 (March, 1875).
[26] The story came out in *Scribner's Monthly*, 12:808–826 (October, 1876). Mrs. Howells, a severe critic, was enthusiastic about this story; Howells to Boyesen, December 6, 1876. Howells would have accepted it if it had been cut.

portant, he falls in love with the dazzling heiress, Edith Van Kirk. Though she admires his taste, Edith is repelled by Halfdan's conversational brilliance "as something odious and un-American, the cheap result of outlandish birth and unrepublican education." She is shocked when Halfdan serenades her, and she assures him that his suit is hopeless. When a trip to Norway fails to cure him of his love for Edith or his preference for the New World, Halfdan returns to New York. There he freezes to death on the girl's doorstep, dreaming that she has relented.

Despite the absurd plot, many parts of "The Man Who Lost His Name" are evidently based on Boyesen's experience in becoming Americanized. The sensitive young Norwegian-American professor who chose to move in upper literary and social circles must have suffered rebuffs that are reflected in a scene from this story. The heroine tells her Norwegian music master that she and her friends are grateful for his help in a Fourth-of-July song fest:

" 'Grateful? Why?' demanded Halfdan, looking quite unhappy.

" 'For singing *our* national songs, of course. Now, won't you sing one of your own, please? We should all be so delighted to hear how a Swedish — or Norwegian, is it? — national song sounds.'

" 'Yes, Mr. Birch, *do* sing a Swedish song,' echoed several voices.

"They, of course, did not even remotely suspect their own cruelty. He had, in his enthusiasm for the day allowed himself to forget that he was not made of the same clay as they were, that he was an exile and a stranger, and must ever remain so, that he had no right to share their joy in the blessing of liberty. Edith had taken pains to dispel the happy illusion, and had sent him once more whirling toward his cold native Pole." [27]

"The Man Who Lost His Name" also points the way to Boyesen's later realistic novels. The hero of the earlier story, "A Good-for-Nothing," was impressed by the "high-minded and refined women" of American society. Halfdan Bjerk, however, came too close to one of these bright stars, and his own pale light was snuffed out. Although Boyesen's attitude toward American girls changed from admiration to criticism and finally to condemnation, the subject never lost its fascination. His later realistic novels invariably dealt with fashionable New York society and its brilliant but heartless young women.

[27] *Tales from Two Hemispheres*, 22, 48–50.

Gunnar to *Falconberg*

With this final story in the collection, Boyesen made the transition from Norway to America. Although he was again to write about Norwegian Americans, the emphasis was usually on the American aspects of their lives. *A Norseman's Pilgrimage* was a rather premature and inconclusive attempt to analyze the author's conversion from a European to an American, from a romanticist to a realist. *Tales from Two Hemispheres* gives evidence of Boyesen's experiments with theme and treatment and thus points the way to later efforts. Though he injected realistic concepts and new ideas into his narratives, the characters retain their romantic coloration and the plots are highly sentimental and melodramatic. This combination was to persist in his fiction.

While Boyesen regarded the last-mentioned volume as his best work, he was far from satisfied with it. "If I could re-edit this book now," he wrote Cable in 1878, "I should cut out a good deal, heighten the effect in many scenes, & subdue it in others." He knew that he was not successful in following Turgenev's advice and example. He outlined his literary creed and affirmed his allegiance to Turgenev when he wrote Cable; but he added: "My preaching, on the whole, is better than my practices. I have written nothing, as yet, that I should wish to be judged by." [28]

"Swart among the Buckeyes," published in *Scribner's Monthly* in August, 1877, was Boyesen's first completely American story. As in his previous efforts, the action and dialogue were theatrical, almost ridiculous, yet the emphasis on environment and character indicated that he was trying to write a serious, realistic story. He was drawing on his memories of Urbana in lampooning Cicero Center, Ohio, and he was recalling his own response to the American small town in relating the experiences of Dr. Fred Swart among the benighted Buckeyes.[29]

The story begins with a letter from the Episcopal clergyman in Cicero Center, the Reverend Luther Norman, to his friend, Dr. Fred Swart. The brilliant and cultured Dr. Swart is persuaded to practice in the little Ohio town, and thereby saves Mrs. Norman from the horrors of tobacco-chewing doctors in the West, who are probably quacks. At a church sociable, Mrs. Norman, a New Englander, indulges in her favorite pastime — making caustic comments about her husband's parishioners. Dr. Swart presumably shares the author's feelings about her snobbery. Mrs.

[28] Boyesen to Cable, February 17, 1878.
[29] For this story, see *Scribner's Monthly*, 14:547–559.

Hjalmar Hjorth Boyesen

Norman, Boyesen observes, feels that "rules of etiquette which prevailed in New England could have no application to the crude society of the West."

The real interest begins when Miss Sylvia Grimsby is prevailed upon to sing several songs at the church sociable. Dr. Swart is interested, for, despite the bad singing, he discovers that the girl has a promising voice. ("His aesthetic judgment was unerring.") Without considering the consequences, he undertakes to coach her; but in learning to become a true artist, Sylvia learns a good deal more than the proper control of her vocal chords:

"It did not occur to him [*Swart*] that he was unfitting her for the life and surroundings among which her lot was cast; that he was daily opening her eyes to the vulgarity of her own immediate associations, that in time she must apply the exalted standard of taste, which he had furnished her, to those whom nature had placed nearest to her. . . . For instance, how could that obtuse little mother of hers, with her impregnable conceit and her blundering cheerfulness, hope to keep her place in the affections of a daughter whose critical acumen had been sharpened by daily intercourse with a highly fastidious and accomplished man?"

To sustain this situation and to justify his harsh judgment of Cicero Center, Dr. Swart has to be a superior person. This Apollolike product of the German universities has an appropriately aristocratic American ancestry, but he has become something of a pagan cosmopolite, apparently through his admiration for Goethe. His is "not what young ladies would call an ideal nature," for he has an unabashed admiration for "blooming and throbbing flesh." Nonetheless, this distinguished being becomes attached to his gentle rural protégée, Sylvia Grimsby, and is self-conscious about it:

" 'It is absurd enough for a novel,' he muttered to himself, 'my entangling myself with that little girl, who has evidently no more in common with me than a butterfly with a rhinoceros.' " And again, " 'I must break loose from these cramping associations,' he continued, half-aloud, 'or my wings will be clipped before I shall have tested their strength.' "

For some reason Boyesen finds it necessary to risk the life of his flying rhinoceros. Sylvia appears at Dr. Swart's office in a state of alarm and dishabille, having dashed through the snow, wearing only one shoe. There are burglars at the Grimsby house. "Her whole figure looked so unnaturally thin and lithe, and her scant drapery clung to her limbs, revealing their form as if they had been cut in marble." Dr. Swart leaves her there while he goes and captures the burglars with proper nonchalance. When he returns:

"As her gaze met his, the blood sprang to her face, she dropped her eyes, pulled nervously at her dress, and made a few spasmodic gestures to smooth her hair. He understood her unspoken thought, and with a quick, silent movement put out the gas. But the burning heap of coals on the grate still spread its vague, red glow through the room."

The scene seems wasted when Dr. Swart wraps Sylvia in a plaid, carries her home in his arms, and kisses her, then departs with the cryptic announcement: "Farewell! I leave tomorrow." Though he has abandoned Cicero Center and Sylvia for a professorship of anatomy in an eastern medical college, locked in the doctor's heart is "the image of a shy and slender little maiden." When a telegram informs him that she is desperately ill of an unidentified ailment, he goes back to Cicero Center to save her: "I verily believe there was healing in his touch."

No doubt Dr. Swart took the bride back to his eastern college, for his (or Boyesen's) antipathy for the little Ohio town was too strong to admit of any compromise. The author directs his sharpest thrust toward a character named Solon Snell: "The outlines of his mouth were loose and indefinite, such as one invariably observes in people who lounge around railroad depots; his brown eyes were soft and watery, suggesting unfathomable depths of crude sentiment." Solon Snell is Cicero Center's town booster.

"Swart among the Buckeyes" and "The Norse Emigrant" never appeared in a book, although all of Boyesen's other writings published during this period were included in short-story collections. Subsequently Boyesen seldom used the American small town as a primary setting, though he often described such places incidentally—and always satirically. The rural village is inevitably a place to escape from. If the small-town boy goes to New York, he becomes rich and successful—and also materialistic and generally unsympathetic. If he goes away to study in Europe, however, he becomes a scientist or an artist, an admirable and superior being; in short, a Dr. Fred Swart.[30]

In Boyesen's later fiction of this sort, he followed the pattern set in

---

[30] A Cincinnati newspaper reported that the town of Urbana was up in arms over Boyesen's gibes. President Sewall of Urbana University denied this charge in a letter to the *New York Daily Tribune*, July 1, 1878.

Hjalmar Hjorth Boyesen

"Swart among the Buckeyes": His stories are encrusted with observations about the ugliness of American small towns and the meanness of their inhabitants. The author's biting observations make lively reading today and impel students to speculate about Boyesen as a forerunner of Sinclair Lewis, to label his satiric thrusts as early examples of "critical realism."[31] Yet the same tales are melodramatic in plot, character development, and dialogue. Since Boyesen's satiric gibes are incidental rather than functional in his early fiction, they must be defined as a cultured European's caustic observations on American life rather than as evidence that American literature was producing a realistic novelist.

Falconberg, Boyesen's third novel, was serialized in nine installments by *Scribner's*, from August, 1878, through April, 1879. It came out in book form in New York in July, 1879, and was reprinted twenty years later.

In Boyesen's "prelude" to *Falconberg*, he invokes Leif Erickson and Thorfinn Karlsefne and announces that he will deal with their latter-day prototypes, now thronging to Vinland by way of Castle Garden. As the novelist watches the Norwegians disembark, he singles out a "sad-faced traveler" whose story he is going to record. This young man is Einar Finnson Falconberg, who is to find his way to the pioneer town of Hardanger, Minnesota. There he redeems his damaged reputation, defeats the Lutheran clergyman who opposes Americanization of Norwegian immigrants, and marries the most beautiful girl in the settlement.[32]

The public's reaction to *Falconberg* varied greatly, in accordance with the reader's point of view. *Scribner's* reviewer was favorably impressed by the book's propaganda: "The contact of slow conservative farmers from Scandinavia with the bustle and stir of Anglo-Saxondom in its American phase cannot fail to offer picturesque situations and these Mr. Boyesen has liberally used." Boyesen himself seemed pleased with the outcry that he must have been expecting from Norwegians on both sides of the Atlantic. Writing to Cable, August 7, 1879, he said: "'Falconberg' is also having a prosperous career & is making a sensa-

---

[31] George L. White, Jr., "H. H. Boyesen: A Note on Immigration," in *American Literature*, 13:363 (January, 1942). See especially "Anastasia," in *Century*, 25:839–852; "The Elixir of Pain," in *Cosmopolitan*, 11:62 (May, 1891); and *The Golden Calf* (Meadville, Pennsylvania, 1892).

[32] Castle Garden, on the southernmost point of Manhattan Island, was the immigrant receiving station in New York City until Ellis Island was established in 1892. Earlier it had been a fort and a theater. In the nineteenth century, writers like Longfellow identified the Vinland of the Icelandic sagas with New England.

Gunnar to *Falconberg*

tion in Norway where it is being attacked on all sides. The alleged anticlerical tendency of the book is naturally looked upon with disfavor among the eminently respectable & conservative Norsemen." In the Scandinavian West the book was still being attacked more than a year later, when Boyesen finally replied to his critics. He contended that some of the leaders of the Lutheran Norwegian Synod were more ridiculous and arbitrary than his caricature of a clergyman in *Falconberg*.[33]

Boyesen's anticlerical bias, which is unmistakable in many of his stories, is most virulent in *Falconberg*. The novel begins with a description of the hero's father in Norway: "The Right Reverend Bishop Falconberg was a man of a truly apostolic appearance, a fact which, as his enemies asserted, constituted his sole claim to the elevated position he at present occupied. He possessed, moreover, in an eminent degree, that peculiarly clerical accomplishment of uttering pious platitudes with a pompousness of voice and manner which, with an uncritical congregation, readily passed for inspiration."[34]

No doubt Boyesen blamed such prelates of the Norwegian state church for ruining the career of his own father, the dissenting Captain Boyesen, but he was even more bitter about the Lutheran clergymen in the immigrant settlements of this country. He had a personal quarrel with the pastors, if his accounts of his experiences with *Fremad* are to be given credence. Boyesen was convinced that the clergy, brought over by the Norwegian Synod, were seriously impeding Americanization; but this bias scarcely justifies his characterization of Pastor Marcus Falconberg, the bishop's brother (and the hero's uncle), who attempts to keep a firm hold on his flock in the pioneer town of Hardanger. Marcus Falconberg is the blackest villain Boyesen ever introduced into his fiction.

To emphasize the pastor's villainy and to draw the line more clearly between the good characters and the bad, Boyesen contrives an alliance between Pastor Falconberg, the uncle, and the corrupt Irish politicians who use liquor and character assassination to further the interests of the Democratic party. Pastor Falconberg has an excellent reason for becoming a Democrat: The progressive Norwegians who are beginning to challenge his temporal authority are all Republicans. Boyesen knew that most Scandinavian Americans were Republicans, and he also under-

[33] *Scribner's Monthly*, 18:472 (July, 1879); Boyesen, in *Budstikken*, February 15, 1881, quoted in Larson, *The Changing West*, 105.
[34] *Falconberg*, 7.

stood the reasons for their party loyalty. He explained later that he himself voted the Republican ticket until 1880, though he had long been in sympathy with the Democratic platform. In his novel, however, right, progress, and political morality are all on the side of the Republicans.[35]

The political campaign in *Falconberg* is subordinated to the workings of the romantic plot, but Boyesen probably thought he was producing realistic fiction by introducing party and church controversy into his story. In later years he found the novels of Howells and James less realistic than they should have been because they did not deal with American politics.[36] In *Falconberg*, Boyesen was unsuccessful in making events function dramatically and realistically. His efforts resulted either in melodrama or in an essay by the author, such as the following description of election day in Hardanger:

"The elections passed off without dramatic incidents. The enthusiastic torch-light processions of the past week with their glaring transparencies and promiscuous cheering from a Babylonic confusion of throats seemed a thing of remote antiquity, and the impartial rain descended in a cold drizzling spray alike upon righteous Republicans and unrighteous Democrats. There was an occasional enlivening of public sentiment whenever fresh bulletins were displayed at 'The Citizen' or 'The Banner' office, the contradictory statements of which, if they served no other purpose, at least stimulated the betting which was understood to be very animated in the bar-rooms of the Franklin and the Hancock hotels. There were also later in the afternoon the usual rumors of Democratic corruption, of which, however, nothing more definite could be ascertained than that the chairman of the state committee had telegraphed somewhere that five hundred votes 'would settle it,' and that an obscure Irishman had called at Norderud's house to inform him that he had sixteen friends who entertained conscientious doubts regarding the merits of the contesting candidates.

"There was the usual number of partisans of Utopian schemes who hung about the polls, button-holing unsophisticated voters and trying to enlist their sympathies for impossible candidates and still more impossible reforms. There were the ardent neophyte voter with ready-made convictions who deemed the exercise of his civic rights a great and glori-

---

[35] Boyesen, "The Scandinavian in the United States," in *North American Review*, 155:527 (November, 1892).

[36] See Boyesen, "Why We Have No Great Novelists," in *Forum*, 2:617 (February, 1887); Boyesen, *Literary Silhouettes*, 46.

ous privilege, the pessimistic citizen who believed that the country was going to the dogs — voted a mixed ticket and held it to be a cheap privilege to choose between two evils; the apathetic voter who would have stayed at home and had yielded only to the importunities of partisans and the offer of a free ride, and at last the political manager and wirepuller who besieged the polls from dawn till sunset, thrusting his ticket into your hand and overwhelming you with a deluge of arguments if you appeared for a moment to be doubtful in your choice." [37]

The background matter in *Falconberg* has drawn attention from the novel Boyesen really wrote: the romantic story of Einar Finnson Falconberg, "an alpine flower among men," who was forced to flee from Norway because of a youthful indiscretion. The political and religious questions are introduced unconvincingly and settled indecisively because they are subservient to the success story of a typical Boyesen hero. The reader is assured that this university man with the delicate hands and classic profile becomes a recognized leader in the Norwegian colony chiefly because he is made of finer stuff than the common herd. The best of the sturdy young pioneers of Hardanger prove their worth by becoming his loyal but helpless followers. Einar's downfall stems from the accidental revelation of his disgrace in Norway, not from any failure or weakness he has displayed in America. Coincidence is added when the villainous pastor learns that Einar Finnson is really his nephew, Einar Falconberg. Einar's ultimate victory, which is primarily a moral triumph, is confirmed by his willingness to remain in Hardanger and live down his past. The chief token of his success is his marriage to Helga Raven, the most desirable girl in town, whose husband, in her words, "must have a strong will, to which everything and everybody instinctively yield, and a lofty purpose." Einar's astonishing beauty is discounted. Given the other qualities that Helga demands, she adds, "It would matter little to me whether his head was bald and he was small." [38]

Falconberg's main theme has led some critics to call the novel Boyesen's first important step toward realism.[39] Because he was a Norwegian-American immigrant author, his story about Norwegian pioneers in Minnesota was the kind of book the critics thought Boyesen should write. The plot sounded promising too: a struggle for authority between secular

---
[37] *Falconberg*, 267.
[38] *Falconberg*, 113.
[39] See B. W. Wells, "Hjalmar Hjorth Boyesen," in *Sewanee* (Tennessee) *Review*, 4:306 (May, 1896).

Hjalmar Hjorth Boyesen

and religious leaders, and a heated political race between Republicans and Democrats. Although *Falconberg* includes these ingredients, religious and political issues are obscured by melodramatic but meaningless events; and the narrative, instead of dealing with the social and economic problems of pioneer settlements, degenerates into a struggle between a good man and a bad one, both highly romanticized figures. The explanation is simple enough: Boyesen wrote the kind of novel he was able to write, and that was not a realistic account of pioneering in Minnesota. He created a genteel hero in his own image and invented a villain whom he invested with the qualities he hated most. For the rest of the ingredients of *Falconberg* he was dependent, not on the close observation of life that Turgenev recommended, but on what he remembered of his visits to the western settlements nearly ten years before, and on second-hand information.

5

A Literary Liaison Man

DURING the seventies Boyesen's nonfictional writing ranged from book reviews and journalistic articles to a scholarly work on Goethe and Schiller. Most of the articles — on European universities, on "Norway and the Norsemen," and on literary men whom Boyesen knew — yield some information about their author and his activities but have little interest otherwise.[1] Boyesen's writings on German literature are the product of a competent scholar whose learning was broad rather than profound. There is little evidence of original thought in any of his work. Some of the longer reviews and articles, however, especially those on Norwegian literature, reveal solid critical competence. These are worth examining, but allowances must be made for some uncertainty and even reversal of direction in so enthusiastic and impressionable a young man. During Boyesen's first decade in America he was still in his twenties, and in the process of changing his nationality. The concomitant shift in his aesthetic and philosophic viewpoint is especially significant.

[1] Boyesen, "Norway and the Norsemen," in *Scribner's Monthly*, 13:291–305 (January, 1877). Boyesen gives a fair idea of Norway's history, government, culture, industries, customs, and the character of its people. He was very proud of his native land, and obviously annoyed by the misconceptions about it that he encountered in America. The heroes of his early stories are often subjected to stupid questions about Norway from obtuse Americans. See, for example, *A Norseman's Pilgrimage*, 107.

Hjalmar Hjorth Boyesen

Boyesen's career as an interpreter and critic of Continental literature — for his adopted country — began before his first fiction and poetry appeared in print. His review of Hans Christian Andersen's travel book, published in the *Atlantic Monthly* in 1871, was a slight affair, but a year later he made a real beginning in the *North American Review* with an article on Kristofer Janson and language reform. Boyesen's title was misleading and his article badly organized: He first discussed the growth of Norwegian nationalism and the movement for Scandinavian unity, and finally came to the Norwegian language reformers, Vinje and Aasen as well as Kristofer Janson. But this was only the first third of his article. Boyesen showed that his primary interest was literature, not philology: The last part of his essay is a résumé and evaluation of Janson's long poem, *Sigmund Brestison*, which was written in New Norse and based on *The Faereyinga Saga* (The Saga of the Faroe Islanders), the account of a great leader.[2]

Although Boyesen's article turned into a review of Janson's poem, he took the opportunity to express his own opinions of life, literature, and morality, and the proper relationship of the three. Janson was a reformer who believed that the humble people of Norway must be made aware of their noble heritage, and thus his hero, Sigmund Brestison, was a prototype of the race, a model of the Norwegian peasant. Boyesen said that this didactic element weakened the poem:

"The author has had an object in his work, a purpose outside of the poem, and not necessarily flowing from it. And such a purpose cannot but hamper his freedom, draw his imagination earthward, and force it into this stereotyped mould, which the moralist and not the poet in him has set up for imitation." Boyesen also objected to being told that Sigmund Brestison was heroic and noble: "The highest art will always avoid explanations of this kind; it betrays a certain want of trust in the

---

[2] See Boyesen, "A Poet's Bazaar," in *Atlantic Monthly,* 28:512 (October, 1871); Boyesen, "Kristofer Janson and the Reform of the Norwegian Language," in *North American Review*, 115:379–401. Kristofer Janson (1841–1917) was an optimistic and prolific author and lecturer, and a Unitarian clergyman in Minnesota. Like Boyesen, he began by imitating Bjørnson, but his works were written in *landsmaal* (New Norse). Ivar Aasen (1813–96) was the first scholar to make a scientific study of Norwegian dialects, with a view toward creating a distinct national language for Norway to replace Danish. Aasmund Olafsson Vinje (1818–70), friend and associate of Ibsen, was a poet, wit, and journalist of considerable importance and influence in his day. He followed Ivar Aasen's lead in writing in *landsmaal*, and in 1858 founded his own paper in Christiania, *Dølen* (The Dalesman). See Beyer, *History of Norwegian Literature*, 143, 152, 162–166, 199.

intelligence of one's readers to label every character, at its first appearance, with his moral testimonials." [3]

Boyesen thought Janson's chief fault lay in "his deep-rooted reverence for the early monuments of his nation." Historical poetry, said Boyesen, must be keyed to the era for which it is written, because "what may have been a strong dramatic or tragical motive in one age, may have altogether vanished from another, and may no longer appeal to the feelings of men, except as a revolting barbarism." He cited an example: "It may be Norse, but it certainly does not enhance either the picturesque or the aesthetic effect of the scene to have Turid so far forget her womanly nature as to mingle with the men, helmet on her head, and axe in hand, and fight like a lioness." And, "[This] is revolting to our sense of aesthetic propriety," he said, and presumably should be omitted from the poem, or at least softened to suit nineteenth-century sensibilities.[4]

This conviction was probably derived from the precepts and practices of the great Swedish poet, Esaias Tegnér. As we have seen, Boyesen received a copy of *Fritiof's Saga* on his twelfth birthday and was soon trying to write romantic poems of his own, based on the old heroic legends. In later years, though he still admired Tegnér, Boyesen changed his mind about the proper treatment of the saga material, but in 1872 he still echoed the Swedish poet. Boyesen's critique of Janson's poem involved the arguments Tegnér had advanced to justify his approach in *Fritiof's Saga*:

"In the saga much occurs which is very grand and heroic, and hence valid for all times, which both might and ought to be retained; but, on the other hand, a great deal occurs which is rough, savage, barbarous. . . . Up to a certain degree it therefore became necessary to modernize; but the difficulty was to find the golden mean. On the one hand, the poem ought not to offend too much our more refined manners and gentler modes of thought; but, on the other hand, the natural quality, the freshness, the truth to nature ought not to be sacrificed." [5]

In Boyesen's review of Thomas Carlyle's *The Early Kings of Norway*, in the October, 1875, *Atlantic*, he looked at the sagas as history. They were not an entirely reliable record, he conceded, but they deserved

---

[3] Boyesen, in *North American Review*, 115:388, 389.
[4] Boyesen, in *North American Review*, 115:388, 389, 397.
[5] Tegnér is quoted in Boyesen, *Essays on Scandinavian Literature*, 265 (New York, 1895).

more respectful treatment than they received in Carlyle's flimsy and slipshod book. Boyesen was obviously angered by this contemptuous and eccentric account of Norway's heroic period.[6]

"Two Norse Sagas," in the March, 1877, *International Review*, consists largely of plot résumés of *The Story of Burnt Njal* and *The Story of Gisli the Outlaw*, translations by G. W. Dasent brought out in America by A. S. Barnes. Boyesen also discusses, however, the characterization and psychological treatment in the sagas and compares these two stories to Greek and Roman heroic legends and to modern fiction. The comparison was particularly attractive to Boyesen: He discovered that Gunnar and Hallgerda in *Burnt Njal* had striking modern parallels in Lydgate and Rosamond of George Eliot's *Middlemarch*.[7]

As Boyesen gained more confidence in his role as American interpreter of Norwegian literature, he became a stronger partisan of the sagas. In 1877 he said, "They are the clear and strong utterances of a warm-blooded and clear-sighted race, which measured the world fearlessly by its own standards." This statement appeared in a review, in the April *Atlantic*, of *Viking Tales of the North*, translated by Rasmus B. Anderson and Jon Bjarnason. Though Boyesen did not condone the savage, lawless spirit which pervaded the sagas, he could now explain it. They were set in a time when "the individual was strong, and society as yet crudely organized and therefore weak." Since there were few moral or legal restraints, animal passions ran wild and personal traits were grotesquely emphasized. Consequently, character delineation was a simple process for the writer, all the figures being in bold relief. Boyesen ended his review with a hope that more such translations would appear: "If the great sagas of the North were generally known among us, they could hardly fail to produce a healthful influence upon the future of American literature." He does not explain what the influence would or should be.[8]

In "Bjørnstjerne Bjørnson as a Dramatist," in the January, 1873,

[6] *Atlantic Monthly*, 36:498–500 (October, 1875). Despite Carlyle's stature, Boyesen's reaction to his book was justified.

[7] Boyesen, "Two Norse Sagas," in *International Review* (New York), 4:209–229 (March, 1877). This was a publication of some distinction, but it lasted only from 1874 to 1883. The Dasent translations were first published in Edinburgh in 1861 and 1866. George Eliot's *Middlemarch* (1859) is an analysis of an English community accomplished through case studies.

[8] Boyesen, review entitled "Viking Tales of the North," in *Atlantic Monthly*, 39:498–500 (April, 1877).

A Literary Liaison Man

North American Review, Boyesen explained the significance of Bjørnson's career. This writer and patriot had taught his countrymen that "the old strong saga-life was still throbbing with vigorous pulse-beats" in the veins of Norwegian peasants. He had been able to overthrow Danish domination of the Norwegian stage and to substitute his own genuinely Norwegian plays. The "fresh naturalism" of Bjørnson's dramas stemmed chiefly from the "pithy and laconic dialogue, which has a distinct national coloring," said Boyesen. Bjørnson's first plays (and Ibsen's also) were based on the sagas, but both dramatists were more concerned with the modern or timeless implications of their material than with a re-creation of the past. Furthermore, Boyesen observed that greater naturalness in expression was being combined with the use of more realistic modern settings.[9]

Norwegian literature had only partially freed itself from the romantic and heroic past when Boyesen first discussed it for American readers in 1872 and 1873. As his Norwegian friends wrote more and more realistically about modern subjects and contemporary problems, Boyesen recorded their progress in American periodicals and tried to keep pace with them in his own attempts at being a realist.

A definite change in Boyesen's critical thinking can be traced in his comments on Norwegian writing. In his first articles and reviews he seemed eager to present the literature of his native land in a favorable light, and was careful to conciliate readers of the *Atlantic Monthly* and the *North American Review* whose taste was for the romantic and genteel. He stated that the sagas should not be handled too literally in translations or adaptations made for these readers: He was eager that the crudeness and naturalness be pruned away until nothing remained which was "revolting to our sense of aesthetic propriety."[10]

After Boyesen's trip to Europe in 1873 his attitude changed. The lectures he heard at Leipzig, relating the sagas to medieval German literature, invested the old Norse legends with a new dignity.[11] At the same time the influence of Bjørnson, Turgenev, and other European literary men modified his view of the prevailing literary taste in the United States. As his confidence increased, he began to defend the sagas,

---
[9] *North American Review,* 116:109–138. Boyesen used this article, with some revision, as part of his long chapter on Bjørnson in *Scandinavian Literature,* 3–104. See especially p. 12, 16.
[10] *North American Review,* 115:397.
[11] Boyesen to Fiske, November 30, 1873.

Hjalmar Hjorth Boyesen

arguing that English and American writers would be improved by familiarity with them. He found that their crudeness could be rationalized and explained, instead of suppressed in deference to the delicate sensibilities of modern American readers. Truthfulness was preferable to the romantically picturesque: strength was a higher good than aesthetic purity.

Still more important for Boyesen's future development was his discovery that modern Norwegian writers were turning away from ancient legends to write about contemporary life. From the saga era they inherited or borrowed a simplicity and directness of expression, a forthrightness and even boldness of approach, which they retained in dealing with modern problems. As a result, writers like Bjørnson, Janson, and Jonas Lie developed a type of realism, with many romantic admixtures, that had a strong appeal for Boyesen. Despite his admiration for Turgenev, he felt a greater kinship with these Norwegians and a more natural affinity for their writing than for the objective realism of Turgenev and Flaubert.

Following Boyesen's appointment to Cornell, and the three months he spent at Leipzig, he gained recognition as a critic of German literature. In October, 1874, and January and April, 1875, he reviewed new novels by Gustav Freytag and Friedrich Spielhagen, and by the Norwegian, Jonas Lie, for the *North American Review*. These detailed critiques, which show the reviewer's wide acquaintance with nineteenth-century fiction, also reveal some of his own theories about the novel, and, once again, about the relationship between literature and life. Boyesen applauded the new spirit that produced earnest writers like Freytag and Spielhagen, and approved the statement of a modern critic: "The novel must seek the German people where it is to be found in its strength, that is, at its labor." Modern Germany was no place for a Goethe: "Whoever expects to maintain an exalted position in the society of today must have other things to do than to roam around the world in pursuit of culture, or to arrange private theatricals for the edification of a family of noble idlers." Yet Boyesen admitted that contemporary standard-bearers of German literature did not rank high when compared to writers of other nations. At least a dozen living novelists (of whom he identified only two, Turgenev and George Eliot) outranked Freytag and Spielhagen, the best of the Germans.[12]

---

[12] Boyesen, "Lie's Lodsen og hans hustru," an unsigned review of Lie's "The Pilot and His Wife" (1874), in *North American Review*, 120:471–474 (April, 1875);

A Literary Liaison Man

Boyesen condemns Spielhagen's *Ultimo* as a melodramatic reworking of the author's usual revolutionary themes, but he praises Freytag's *Die Ahnen* (The Ancestors) series, which traces the development of traditional virtues from the fourth century to the present day. Freytag, unlike the usual German imitators of Walter Scott, steered clear of supernaturalism and gave this type of novel a new dignity: "The historical novel, if written with the minute scholarly conscientiousness which Freytag displays, still has its mission, or, to speak more strictly, this new phase of the novel which he has been the first to develop has given it a mission which it could not formerly boast. Freytag's romances, in a manner, clothe the dead skeleton of chronology and statistics with living flesh and blood; they give it a form and a distinct physiognomy, and make it breathe and move in our presence."

Freytag's medieval narratives are better than Victor Hugo's, says Boyesen. Hugo "regards only those features as characteristic of a past period which are impossible in our own," but Freytag "strives to make his tales appeal to us by their human interest, and draws into prominence those traits in the lives and characters of his heroes which prove the psychological unity of the race through all the changes of time."[13]

Boyesen respected Freytag's *Die Ahnen* novels for their historical authenticity, and he was careful to point out what made them acceptable as fiction: "It is the realism of the nineteenth century which has invaded the graveyard of the dead centuries." Freytag's heroes were not always convincing as human beings, Boyesen admitted, and he knew why: they were embodiments of traditional German virtues, not real men. Yet he does not object to the philosophical burdens these novels bear; in fact, he thinks the didacticism of Freytag and Spielhagen is a point in their favor. But, Boyesen adds, Americans would find reading these novels more of a task than a pleasure.[14]

Three articles on the German romantic school that appeared in the

---

Boyesen, review entitled "Freytag's Ingo and Ingraban," in *North American Review*, 119:476–482 (October, 1874). The critic quoted was Dr. Julian Schmidt. Gustav Freytag (1816–95), Friedrich Spielhagen (1829–1911), and Jonas Lie (1833–1908) were all realists, although there was a strong visionary and fantastic streak in Lie. Boyesen was acquainted with these writers.

[13] Quotations in these two paragraphs are from Boyesen, review entitled "Spielhagen's Ultimo," in *North American Review*, 120:446 (April, 1875). Boyesen is quoting Dr. Julian Schmidt on Hugo.

[14] Boyesen, review entitled "Freytag's Die Ahnen," in *North American Review*, 120:444–452 (January, 1875). See also Boyesen, *Essays on German Literature*, 213–263.

Hjalmar Hjorth Boyesen

Atlantic in 1875 and 1876 are properly the work of Professor Boyesen, the German scholar, not of the popular novelist and literary critic. Yet the distinction is not absolute. These essays have a bearing on Boyesen's own literary theory and practice. It has been argued that the *Atlantic* articles stem from Boyesen's stay in Leipzig in 1873 and that, while studying Novalis and his brethren, he suffered a revulsion against the whole romantic doctrine. He admitted later that the German romantics had once appealed to him, and he said that Thackeray's cynicism had cured him of their unhealthy influence.[15] Now he found the fiction of Tieck, Brentano, Von Arnim, and Hoffmann inferior to the novels of his own day:

"It is difficult to read a novel of the eighteenth century without feeling what great strides we have made in that branch of writing during the last ninety years. How much more entertaining, how much truer, stronger, and more artistic is the work of those whom we call the average writers of the present day, than were those clumsily moral or lasciviously virtuous romances in which our slim-waisted grandmothers delighted! In the course of one's reading one is constantly astonished to see what an amount of space the literary histories devote to books which, if they had been written today, would hardly have been honored with a notice in the monthly reviews. Characterization of the kind which we find even in the minor novelists of our day is seldom attempted in these romantic extravaganzas. Everybody moves about as in a fever-dream, the most unheard-of things are continually happening, and nobody is really responsible either for himself or for anybody else. The fact that a man determines to do something is no reason why he should do it; it is rather a reason why he should leave it undone or do the very opposite. Human will is at the mercy of mysterious powers, which thwart it, play with it, and urge it on to the most arbitrary acts."[16]

The three essays on German romanticism should be considered along with *Goethe and Schiller*, which Boyesen began writing at this time. In

---

[15] "Social Aspects of the German Romantic School," "Novalis and the Blue Flower," and "Literary Aspects of the Romantic School," in *Atlantic Monthly*, 36: 49–57, 689–698, 37:607–616 (July, December, 1875, May, 1876). These essays were incorporated, without revision, into *German Literature*. Boyesen discussed German romanticism without making any clear distinction between the two separate movements that are now commonly called the first and second German romantic schools. See also Larson, *The Changing West*, 99; Boyesen, "The Great Realists and the Empty Story-Tellers," in *Forum*, 18:726 (February, 1895).

[16] *German Literature*, 347.

the preface to this volume, he says that the book grew out of his Cornell lectures on German literature; his treatment of the romantic movement probably had a similar origin. Boyesen's three chapters read like a segment of a complete survey of German literature. He never wrote such a book, but these early articles were eventually republished, without revision, in *Essays on German Literature* (1892).[17]

On the whole, Boyesen maintained a scholarly detachment about German literature. Nevertheless, his efforts to explain the romantics brought the accusation that he was a partisan of the movement, and his study of Goethe drew the charge that he prostrated himself uncritically before his subject. This was the *Atlantic Monthly's* only adverse criticism of *Goethe and Schiller*. The *Nation* and *Scribner's* indicated that Boyesen was in awe of both Goethe and Schiller. The reviewers would have preferred more criticism, with less exegesis and fewer pages devoted to plot summaries. They joined in praising the book's graceful style and general readability.[18]

Some of this criticism is due to a misunderstanding of Boyesen's purpose in writing *Goethe and Schiller*. It was intended as a college text and was widely used for that purpose. The 135-page section entitled "Commentary on Goethe's *Faust*" was an especially popular feature, even though the *Nation* found it elementary and discursive. Boyesen admitted that this part, as well as the book proper, was largely a compendium of facts and opinions derived from German sources. The inclusion of such material explains the charge that he praised Goethe and Schiller too highly. American reviewers, whose bias was essentially English, were not likely to accept the German evaluation. Boyesen, of course, did not judge this literature from a British point of view. When he published his second book on the subject in 1892, a far more confident Boyesen openly attacked the English for their unwillingness or inability to understand Goethe.[19]

If Boyesen's two articles on Turgenev, published in 1874 and 1877, do little to enhance his reputation as a critic, they are worthy of con-

[17] When Boyesen began working on *Goethe and Schiller*, it was scheduled for publication by Osgood, in the spring of 1878. See Boyesen to Howells, October 30, 1877, quoted *ante*, chapter 2. *Goethe and Schiller* was finally brought out by Scribner's early in 1879.
[18] See reviews of *Goethe and Schiller*, in *Atlantic Monthly*, 43:541 (April, 1879); *Nation*, 28:189 (March 13, 1879); and *Scribner's Monthly*, 18:147 (May, 1879).
[19] See preface to *Goethe and Schiller*, v–ix; Boyesen, "The English Estimate of Goethe," in *German Literature*, 85–108.

Hjalmar Hjorth Boyesen

sideration for other reasons. Properly speaking, they are not criticism. A recent writer has labeled them "overwritten journalistic patchwork of personal description, summaries of novels, and general enthusiasm," but even this harsh judge would allow that "such literary journalism does play a part in the making and reading of books." And if Boyesen made no observations of his own to match the criticism Henry James was writing at this same time, he did draw from Turgenev a statement of his literary creed: "I never try to improve upon life; I merely try to see and understand it. . . . Every line I have written has been inspired by something which has happened to me or come within my observation. . . . I cannot pride myself on strength of imagination; I have not the faculty of building in air." [20]

Boyesen was impressed by Turgenev's objectivity, his "delight in reality for its own sake." Despite this Russian's strong sympathies, he was a novelist, not a reformer. In the article of 1874 Boyesen quotes Julian Schmidt's comparison of *Uncle Tom's Cabin* with Turgenev's *A Sportsman's Sketches:* Schmidt stated that Turgenev's fidelity to fact produced a far more devastating indictment of serfdom, or slavery, than Mrs. Stowe's abolitionist propaganda, which sacrificed artistic integrity to the purposes of reform. Boyesen picks up this argument in the article of 1877 on Turgenev:

"A reformer is always primarily an idealist; he views his subject abstractly, and, in case he is a writer, constructs his plot, with all its minor machinations, in conformity to some leading purpose which he wishes to accomplish. With Tourguéneff, the moral tendency is not the leading motive; his works would have the same right to be, even if they had no bearing upon the social abuses of the day. As an artist, he takes a keen delight in reality for its own sake; he notes with unerring accuracy every characteristic detail; and then, calculating the finest *nuances* of shade and color, fashions his plot so as to bring these details into their proper relief and proportion. But this very reality which he portrays is so deplorable that no man can fail to see the need of a reform." [21]

It is difficult to judge how seriously Boyesen regarded his function as literary liaison man between Europe and America. He had first assumed and played that role in Scandinavia during his visit there in 1873.

---

[20] The quotations are from Gettman, in *Illinois Studies in Language and Literature*, 27:103, 180, and Boyesen, in *Galaxy*, 17:461.
[21] Boyesen, "Ivan Tourguéneff," in *Scribner's Monthly*, 14:200 (June, 1877).

A Literary Liaison Man

In 1878–79 he sought out the literary men of Germany, Italy, and France, and tried to interpret the new American literature to Daudet's circle, as he had already done with Turgenev.[22] Boyesen was aware that his personality and knowledge of languages gave him a unique advantage in meeting literary lights of other lands. He knew from past experience that reminiscences involving famous foreign writers could be sold to American magazines. The contacts he made in 1878 and 1879 were to furnish him material for articles written over a period of years. One is tempted to call him an opportunist, who rushed his "Reminiscences of Bayard Taylor" into print soon after his friend's death, and wrote a sketch of Victor Hugo, not because he cared about the man's ideas but because the American public put a high valuation on Hugo's work and would read such an article whether it was any good or not.

There is some truth in this judgment, but Boyesen's articles, even though never profound, are not without value. At worst they are readable, sane, cosmopolitan critical appraisals of men, literature, and ideas. Fifteen years later Boyesen was called "An International Boswell." He had begun to merit that title much earlier.[23]

"Two Visits to Victor Hugo," published in *Scribner's Monthly* in December, 1879, is a fair example of Boyesen's "literary journalism." He was self-conscious about visiting a celebrity whose work he did not admire, even though he carried a letter of introduction to him from Turgenev. A good deal of an enthusiast himself, Boyesen was plainly skeptical of Hugo's extreme optimism. He told him that he had much in common with the American idealist, Ralph Waldo Emerson. Hugo had never heard of Emerson! His favorite scheme to guarantee progress and prosperity was a colonization of Africa on a grand scale. Boyesen, however, was worried about what would happen to the aborigines: "In our Southern states . . . the result seems to be that the blacks, although they have the support of the general sentiment of the people of the North, will either have to emigrate or to accept the yoke of political thralldom and social inferiority and dependence." This did not worry Hugo. Eventually they would all become white, he said. Boyesen secured permission to publicize Hugo's views in the United States, indicating that he had hoped all along to turn these interviews into an article.[24]

---
[22] Boyesen, in *North American Review*, 161:532.
[23] *Critic*, 23:131 (August 19, 1893).
[24] *Scribner's Monthly*, 19:184–193 (December, 1879).

Hjalmar Hjorth Boyesen

As an American professor who had been educated in Europe, Boyesen felt qualified to comment on education and scholarship from an international point of view, and he did so on a number of occasions. Before going abroad in 1878, he had been commissioned by *Scribner's* to write a pair of articles on European universities. "The University of Rome," published September, 1879, is, in large part, a warning against either state or church control of education: both stifle scholarship. Boyesen thought that the establishment of a national university in Washington, D.C., would be a mistake. In "The University of Berlin," published in June, 1879, he made some observations on American colleges. Student-teacher relationships were much better in Germany, Boyesen found, and the brilliance of the German faculties suggested one reason for this. The young Cornell professor had a poor opinion of his American colleagues:

"A man who sits year after year at a desk, droning out the same commonplace lectures, interspersed with feeble jokes, or hearing lessons in a half mechanical way, even if his moral character be ever so estimable, can hardly chain the attention of twenty or a hundred lively young men, overflowing with animal spirits. He is merely a school-master, and school-masters have proverbially a hard time in trying to enforce discipline.

"Then again, the American professor is too often, in our smaller colleges, a man who has failed in some other pursuit, and falls back on teaching as a last resort. Real scholarship, in the German sense, has certainly been the exception, and respectable mediocrity the rule. No one has ever thought of demanding prominence as an original investigator as a necessary qualification for a professorship." [25]

The United States had some able scholars and competent teachers, Boyesen conceded, citing other reasons for the comparative inferiority of American colleges: "The board of trustees—in most cases a very miscellaneous body, consisting largely of men who have no idea of what a university is or ought to be—come together and deliberate concerning the needs of the institution." In some American colleges the influence of wealthy trustees was responsible for the appointment of a "worthless polyglot" with no better claims to their faculty chairs than suitable family relationships or connections. Boyesen felt that the self-governing privileges enjoyed by the German universities suggested the proper

---

[25] *Scribner's Monthly*, 18:210 (June, 1879).

A Literary Liaison Man

remedy: "It is a very curious notion, however, which seems to be prevalent among us, that professors, who certainly know the needs of a university better than anyone else, and have its interests more at heart, must be excluded from all direct participation in its government."[26]

Perhaps such articles were literary hack work, but if they were topical and ephemeral they were also lively and pertinent. Boyesen was a good journalist, and he carefully aimed his essays on Europe at American magazine readers. Yet he was no sycophant: His criticism of the manners and mores of his adopted land is sharply pointed and seriously intended.

The reviews and critical articles Boyesen wrote during the seventies gave him little opportunity to expound a coherent literary creed, even if he had been ready to do so. Nearly all of his early essays dealt with European writings and authors. Not until the end of the decade did he have sufficient confidence to discuss American literature in print. He was never entirely sure of himself during the seventies, and some of his ideas had not yet taken definite shape. Nevertheless, this period was important in Boyesen's career as novelist, critic, and scholar. If a positive critical stand cannot be found in his writings, the forces that influenced him can be observed and some important trends recognized.

Gunnar, which Boyesen wrote before he had made any literary alliances outside his native land, shows clearly that his first master was Bjørnstjerne Bjørnson. Later, when Bjørnson turned from romanticism to realism, Boyesen kept pace with him. Although Boyesen was now subject to new influences, he discovered that Norwegian writers were in harmony with the realists of other lands. In February, 1881, he stated the following conclusion after considering the new works by Bjørnson, Lie, and Janson: "The absence of dramatic incidents is the rule rather than the exception in Norse literature. Life in Norway is externally monotonous, and the poets represent it as it is. On the other hand they concentrate their energy on the inner soul life of their characters, and often produce psychological studies of rare excellence." This sounds very much like Howells' "realism of the commonplace" and like the "psychological realism" of Henry James.[27]

---

[26] "The University of Berlin," and "The University of Rome," in *Scribner's Monthly,* 18:205–217, 654–667 (June, September, 1879). The quotations are from the former.

[27] Review entitled "The Spell-bound Fiddler by K. Janson," in *Atlantic Monthly,* 47:287 (February, 1881).

Hjalmar Hjorth Boyesen

Howells' influence on Boyesen was so extensive that it cannot be measured accurately. Howells was friend, editor, and literary adviser. He "Americanized" Boyesen, persuaded him to read Turgenev, corrected his English, suggested revisions, explained why he rejected contributions, sympathized with him, encouraged him, and predicted that he would have a bright future. Howells' early faith in the immigrant writer seems never to have left him.

Before Boyesen met Turgenev for the first time, he had spoken of him as "the world's greatest novelist." After that encounter Boyesen was an avowed disciple and a realist in theory, even though in his own practice he did not break away from romanticism quite so readily. He sent his stories to Turgenev for criticism, and the Russian concluded that the enthusiastic young man was incurably romantic in temperament. This quality was a guarantee of popular success, said Turgenev, but Boyesen was chagrined rather than pleased. He finally succeeded in writing a story that was realistic enough to satisfy Turgenev: It was "A Dangerous Virtue," published in *Scribner's Monthly* in March, 1881.[28]

Both Howells and Boyesen accepted Turgenev's dictum that a novelist should record his own observations of life and shun the inventions of the imagination. This usually meant that psychological study of character replaced plot complication as the chief ingredient of fiction. A favorite target of this early realism was the "abnormality" of romantic fiction. Howells was especially insistent that spectacular events be avoided. Boyesen thought that normal situations could best be depicted if the novelist could find typical characters. Here, he maintained, Turgenev pointed the way for American writers:

"I have often heard it said, and probably with good reason, that the Russians have much in common with Americans. Both are patrons of the future; both feel great possibilities within them. We have long accustomed ourselves to think that our society presented *no fixed or striking* types, and that the mobile, ever billowing surface of our life is unfavorable to artistic effects, if not incapable of artistic treatment. No doubt the Russians thought the same until Tourguéneff came and showed them that this so-called dreary monotony of their existence was, on the contrary, a grand, striking, and animated picture. And when our great novelist comes — as surely he will — he will teach us a similar lesson.

---

[28] Boyesen, in *Philadelphia Inquirer*, October 1, 1893; *Scribner's Monthly*, 21: 745–759. "A Dangerous Virtue" was included in *Queen Titania* (New York, 1881).

A Literary Liaison Man

But as yet Russia is one step in advance of America, for we have no Tourguéneff." [29]

Boyesen was impressed by Turgenev's emphasis on the seriousness of fiction, on the novelist's obligation to make his readers think about important matters. He encouraged Cable to read Turgenev's novels: "They will give you many superb hints of how to manage dramatically a social problem." It was this high seriousness, this willingness to grapple with large subjects, that recommended the contemporary German novelists to Boyesen. Though he saw the faults of Spielhagen and Freytag, he was obviously impressed by their far-reaching aims. He paraphrased the explicit statement of those aims in Spielhagen's *Theorie und Technik des Romans:* "The business of novelists is to give word-pictures — pictures of their nation and its aspirations during a certain period." He was impressed both by Spielhagen's purpose and by his faithful adherence to it: "The profound pleasure which I have found in reading his works is perhaps also due to the fact that I have recognized their typical quality and their direct bearing upon the great questions which agitate the century."

When Cable sent Boyesen his draft of *The Grandissimes* early in 1877, the response was: "Yours is going to be the kind of novel which the Germans call a 'Kulturroman,' a novel in which the struggling forces of opposing civilizations crystallize & in which they find their enduring monument." In reviewing this book for *Scribner's* four years later, he especially commended the author for dealing with a large and serious theme, "the conflict of two irreconcilable civilizations." Even failure in such an ambitious undertaking would be preferable to success in more trivial efforts, he said.[30]

Boyesen's most complete expression of his literary beliefs during this period is in a letter to Cable of February 17, 1878. Cable had evidently asked for such a statement.

"I write to-night only for the purpose of giving you, however vaguely, my present creed or rather theory of novel writing. I hope you won't attach much value to it; for probably it isn't worth much. And still I can't help wishing I had arrived at these conclusions three years earlier. First then, I believe that to be a second class novel where the chief

---

[29] Boyesen, in *Galaxy*, 17:466.
[30] Boyesen to Cable, March 17, 1877, February 17, 1878; Boyesen, *German Literature*, 253; Boyesen, in *Scribner's Monthly*, 21:159.

interest hinges upon the complications of the plot. The plot should be merely a frame-work so arranged as to bring the problem of the story into the strongest possible relief. Extreme complications, according to my notion, are only allowable within the strictest limits of probability; thus in an historical novel or one dealing with remote ages there is a much wider scope for complication than in one dealing with the present age. How far this is sound, I don't know; & you must judge for yourself; you understand I offer these remarks merely in a humble tentative manner. Further, it is the typical quality of the novel which gives it its chief value in my eyes; & it was the mastery with which you seize typical characters & situations which especially charms me in your short stories. There should be no element of the accidental; the *denouement* & the whole progress of events must be as inexorable as Nature herself. A winding up which appears as an accident, a *deus ex machina*, always weakens the effect of a work, however excellent its quality in other respects."

6

The Move to New York City

IN THE spring of 1880 Boyesen looked back nostalgically on the decade that had passed. Writing Howells, April 2, he indicated, not at all paradoxically, that he had fallen short of his ambitions and yet was proud of his attainments: "I am tempted once more to try your editorial patience, this time with a poem which, just this moment, appears to its prejudiced author to have a spark of immortality in it. When I read my early Norse ballads, which are from time to time being resurrected from their sepulchers in the old Atlantic volumes, & when I reflect upon your indefatigable kindness . . . I often ask myself if without your advice & criticism I should ever have amounted to anything. . . .

"I intend, by the way, to bring out a volume of my poems this autumn & should therefore be obliged, if (in case you accept the enclosed elegy) you could publish it before October.—I am having quite a triumph in Germany at present, occasioned by the publication of 'Gunnar' & 'Tales from Two Hemispheres' & have been engaged to write for several well-known German magazines, at good prices. My other books are also to be translated in the course of the year.

"My little boy is physically a splendid specimen of the genus 'homo' & has by this time nearly eaten up his poor mother who at present is ill, though, I hope, not seriously."[1]

There were then no international copyright laws, and Boyesen derived more satisfaction than financial return from his European successes. He

---

[1] Hjalmar Hjorth Boyesen, Jr., was born July 7, 1879.

was able at times, however, to realize some income from his German affiliations. The novelist Friedrich Spielhagen, who edited a literary periodical, had engaged him "as a regular contributor to Westermanns Monatshefte [*Westermann's Monthly Magazine*] at a very good pay," Boyesen wrote Willard Fiske on May 2, 1880. But he also mentioned, in the same letter, that "piratical editions of 'Gunnar' . . . have appeared in Germany, besides the authorized one." In the previous year, Spielhagen had translated and printed in his magazine a couple of stories from *Tales from Two Hemispheres*, along with a biographical sketch of Boyesen. All of the stories had been translated earlier in Vienna, where they appeared in both periodical and book form.[2]

By 1881, when the fourth American edition of the *Tales* appeared, one of the stories had been "put into Russian," and a new literary magazine, the *Critic,* reported an even more curious proof of Boyesen's popular success: "Mr. Boyesen has had the singular experience of seeing his stories translated into his mother tongue. Three German translations of the 'Tales from Two Hemispheres' have been made for as many publishers, and from the German they have been put into Danish, the literary language of Norway." Subsequently the *Critic* announced that "Prof. Boyesen's complete works, except his poems, are about to be published by the firm of Cammermeyer, in Christiania, in a Norwegian translation by Otto Anderson."[3]

Although Boyesen was pleased by this popular success, he was uneasy about the approval of critics and fellow authors. When Willard Fiske wrote of a meeting with Henry James in Europe that included some discussion of Boyesen's work in talk about mutual friends, Boyesen immediately assumed a defensive attitude: "Whatever Henry James may think of my writings (& I have a strong suspicion that he abused them or damned them with faint praise) they are genuine, as far as they go, & they seem at present to be in demand."[4]

Certainly Boyesen's activities during this period gave the impression that popular success, and the financial rewards of such success, were his chief goals. Two collections of his stories were published by Scribner's in

---

[2] Boyesen to Fiske, November 8, 1879, May 2, 1880. The quotations are from the second letter.

[3] *Critic* (New York), 1:53, 109, 9:23 (February 26, April 23, 1881, July 10, 1886). As Boyesen was a close friend of Richard Watson Gilder, then editor of the *Century,* he knew Gilder's younger brother and sister, Jeanette and Joseph Gilder, who published and edited the weekly literary magazine and review, the *Critic* (1881–1906).

[4] Boyesen to Fiske, May 2, 1880.

The Move to New York City

1881, *Ilka on the Hill-Top and Other Stories* first and *Queen Titania* later. Seven of the nine pieces in the two volumes had been previously printed in *Scribner's Monthly*. With the exception of "A Dangerous Virtue," a stark tale apparently written to gain Turgenev's approval, the stories are sentimental and melodramatic. They are also derivative: Even a casual reading reveals Boyesen's debt to Hawthorne, Bret Harte, and Henry James; and although he may have been experimenting with both theme and subject matter, it is difficult to detect any seriousness of purpose or artistic integrity in this fiction.

Writing Howells in September, 1880, Boyesen explained that he had left Cornell and intended to make his living in New York City. The letter also points up his estrangement from the *Atlantic* and his concern for his poetry. He apparently wanted one poem to appear in the *Atlantic* about the time the complete volume was advertised for sale:

"I suppose I ought to be discouraged, for I had great hopes of the last poem (on Hellas) which you returned. But as I cannot make up my mind to relinquish my last hold on the Atlantic, I come back once more. . . . The theme is a Norwegian legend which I heard in my childhood & which undoubtedly must have been treated by ballad writers before. Of course the final tableau is wholly conventional as a romantic situation, but this very thing makes it (to my mind) more available in a ballad like this.

"We have now at last taken the bold step which I have meditated so long. We have abandoned Ithaca (which Mrs. B. never liked & which I had ceased to like) & I am now wholly dependent upon my literary income. 'Scribner's' gives me a great deal to do & 'The Nation' and 'St. Nicholas' are also old customers. I feel rather hopeful & am jubilant at the daily thought of being independent of that tyrannical University bell. The president, however, will not consent to release me altogether; & in accordance with his request, I am to return for one month every year & deliver daily lectures.[5]

"I need not say that if you have any books which you care to send me for review I shall be happy to receive them & shall send you the notices promptly." [6]

---

[5] The president of Cornell was Andrew D. White. Boyesen gave these lectures the first year after he left, but as he was teaching at Columbia from then on, the arrangement must have ended. See W. T. Hewett, *Cornell University: A History*, 2:27 (New York, 1905).

[6] Boyesen to Howells, September 15, 1880.

Hjalmar Hjorth Boyesen

Howells turned down the new poem, but Boyesen still had faith in his verses. When his book of poetry finally appeared late in 1882, "The Lost Hellas" was the opening piece. *Idyls of Norway and Other Poems* was published by Scribner's two years later than its author had anticipated. During the early eighties his output of verse almost ceased. His new poems were not so well received as the simple rhymes on Norwegian themes printed in the *Atlantic* and the *Galaxy* in the early seventies had been. Besides, the urge to compose verse came on him less often. After one particularly long interval, Howells inquired about Boyesen's silence: "He answered, as if still in sad astonishment at the fact, that he had found life was not all poetry." Remembering their first meeting in Cambridge in 1871, Howells added: "In those earlier days I believe he really thought it was!" [7]

Mrs. Boyesen's poor health had been a constant worry when her husband gave up his position at Cornell to try free-lance writing. He wrote to Willard Fiske that he was taking "the bold step" of abandoning Ithaca for New York because "my interest & especially my wife's health positively demand the change." Lillie Boyesen, who was pregnant again, was ill for two months in the spring of 1880. Their second child, Algernon, was born in New York City October 13, 1880, fifteen months after the first son. The extent of Boyesen's concern for the health of his family was reflected in a new book published three months after Algernon's birth. He dedicated *Ilka on the Hill-Top* to Dr. Egbert Guernsey, a well-known homeopath, with the inscription: "I can never expect adequately to repay you for your many valuable services to me and mine." [8]

A letter to Howells of September 15, 1880, shows that Boyesen began the experiment of living by his pen with a good deal of confidence and hope, but the venture was not a success. Besides writing for *Scribner's*, the *Nation*, and *St. Nicholas*, he sold an article to the *American*, which began publication in Philadelphia in 1880; a short story and a poem to *Harper's*; two sonnets to *Lippincott's*; and a short article to the *Critic*. Several other contributions to the latter appeared as letters to the editor and were probably not paid for.[9] While Boyesen was teaching at Ithaca,

---

[7] Boyesen, *Idyls of Norway*, 1–7; Howells, *Literary Friends*, 257. Most reviewers shared Howells' opinion of "The Lost Hellas."

[8] Boyesen to Fiske, May 2, 1880. Scribner's published *Ilka on the Hill-Top and Other Stories* on January 14, 1881. For information about Dr. Guernsey, see *National Cyclopedia of American Biography*, 2:484.

[9] The number of editorials and unsigned reviews Boyesen did for periodicals can-

The Move to New York City

he had written reviews for the *Atlantic* and the *North American Review*, but during his first year in New York Howells was able to give him only one book to review. If he did any work for the *North American*, the results have not been identified. It is possible that other stories, poems, or articles were sold to more obscure periodicals and have not come to light.

Boyesen worked "desperately hard," staying at his desk from nine to six each day. But his efforts were not sufficiently rewarded, and he felt the loss of the assured, if meager, salary of a professor. Lillie Boyesen, daughter of a wealthy father, was not accustomed to living meanly, and the medical and other expenses incidental to childbirth were considerable. At the end of a year Boyesen was convinced that an American writer could not make an adequate living by his pen alone, and he accepted an appointment at Columbia College. Some time later, when a young teacher wrote for advice about devoting his time exclusively to writing, Boyesen emphatically urged him to think better of the idea, citing his own unfortunate experience: "Will you pardon me if I say that I think you are very sanguine, and take rather unwarrantable risks, in giving up a safe and sure position as a teacher for the very uncertain chance of making a success in journalism. . . . In 1880 I gave up my Cornell professorship for the very same reason that you adduce; and I was very glad to resume the same harness at Columbia in 1881. . . . I have never since contemplated the possibility of getting rid of it." [10]

The appointment at Columbia was made in June, 1881, and Boyesen's duties began that fall.[11] The position was only an instructorship, but, harassed as he was by financial obligations and his wife's continued ill health, he was happy to be back in harness on any terms. A third son, Bayard, was born January 30, 1882.

During the Boyesens' first two years in New York City the family lived at 353 West Fifty-first Street, "in a comfortable flat whose only disadvantage is that it is a little too far over on the West Side." The

not be accurately estimated. For signed articles published during these years, see the bibliography.

[10] Barry, in *New York Illustrated American*, 17:179. Boyesen's letter, dated May 29, 1894, is quoted by G. M. Hyde, in "In Gratitude to Professor Boyesen," in *Dial* (Chicago), 19:323 (December 1, 1895). The recipient is identified only as "Nicodemus."

[11] *Critic*, 1:166 (June 18, 1881). The name Columbia University was not adopted until 1896, after Boyesen's death. Columbia College continues as a separate school within the university.

summers of 1881 and 1882 were spent at Stockbridge, Massachusetts, and when the family returned to New York after the second summer, they moved into an apartment at Park Avenue and Sixty-third Street that Boyesen described as "large and commodious." [12]

By the fall of 1882 the Boyesens were healthy, happy, and comparatively prosperous. Writing to Fiske November 26, the head of the household could report, "The Norse trio are flourishing & their mother too is better than she has been for years." He had been made a professor.

Boyesen's early promotion at Columbia came partly because of his merit and qualifications, and partly because of circumstances. If he needed the appointment badly, the college also needed Boyesen. A new modern-language program had been authorized by the trustees June 7, 1880, but when the next school year opened, only Schmidt, an elderly professor of German, and a new instructor in Italian and Spanish were available to do the teaching. A part-time French instructor was borrowed from the affiliated school of mines, but ill health forced Schmidt's resignation that same fall. Two new instructors were hired in November, 1880, but neither survived the first two years of the program. One of them reported "unpleasant conflicts with certain students": The Columbia boys, especially the upperclassmen, were not serious about their language courses. This had been the situation when Boyesen joined the faculty in the fall of 1881, on a one-year appointment as instructor in German.[13]

By May 1, 1882, President F. A. P. Barnard could survey the situation with more confidence. C. S. Smith, hired as an instructor in Italian and Spanish, found himself teaching French, German, and Danish, too, during the first year, but he had been conspicuously successful in getting the program under way. Smith had inherited the Gebhard Professorship in German when Schmidt retired in the fall of 1880. "Practically," said the president in 1882, "Professor Smith is discharging the duties of a Professor of the Modern Languages and Foreign Literature generally. It would . . . be a very fitting arrangement to transfer the Gebhard professorship to Prof. Boyesen, who actually gives the largest part of the instruction in German." Barnard went on to justify this recommendation:

---

[12] Boyesen to Fiske, September 12, 1881, September 25, November 26, 1882.

[13] F. A. P. Barnard, "Instruction in Modern Languages," in Columbia College, *Annual Report of the President, May 1, 1882* (New York, 1882). See also *Annual Report, June 6, 1881* (New York, 1881). Henry Immanuel Schmidt was Gebhard Professor at Columbia, 1847–80.

The Move to New York City

"Professor Boyesen is, moreover, a very thorough German scholar, fully versed in the literature as well as the language of Germany, as he has demonstrated by his published writings, and as is made evident by the fact that, during the past winter, he has delivered, on invitation, a course of lectures on the poetry of Goethe and Schiller before the Lowell Institute of Boston. These lectures were largely attended, and were received with evidences of marked approbation. Prof. Boyesen is, moreover, an accomplished English writer and a popular contributor to the literature of our language. On every account he is eminently fit for the position to which it is proposed to promote him. The term of office of Prof. Boyesen under his present appointment expired with the close of the present year." [14]

Barnard told the trustees that interest in the Scandinavian languages at Columbia was less than had been expected, Danish being the only one elected by any students. He hoped an arrangement could be made for Professor Boyesen to teach Danish, "which he is quite competent to do, being himself a Dane by birth, and quite familiar with the languages and literature of Denmark, Norway, and Sweden." The plan was carried out, but Danish did not become popular at Columbia. In Boyesen's first or second year, he lectured on modern Scandinavian literature, officially "in Danish"—but the class included only two students. He made it clear that he was not a Dane and that the language he was speaking was Norwegian. He offered courses in Scandinavian literature in later years, but the lectures were in English.[15]

The student who described the "Danish" lectures also remembered "the privilege" he had enjoyed in 1881–82 of hearing Boyesen lecture on *Faust*: "To me, as I imagine to the rest of the fourteen or fifteen composing the class, those lectures were a revelation; they opened my eyes to the true meaning of the word culture. As poet, scholar, and man of the world himself, Professor Boyesen understood the man Goethe as few have understood him. He offered to the interpretation of the German masterpiece a variety and breadth of scholarship that were truly marvelous. Everything was brought into requisition, from the poems of Homer, which were recited with true Hellenic enjoyment, to the delicate sonnets of the lecturer himself." Boyesen gave little attention to textual

---

[14] *Annual Report, May 1, 1882*. Barnard was in error about the subject of Boyesen's Lowell lectures.

[15] *Annual Report, May 1, 1882*; Daniel Kilham Dodge, "Hjalmar Hjorth Boyesen the Teacher," in *Bachelor of Arts* (New York), 2:822–825 (May, 1896).

criticism, the student remembered, but the exclusion "of grammatical and philological explanation" allowed more time for what really interested the lecturer: Goethe's ideas, especially as applied "to the intellectual and social conditions of the present time." Together, Boyesen and Goethe made a very strong impression: "We were brought face to face with the great questions of life, and if we failed to grasp these firmly then, many of us undoubtedly owe much of what maturity of thought we may now possess to those classroom interprctations."[16]

A colleague, Brander Matthews, mentioned Boyesen's teaching methods in a letter on "Literature at Columbia College" written to the *Dial:* "At Columbia the literary spirit also dominates the teaching in other languages than English, as those know who are familiar with the way in which Professor Boyesen expounds Goethe and Schiller." Later, Matthews acknowledged that Boyesen was also responsible for instruction in philology: "In the department of the Germanic languages, of which Prof. H. H. Boyesen is the head, he and Prof. W. H. Carpenter offer courses in Icelandic, in Gothic, and Middle High German and in Old High German, — all of which would be useful to a student of English philology." Carpenter, a Cornell graduate whom Boyesen had persuaded Columbia to hire in 1883, was a bona fide philologist. The department head at Columbia left this phase of the German program to his colleague as far as possible. In speaking of one of the distinguished men at the University of Berlin, Boyesen said: "Like most German professors, he dwells with preference on the philological phase of the text, and illustrates it abundantly with historical and philological comments. He rarely seems to regard his author from a literary point." Though Boyesen respected philology, he emphasized literary quality and ideas.

At Cornell Boyesen had been a skillful lecturer, although his efforts were limited to the classroom. A gifted raconteur, he always gave a lively and enthusiastic performance; consequently, although he demanded much of his students, his Cornell courses increased in popularity until seventy students were enrolled in his German literature course in 1879–80, with eighty to a hundred attending each lecture.[18]

[16] Dodge, in *Bachelor of Arts*, 2:822.
[17] Brander Matthews, "Literature at Columbia College," and "English at Columbia College," in *Dial,* 14:206, 16:101 (April 1, 1893, February 16, 1894); Boyesen to Fiske, March 29, April 17, 1882; Boyesen, in *Scribner's Monthly,* 18:213 (June, 1879).
[18] Boyesen to Fiske, May 2, 1880.

The Move to New York City

Before beginning his work at Columbia, Boyesen had been engaged by the Lowell Institute of Boston to give a series of addresses the following season on "Saga Literature of the North."[19] Boyesen had prepared thoroughly for these appearances, he wrote Fiske on September 12, 1881, explaining why he had borrowed some of his friend's books while Fiske was in Europe.

The six Lowell lectures were given Tuesday and Friday evenings from February 21 through March 10, 1882, in Huntington Hall, Boston. The *Boston Evening Transcript*, faithfully noting the main points of the lectures, called them an "interesting series"; "a fine audience" was in attendance. Boyesen carefully covered the usual material, but he found opportunities to compare the moral point of view of the sagas to Christian ethics, and their sociological aspect to the theories of Herbert Spencer.[20]

The pleasure and satisfaction he derived from lecturing is clearly reflected in a letter to Fiske of September 25, 1882: "The college work will commence on Monday & I am eager to get back into the harness. I am also to deliver a course of public lectures on German literature, & have a most tempting program laid out for the winter."

Boyesen soon became one of Columbia's best-known professors, but his literary efforts of the eighties lack quality and direction. Only two or three of some two dozen short stories written during the decade have any real significance, and the three novels he produced do not appear to be "serious" efforts. He published a collection of his earlier poems, but wrote so few new ones that he was no longer a truly active poet. Nor could he be called a playwright on the basis of a single play, to be mentioned later. His new literary ventures were a young people's history of Norway and a first volume of juvenile fiction.

One inference is inescapable: He was writing to increase his income and was willing to try any medium that offered a promising financial return.

Scribner's, Boyesen's regular publishers, brought out four of his books during the eighties: two collections of short stories, a selection of poetry, and a volume of tales for boys. During the same period four other publishers issued single volumes. Boyesen's history of Norway for juveniles was commissioned by Putnam for its *Story of the Nations Series*; his

---

[19] *Critic*, 1:10 (January 15, 1881).
[20] *Boston Evening Transcript*, February 21, 24, 28, March 3, 7, 1882.

Hjalmar Hjorth Boyesen

novels were published by Roberts Brothers in its *No Name Series,* and by Appleton in its *Town and Country Library.* And D. Lothrop Company brought out *Vagabond Tales,* the only collection of Boyesen's stories to be published after 1881.[21]

Boyesen's magazine offerings of the same period were scattered even more widely than his books. During 1882–84 he published five short tales, in as many magazines. None of these had any great merit or significance, although "A Daring Fiction" was included in the ten-volume *Stories by American Authors* put out by Scribner's in 1884–85.[22] Boyesen published three stories in 1885: two very short ones in *Harper's Weekly* and a more ambitious effort in *Century.* His only contribution of 1886, "The Story of a Blue Vein," a sentimental tale with a German setting, was the opening piece in the first issue of a new magazine, *Cosmopolitan.*[23] While this record may prove that Boyesen was eager to sell his wares in any market, it also indicates that his name was a popular drawing card. Several years later, after *Cosmopolitan* had changed hands, it became Boyesen's chief outlet, printing a large proportion of his work during the nineties.

In the eighties, Boyesen welcomed these new outlets, for some of his old markets were failing him. After William Dean Howells resigned the editorship of the *Atlantic Monthly* in February, 1881, Boyesen's writings ceased to appear in the magazine. Even earlier, between 1876 and 1881, Boyesen had submitted, and Howells had rejected, many stories and poems. Two groups of sonnets in 1878 and 1879 and a single sonnet in 1880 had been Boyesen's only contributions to the *Atlantic* since the essays on German romanticism of 1875–76. Although he was on good terms with Thomas Bailey Aldrich and Horace E. Scudder, who succeeded Howells as editors, they did not use any of his work. Under

[21] For more information on these books, see the bibliography.

[22] "A Daring Fiction," in *New York Commercial Advertiser,* November, 1884. The Scribner series was apparently a publisher's venture, as no editor is listed. The fifty-odd stories were by James, De Forest, Bellamy, Bunner, Stockton, and other authors well known at the time, but it is difficult to see any guiding principle behind the selection. Boyesen's story is one of his worst. See *Stories by American Authors,* 10:112–153 (New York, 1885).

[23] "Mr. Block's One Glorious Night," and "In the Wrong Niche," in *Harper's Weekly,* 29:154, 330 (March 7, May 23, 1885); "A Child of the Age," in *Century,* 31:177–192; *Cosmopolitan* (Rochester, New York), 1:3–11 (March, 1886). *Cosmopolitan,* founded by Joseph N. Hallock, was moved to New York City and, in 1889, sold to John Brisben Walker, who became one of Boyesen's closest literary associates.

COURTESY COLUMBIA UNIVERSITY LIBRARIES

Hjalmar Hjorth Boyesen

The Royal Fredrik University, Christiania, about 1860

Systrand and Sognefjord

COURTESY COLUMBIA UNIVERSITY LIBRARIES

Columbia College about 1880

A page of Boyesen's lecture notes

The Move to New York City

Aldrich the *Atlantic* had returned to its conservative Boston Brahmin tradition. In 1891 a letter to Scudder from Boyesen, offering an article on Ibsen, showed that he was still interested in the *Atlantic*, but also indicated that he was even more interested in selling his work for the best price he could get.[24] New magazines paid higher rates to attract established writers; the *Atlantic* saw no need to do so.

In the fall of 1881 Boyesen lost his chief magazine outlet, *Scribner's Monthly*. The elder Charles Scribner had founded the magazine in 1870, with Dr. J. G. Holland as editor. Holland and Boyesen got along very well. Over a seven-year period from November, 1874, through October, 1881, *Scribner's Monthly* had published nearly all of Boyesen's fiction, and most of his poems and articles. In October, 1881, Dr. Holland died, and the company sold the magazine; in November it appeared as the *Century* under the editorship of Richard Watson Gilder. Gilder, too, was a friend of Boyesen's, but the *Century* published a much smaller proportion of his output than *Scribner's* had. "Anastasia," a short story, appeared in April, 1883, and "A Problematic Character," a book-length serial, ran from August through October, 1884.

In 1883 Boyesen wrote a novel that had both merit and significance; yet this book, *A Daughter of the Philistines*, was published anonymously, as one of the Roberts *No Name Series*. This, Boyesen's first purely American novel, was critical of many phases of life in the United States, especially of New York society, but the attacks in it hardly seem pointed enough to warrant concealment of the author's identity. Boyesen must have been pleased by a paragraph that appeared in the *Critic*: "The No Name novel, 'A Daughter of the Philistines' is said to be in its 5th thousand. By some reviewers this book is attributed to Robert Grant, by others to Prof. Boyesen, of Columbia, and one critic has been found who would suspect Henry James of having written it, if there were any reason for him to publish an anonymous novel. It has been argued that Prof. Boyesen, being a Norwegian, could not have written a book showing such a clear comprehension of the spirit of American life."[25]

Boyesen might have quoted this conjecture to those critics who challenged the accuracy of his portrayal of the American scene and Ameri-

---

[24] Boyesen to Scudder, October 8, 1890, in Houghton Library, Harvard University. Howells' letters to Boyesen indicate that the *Atlantic* would have published some of the stories that Boyesen sold to *Scribner's*, if they had been cut drastically. Apparently he found it financially impossible to do this.

[25] *Critic*, 3:246 (May 26, 1883).

can character. He was certainly pleased by the brisk sale of his book. The financial inducement offered by Roberts Brothers, rather than a desire for anonymity, probably accounts for the appearance of the novel in the *No Name Series,* for *A Daughter of the Philistines* was listed among Boyesen's writings in 1885. He was proud of his growing reputation, even though he acknowledged the shortcomings of certain works; and he was well aware that an author could get better terms from publishers if his books were selling well.

The popularity of Boyesen's books may be inferred from his answers to a query conducted by the *Critic* in 1884, on the proper distribution of book profits. Under the heading "Cash Down, or a Percentage?" the magazine printed the opinions of a number of writers. Boyesen thought an author should be paid a 10-per-cent royalty on the first and second thousand copies of his book, then progressively more. The publisher could well afford to pay 20 or 25 per cent on the fifth and sixth thousand. "I have always had this plan much at heart," said Boyesen. Despite the arguments he had heard to the contrary, he was convinced that this was the only fair way to "enable an author of established reputation to reap a proportionate benefit from the growth of his popularity." [26]

In the early eighties Boyesen made his debut as a playwright. Perhaps he had read the lead editorial in the *Critic*, which expressed regret that Howells was leaving the *Atlantic Monthly* and the hope that he would now give more attention to writing plays. The article ended with the suggestion that other American novelists could do better than the current professional dramatists:

"When one contemplates the sort of thing that has been produced, as a rule with honorable exceptions, by the successful American playwright for a generation past, one cannot but desire that a few more 'amateurs' may rush in where angels fear to tread, to the end that something may be done — even if by accident only — to make theatre-going a rational enjoyment. If Mr. Howells, Mr. James, Mr. Aldrich, Mr. Cable, Mr. Boyesen, Mr. Harte, or Mrs. Burnett (who, 'tis said, has been working lately on a play) — if all or any of them would devote themselves to the writing of plays for a reasonable length of time, it is safe to say that something would come of it." [27]

[26] *Critic*, 4:62 (February 9, 1884). A sliding scale of royalties is now an established procedure in American publishing.
[27] *Critic*, 1:50 (February 26, 1881).

The Move to New York City

Whether or not Boyesen was consciously acting on this advice, he had a play ready in 1883. *Alpine Roses*, based on his short story "Ilka on the Hill-Top," opened at the Madison Square Theatre on January 31, 1884. William Winter described the play as "a sentimental comedy . . . the love story of two blooming peasant girls, resident in the mountains of Tyrol." Most of the interest shown in the play was aroused by the acting of Richard Mansfield, then just beginning his career. Mansfield, recently returned to New York after the disastrous failure of his first starring tour, did not play a leading role, but his acting of Count von Dornfeld won the praise of critics who would have been happy to damn him: "Mr. Richard Mansfield, to whom was assigned the thankless part of the Count, sacrificed himself to the exigencies of probability. He played the character as written: a colorless lounger with nothing to recommend him but courage and honourable instincts. He is not likely to get much credit for the performance. . . . Mr. Mansfield's conceit is always too obvious, but he is a very bright young actor and will have a career when he has learned to put a less extravagant estimate upon himself." [28]

Mansfield remained with the production for more than fifty performances. *Alpine Roses* ran a hundred times in New York, closing April 10, 1884; a successful road tour followed.[29]

"It has been my ambition for many years to write a history of Norway, chiefly because no such book, worthy of the name, exists in the English language. When the publishers of the present volume proposed to me to write the story of my native land, I therefore eagerly accepted their offer." So began Boyesen's preface to *The Story of Norway*, a volume included in Putnam's *Story of the Nations Series*.[30] It had been his conviction, arrived at soon after coming to the United States, that Americans should be better informed about Norway. Throughout his career he tried, in fiction and nonfiction, to correct misconceptions about Norway and to present a true picture. He discovered, moreover, that poems, stories, and articles about his native land found a ready market in

---

[28] George C. D. Odell, *Annals of the New York Stage*, 12:220 (New York, 1940); William Winter, *Life and Art of Richard Mansfield*, 51 (New York, 1910). The review is quoted in Paul Wilstach, *Richard Mansfield: The Man and the Actor*, 120 (New York, 1908). Copies of *Alpine Roses* are in the library of Tulane University and the archives of the Norwegian-American Historical Association.
[29] Odell, *Annals of the New York Stage*, 12:220.
[30] *The Story of Norway*, v (New York, 1886).

Hjalmar Hjorth Boyesen

American magazines. Boyesen's eager acceptance of Putnam's offer was certainly stimulated by the assurance of a good financial return more than by the hope of enhancing his stature as a writer.

"In this work the romanticist had his final inning," a modern critic has said of Boyesen's *Norway*. "The glamorous heroes of the Viking Age receive far more attention than the more commonplace actors of the modern stage. The book is consequently not outstanding as history; but it makes delightful reading and in the author's own day it enjoyed high favor." The designation "romanticist" would not have pleased Boyesen in 1886. He could point to his statement in the preface that this was to be a "story" of Norway, that it was intended "to differ in some important respects from a regular history." In accordance with the publisher's plan, it "was to dwell particularly upon the dramatic phases of historical events, and concern itself but slightly with the growth of institutions and sociological phenomena. It therefore necessarily takes small account of proportion." [31]

In spite of this disclaimer, reviewers of 1886 felt that Boyesen should have given more space to contemporary Norwegian history. The *Nation* remarked that "the interesting final chapter, containing the history of Norway since 1814, might with advantage have been allotted more than barely eighteen pages of text." This statement, and the extensive treatment the *Nation's* reviewer gave the book, is a tribute to Boyesen's work. The history was evidently taken more seriously than he or the publishers had intended. Another reviewer spoke of the author's "limpid English style." Most of the critics agreed with the *Nation* that "Prof. Boyesen's manner of writing is at once dignified and entertaining, and he has produced a valuable and interesting book, which deserves to find a host of readers, old and young." [32]

Norway was dedicated to "Christian Bors, Knight of St. Olaf, Wasa, and the North Star, Consul of Norway and Sweden in New York." Boyesen, in one of his articles, mentioned a sore point for immigrant Norwegians: Because a Swedish consul usually represented the dual monarchy, the tendency was for Norway to be considered a Swedish province or dependency. "Twice in my life," he wrote later, "have I been

---

[31] Larson, *The Changing West*, 107; Boyesen, *The Story of Norway*, v.
[32] *Nation*, 43:276 (September 30, 1886); *Critic*, 9:27 (July 17, 1886). The book contains 538 pages and includes many illustrations and maps. New printings appeared as late as 1904; after Boyesen's death a chapter by C. F. Keary, on the recent history of Norway, was added.

pronounced a boor and a savage because I declined affably to accept the Swedish nationality, and contradicted the Swedish brother who had the kindness to claim me as a countryman; and I scarcely know a single Norwegian abroad who has not had similar experiences."[33] When Boyesen wrote in the book, "To Christian Bors . . . this history of his native land is dedicated by his friend the author," he was saluting an exceptional Scandinavian consul.

Although Boyesen was trying, in the eighties, to make his serious adult fiction as realistic as possible, he did not discard completely the romantic materials he had used earlier. Descriptions of Norwegian scenery, accounts of daring deeds, and old legends and superstitions now became the stock ingredients of dozens of tales for boys. These stories, which have a strong kinship with *Gunnar* and some of the *Tales from Two Hemispheres*, provided a natural outlet for his romantic tendencies and for his storytelling skill. Many of the tales were invented to entertain his own sons, who were eight, seven, and five years old when the first volume came out. *The Modern Vikings* is inscribed "To the Three Vikings: Hjalmar, Algernon, and Bayard." The verses conclude:

> For my Vikings love song and saga,
>   Like their conquering fathers of old;
> And these are some of the stories
>   To the three little tyrants I told.[34]

Many tales in this and subsequent volumes had appeared earlier in such magazines as *St. Nicholas, Harper's Young People,* and the *Youth's Companion.* Two short novels for boys came out in 1890, *Against Heavy Odds* and *A Fearless Trio.* Two more collections of short stories followed, *Boyhood in Norway* in 1892 and *Norseland Tales* in 1894. Obviously most of this fiction was turned out very hastily, and none of it has any real merit even as juvenilia. Yet the books sold well and may have been Boyesen's most profitable ventures. Scribner's continued to bring out new editions as late as 1921, long after Boyesen's other works were out of print.

The rest of Boyesen's writings of the late eighties are hardly more significant than these juvenile tales. He published two poems in the

---

[33] Boyesen, "Norway's Struggle for Independence," in *Harper's Weekly,* 39:390 (April 27, 1895).
[34] *The Modern Vikings: Stories of Life and Sport in the Norseland,* v–vii (New York, 1887).

Hjalmar Hjorth Boyesen

Chautauquan in 1889, the first in seven years, but they did not raise his stature as a poet. Two short stories printed the same year in *Scribner's Magazine* are equally ephemeral. He wrote articles for *Cosmopolitan* on the two American universities he knew best: "Cornell University" appeared in November, 1889, and "Columbia College," in January, 1890. *The Light of Her Countenance*, his first novel in five years, was a reworking of an anonymous novelette, "The Old Adam," published in *Lippincott's Magazine* the previous year.[35]

Boyesen's first critical efforts during the early eighties were even less promising than his fiction: He wrote articles on Turgenev and Bjørnson that had almost no connection with literature, and little enough with the persons under consideration. For example, "Tourguéneff and the Nihilists" is really an essay about the young Russian extremists whom Boyesen had "met and talked with . . . in Parisian cafes." The mention of Turgenev served merely as an introduction to this interesting subject.[36]

---

[35] "The Poet's Vocation," and "Nirvana the Blest," in *Chautauquan*, 9:222, 10:166 (January, November, 1889); "The Two Mollies," and "A Pagan Incantation," in *Scribner's Magazine*, 6:116–120, 200–215 (July, August, 1889); "The Old Adam," in *Lippincott's Magazine*, 41:573–642 (May, 1888). *The Light of Her Countenance* (New York, 1889) was published under Boyesen's name by D. Appleton and Company in the *Town and Country Library*, a collection of light reading.

[36] *Critic*, 1:81 (March 26, 1881).

7

A Bolder Champion

IN A pair of articles on Norwegian writers visiting the United States, Boyesen renewed his old feud with the clergy. *Falconberg* was still a bone of contention in the West, and on February 15, 1881, he had a letter in *Budstikken,* a Norwegian-language weekly published in Minneapolis, admitting that he had deliberately attacked the Norwegian Synod in the novel. His defense was that the actual facts were worse than those he presented. In "Bjørnson in the United States," a letter to the editor of the *Critic*, March 12, 1881, Boyesen was able to get in some more blows at the western pastors.

Bjørnson made his long-contemplated visit to the United States in the fall of 1880, and spent the first three months in Cambridge as the guest of Mrs. Ole Bull. He was wined and dined in the fashionable circles of Cambridge and Boston, but the great Norwegian was dismayed by the conservatism of the Americans he met. "He had half expected to find a nation of thinkers, wide-awake and progressive, and strongly inclined to radicalism." When he arrived in New York, Bjørnson ruled out any social functions. He was more interested in exploring and taking notes than in meeting Hamilton Fish or Cornelius Vanderbilt. "The plutocrats and scions of ancient houses have a family resemblance the world over," said Bjørnson.[1]

---

[1] Boyesen, "Bjørnson in the United States," in *Critic*, 1:58 (March 12, 1881). Boyesen said Bjørnson had met the wrong people in Cambridge: He should have spent his time with John Fiske, James Freeman Clarke, and Henry James, Sr.

Hjalmar Hjorth Boyesen

When Boyesen wrote his article, the Norwegian author-reformer was completing a stormy tour of the Scandinavian West, where a hostile reception awaited him: "The clergy, as usual the representatives of obscurantism and bigotry, began a fierce and determined warfare upon him the moment his arrival was announced: but they have so far accomplished nothing, except to stimulate the universal curiosity to hear him." Boyesen was torn between indignation at the intolerance of the Lutheran clergy and exultation over Bjørnson's fearless speeches: "The Scandinavian press in the West is discussing with great vehemence and animation the questions and problems which he has broached in his lectures, and there are, amid much bigotry and foolishness, frequently a vigor and sincerity in these discussions which are the direct reflections of Bjørnson's sincere and vigorous speech. It is evident that even though he has often been misunderstood, he has roused to thought the great priest-ridden masses in the Scandinavian West, and for years to come his mighty voice will be reverberating in their memories." [2]

The following year Boyesen hailed the coming of another Norwegian liberal writer who would help alleviate the intellectual stagnation and spiritual servitude of the western Scandinavians. In a second letter to the *Critic*, he announced that Kristofer Janson was going to become a Unitarian clergyman. Boyesen said Janson was not abandoning his life-work — awakening and educating the Norwegian peasant — in making this move:

"He wishes merely to transfer his labors to a new field, working in the same spirit as before among his Scandinavian countrymen in the Northwest. These number, at present, about 600,000; and they are sorely in need of the liberalizing influence of just such a man as Mr. Janson, having been too long shut off from intellectual contact with the Nineteenth Century by their 'evangelical' Norse Lutheran Synod. It speaks very poorly, in fact, for the culture and the intellectual status of the Norwegians that they have allowed themselves to be ruled so long by a corporation which would find its proper place in a museum of antiquarian remains. It is the soul-paralyzing tyranny of this body of clergymen that Janson is endeavoring to break, apparently with encouraging success. He is an eloquent and forcible speaker, and has a great future before him in the field which he has chosen." [3]

[2] *Critic*, 1:58.
[3] "Kristofer Janson and the Norse Lutheran Synod," in *Critic*, 2:8 (January 14,

A Bolder Champion

Despite these flare-ups, Boyesen remained generally indifferent to his fellow Scandinavian Americans. Since his brothers were practicing law in the West — Alf in St. Paul and Ingolf in Chicago — he had some contact with these people, but it was very slight.[4] No native-born American could have spoken more condescendingly of the "priest-ridden masses" than Boyesen did. He was willing to write about his fellow immigrants, if American magazines would buy such stories or articles, but he never wrote as one of them. As a Columbia professor and New York man of letters he was far removed in spirit and sympathy from the western Scandinavian Americans, a fact which both he and they fully appreciated.

Except for the outbursts that Boyesen's strong prejudices and partisanship produced, his best and most significant writing during the eighties was in his critical articles. If his poetry and one play are sentimental, romantic, conventional, and derivative, a half dozen reports on the new literature of Germany and the Scandinavian countries are clearly the work of a dedicated realist and a literary and social insurgent. He took special pride in the boldness of the Norwegian writers, and noted with satisfaction their defiance of critics and public. No question was forbidden ground for Bjørnson, Kielland, and Ibsen; these men would continue to search out humanity's ills and sound even lower depths, Boyesen prophesied. He himself gained courage and confidence from his former countrymen, who had become such fearless and uncompromising realists: "The scientific spirit which regards truth rather than beauty has taken possession of them, and has made them scorn the path of delectable trifling which they trod before."[5]

Boyesen's personal life was comparatively uneventful after he settled into the routine of a Columbia professor. The responsibilities and problems of a family that included young children kept him tied to his position and ruled out trips abroad, though he was making plans for a tour in Europe at the end of the decade, when his youngest son would be eight years old. When Columbia was not in session, he had some freedom of movement, and he took his family out of the city during the hottest months. In 1881 and 1882 they summered at Stockbridge, Massachusetts; the only noteworthy event was a meeting with T. R.

1882). In 1873 Boyesen had stated in a letter to Howells that there were 800,000 Norwegians and Danes in the United States. His figure of 600,000 Scandinavians in 1882 is a more accurate one.
[4] See Nelson, *Scandinavians in the United States*, 1:348.
[5] "Social Problems in Norwegian Novels," in *Critic*, 7:134 (September 19, 1885).

Lounsbury, professor of English literature at Yale. During the summer vacation of 1883, spent at Westhampton, Long Island, an incident occurred that was to give Boyesen some uneasiness. To stop a seven-year-old from "bullying and beating his [*Boyesen's*] son and other small boys," he slapped the offender on the cheek. Two years later, the father of the boy sued Boyesen for $5,000 damages, claiming that the blow had brought on deafness. Although Boyesen produced the hotel manager and a doctor to testify that the child's deafness was probably the result of excessive ocean bathing, he lost the suit, and a New York City jury awarded the plaintiff $400.[6]

In 1883 a Russian professor, Waldemir Kowaledsky, wrote an article that threatened to cause a rift between Boyesen and G. W. Cable. Kowaledsky, visiting America the previous year, had presented a letter from Turgenev to Boyesen and received from him a letter to Cable in New Orleans. Upon his return to Russia, Kowaledsky published an article on Cable in *Viestnik Europii;* the *Critic* printed it in translation. The embarrassing paragraph read: "Of Boyesen, Cable said to me that he considered him a learned man, but not an artist. He is a purist in the matter of language and in literary methods; but he is a man without the imaginative faculty, and at the same time with an obstinate desire to create types. Howells seemed to Cable a much greater talent."[7]

Cable wrote an indignant letter of denial to the *Critic*: "I have no idea that anybody doubts Professor Boyesen is learned; but if I must acknowledge the truth, I have not learning enough to know whether he is learned or not. But I am no critic. But if I am artist enough to know, then I know he is an artist. Even to say this seems hardly modest; for his literary work had secured him the recognition both of critical writers and of the reading world before I had had the pleasure to read them. Later, they had delighted me before I could presume to express for them the interest of a fellow-author; and his deserved fame as a literary artist, for some of whose qualities I think it no harm to envy him, was secured (though not complete) before he, almost first among critics, kindly rec-

---

[6] Boyesen to Fiske, September 12, 1881; "Professor Boyesen Sued," in *New York Times*, May 6, 8, 1885. Thomas Raynesford Lounsbury (1838–1915) was professor of language and literature at Yale from 1870 until his death. After he published *A History of the English Language* (1879), he became an acknowledged leader in his field in American academic circles.

[7] "My Acquaintance with Cable," in *Critic*, 3:317 (July 28, 1883). The article, translated by Charlotte Adams, was printed as a letter to the editor.

A Bolder Champion

ognized what he believed to be an artist's work in the productions of my tardy pen.

"Whether the next sentence in the paragraph to which I am replying is put forward as my utterance its construction does not indicate with certainty; but it certainly is not my words, expresses but feebly my admiration for Prof. Boyesen's wonderful command of modern languages, and does not agree with my opinion of his imaginative faculty or of his 'desire to create types.'

"The paragraph ends with the following short sentence: 'Howells seems to Cable a much greater talent.' I do not think I ever instituted a comparison between Boyesen and Howells; but the sentence is not so far wrong but a word will correct it. If you will substitute the word 'than' for 'to' your printer may put me down among his grateful friends." [8]

Boyesen was mollified; by fall the two men were on good terms again. On October 28, 1883, Cable wrote in his diary: "Last evening dined with Johnson and wife and met Boyesen as my vis-a-vis. Never enjoyed Boyesen's company so much. Went thence with Johnson and Boyesen to the Matthew Arnold reception at the Windsor Hotel." [9]

In the summer of 1884 Boyesen made one of his rare visits to "the Scandinavian West." Once again a literary magazine offers the clue to his whereabouts and activities. The *Critic* was fond of observing anniversaries, and of utilizing any other opportunity for soliciting opinions and tributes from prominent American authors. The seventy-fifth birthday of Oliver Wendell Holmes was one such occasion. Boyesen's letter, written from Lake Geneva, Wisconsin, on August 21, 1884, announced that a poetic tribute would have been included "if my muse were not on a fishing excursion in the wilds of Wisconsin . . . in search of black bass." While engaged in this pursuit the writer "had an involuntary ducking, caught an awful cold, and can therefore only croak in prose." [10]

Boyesen knew the value of publicity and did not overlook opportunities to get notices in literary journals. His Norwegian name received a good deal of attention from professional funny men. "The Lounger," Jeanette Gilder's column in the *Critic*, carried the following item: "It is at this season of the year that the newspapers, having nothing of importance to chronicle save the fishing adventures of the President and the

---
[8] *Critic*, 3:348 (August 25, 1883).
[9] L. L. C. Bikle, *George W. Cable: His Life and Letters*, 103 (New York, 1928).
[10] *Critic*, 5:98 (August 30, 1884).

Hjalmar Hjorth Boyesen

(sometimes) bloodless victories of the baseball field, turn their attention for a moment to Prof. Hjalmar Hjorth Boyesen, of Columbia. Not that Mr. Boyesen is particularly active in these days; but, everything else being so quiet, this is accepted as the best time to consider the peculiar spelling of his name. One paper, at its wit's end for news or gossip, has recently announced that the Norwegian novelist and poet is in receipt of $10,000 a year, Columbia College paying him $5,000 for his professional services and Messrs. Charles Scribner's Sons, his publishers, a like sum for the use of the j's in his name. This paragraph has been quite widely circulated; the result being that Mr. Boyesen has suddenly become conscious of the existence of a vast army of needy relatives, scattered over every county in the Union." [11]

An earlier paragraph must have been "planted" deliberately: "Prof. Boyesen spent his summer vacation on Nantucket. . . . Knowing the reputation of the place for backwardness, Mr. Boyesen was surprised to find a native who seemed to take an interest in Norwegian politics, and who not only talked intelligently on the subject, but even corrected the visitor's figures concerning the size of the Government's minority in the *Diet*. When he quoted as his authority an article by Prof. Boyesen in *The Christian Union*, all the visitor could do was accept the correction, and confess the authorship of the article. 'Then you are a Norwegian?' enquired the native. Mr. Boyesen nodded assent. 'It's odd,' the Nantucketer went on, 'but you're the first one I ever saw here who hadn't come on a wreck.' 'O,' exclaimed Mr. Boyesen, 'I came as a wreck, so the difference isn't so great after all.'" Nantucket is the model for the island of Poltucket in "Charity," a short story Boyesen published two years later.[12]

Parallels between Boyesen's personal activities and his fiction are plentiful. He never ceased to take a lively interest in every phase of American life, and he gleaned much material for his stories from personal experiences. Even his own religious activities furnished grist for his mill. Early in his career he had attacked the Norwegian Synod; but when he himself became an Episcopalian, perhaps for the sake of family unity and solidarity, he abandoned his old target and instead lampooned the fashionable American clergyman in a number of novels.[13]

---

[11] *Critic*, 10:297 (June 11, 1887).

[12] *Critic*, 9:198 (October 23, 1886); *Scribner's Magazine*, 4:490–506 (October, 1888).

[13] Boyesen became an Episcopalian in 1886; Austa Boyesen to Larson, April 19,

A Bolder Champion

Boyesen gave the first series in a new program of free public addresses offered by Columbia College in the spring of 1886. The *Critic* carried the announcement: "Prof. H. H. Boyesen will commence the delivery of a course of six free public lectures at Columbia College today (Saturday) on the tendencies of contemporary literature. The subject of the first will be 'The French Novelists,' and of the subsequent ones 'French Poets and Critics,' 'The German Novel,' 'The English Novel,' 'Russian Novelists and Nihilists,' and 'Scandinavian Poets and Novelists.' The lectures will be delivered on successive Saturday mornings, from 11:30 to 12:30 o'clock. Tickets may be had by addressing Prof. Boyesen at Columbia College, Madison Avenue and Forty-ninth Street."[14]

The public's response was better than the college had expected. These Saturday morning addresses were given in a lecture hall seating four hundred, but many applications for tickets had to be turned down. Boyesen wrote to a friend after the first lecture, "I . . . had such an audience that about a hundred had to go away. I stood on the platform surrounded by fair damsels, who literally 'sat at my feet.' It was a delightful situation."[15]

The following year Columbia hired the Lyceum Theatre for Boyesen's new series of talks. The *Critic* gave his lectures a paragraph after they were already under way: "Prof. H. H. Boyesen, of Columbia College, gave his third lecture on 'The Modern English Poets' on Monday in the Lyceum Theatre. Keats was the poet chosen for criticism. The lecture on Browning, to be delivered on the 21st, promises to be the most interesting of the course. Browning has been a subject of study with him for 15 years, and what he will have to say about the poet at whose shrine he has worshipped for so long cannot fail to be worth hearing. In the lecture on Tennyson set down for the 28th, he will criticize the tendency of the Modern school toward over-elaboration of technique, and the subordination of sense to sound. The last lecture, on Monday, April 4, will be devoted to 'Swinburne and the Later Lyrists' (particularly Austin Dobson and Andrew Lang)."[16]

1936. He was confirmed April 3, 1888, according to a certificate in the Boyesen Papers. For Boyesen's caricatures, see "A Candidate for Divorce," in *Cosmopolitan*, 8:596, 608 (March, 1890); and the character Dr. Gunn, in *The Golden Calf*.
[14] *Critic*, 8:124 (March 6, 1886).
[15] Boyesen to Robert Arrowsmith, March 12, 1886, Columbia University Library. See also William F. Russell, *The Rise of a University*, 1:389 (New York, 1937); *Critic*, 8:171 (March 27, 1886).
[16] *Critic*, 10:146 (March 19, 1887).

115

Hjalmar Hjorth Boyesen

In 1889 Boyesen appeared on the largest and most celebrated of all American lecture platforms, at Lake Chautauqua, New York. The *New York Daily Tribune* writer, who sent in daily reports on the activities, was much impressed by Boyesen. After the professor's debut on July 22, the *Tribune* carried a report of his talk under the heading "Boyesen at Chautauqua." The article began with a description of the speaker: "A sturdy, thick-set gentleman, bronzed and bearded, wearing a red-barred necktie and a horse-shoe pin, and looking not unlike the first mate of a California packet ship, has been roaming about the grounds for the last day or two, and this afternoon surprised everybody by ascending the platform in the Amphitheatre to deliver a lecture on the French novel. He was H. H. Boyesen, the Norwegian writer and professor at Columbia College, who speaks English as well as his native tongue, and writes it even better."

The *Tribune* reporter was equally impressed by the addresses themselves. From the paper's full accounts, Boyesen evidently gave the same series he had delivered at Columbia in 1886: After two sessions devoted to the French novel, he discussed the current fiction of Germany, Russia, the Scandinavian countries, and England. But he got his heartiest applause "when he abandoned his manuscript to tell some good stories." Following the third address, the *Tribune* reported, "Professor Boyesen is proving a great success. His lectures are admirably adapted to a popular audience, being full of personal allusions and racy anecdotes." The same day, under the heading "Men of Chautauqua," the paper stated, "Of the visitors here Prof. Boyesen has so far achieved the most enviable reputation as a storyteller." And, after the final talk on Saturday, July 27: "Professor Boyesen's last lecture was on George Eliot, and was even better than its predecessors. The series has been an exceptionally good one and when Mr. Boyesen left this afternoon for his summer home at Southampton, he was parted from with genuine regret."[17]

No activity of Boyesen's is more revealing than his close connection with the Authors' Club, a social organization that held its first meeting November 23, 1882. The club elected thirty-six members and met twice a month, each member being privileged to bring one guest. The executive committee consisted of H. M. Baird, Noah Brooks, Edward Eggleston, E. L. Godkin, Laurence Hutton, Charles De Kay, C. T. Lewis, E. C.

---

[17] *New York Daily Tribune*, July 23, 25, 26, 29, 1889. See also issues of July 24 and 27.

A Bolder Champion

Stedman, and Richard Grant White. Among the members were Boyesen, John Burroughs, H. M. Alden, G. W. Curtis, R. W. Gilder, Bronson Howard, Clarence King, H. W. Mabie, Brander Matthews, Frederick Law Olmsted, and R. L. Stoddard.[18]

This club meant a great deal to Boyesen. There he saw the literary friends whom he did not entertain at home because "they were not congenial to his wife." His skill as a storyteller made him a popular figure at the meetings. Boyesen's letter to Horace Scudder, written a few months before Scudder succeeded Aldrich as editor of the *Atlantic* (in 1890), gives some information about the nature of the club at the close of the decade: "I write unofficially to ask you whether you would care for an election as a non-resident member of the Authors' Club. We have now, either as honorary or as active members, nearly all the literary men of any consequence in the country & the absence of your name leaves a lacuna in our catalogue which I for one (& which many beside me) would like to see filled. The dues for non-resident members are $10.00 —ten dollars—a year & the initiation fee is $25.00. I shall be glad to find a good proposer & seconder, if your reply is favorable. I am unhappily debarred from the privilege of proposing you myself, as I am a member of the committee on admissions." [19]

Although the Authors' Club remained purely social as a group, its members led the fight in the United States for an international copyright law. R. W. Gilder and Edward Eggleston drew up the platform for the American Copyright League, which was organized formally in 1883. Boyesen became a member of the council of the league, along with Gilder, Brander Matthews, C. D. Warner, S. L. Clemens, and others.[20]

In 1886 the *Century* devoted eight pages in its "Open Letters" section to authors' statements on international copyright. Boyesen wrote: "I find it difficult to speak dispassionately on the subject of 'International Copyright,' because my experience has made me feel the injustice of the present state of things most keenly. A man who constructs an improved

---

[18] *New York Daily Tribune*, November 24, 1882; "Authors' Club," in *Critic*, 2:328 (December 2, 1882).

[19] Austa Boyesen to Larson, May 3, 1936; Boyesen to Scudder, December 23, 1889, Houghton Library, Harvard University. Horace Elisha Scudder (1838–1902), general editorial assistant at Houghton, Mifflin, and Company from 1880 until his death, was responsible for the publication of many studies in English and American literature.

[20] *Publishers' Weekly* (New York), 33:59–64, 39:365–370 (January 21, 1888, May 7, 1891).

Hjalmar Hjorth Boyesen

button-hook or darning-needle may patent his invention in nearly every country of the civilized world, while the man who embodies the best of his thought and culture in a book is exposed to depredations from anyone (outside his own country) who chooses to steal from him. In the space you have allotted me there is no opportunity for arguing the question. All I can do is give an expression of sentiment in favor of International Copyright, and this I do with all possible emphasis; first, because the present system of mutual stealing is ethically wrong, and will in the end benefit nobody; and secondly, because I have myself suffered in many ways from the liberties taken with my writings in foreign countries." [21]

In spite of the league's efforts, the copyright bill failed to get through Congress in 1886. Two years later, another concerted effort was under way. Boyesen approached a dozen congressmen on behalf of the measure, and wrote a full-length article in the February, 1888, *Cosmopolitan*. In "A Defense of the Eighth Commandment," he insisted that an essentially simple moral question was being obscured by the economic forces involved:

"As we grow big, and our enormous capital gets invested in all sorts of enterprises, our conscience gets ossified, and we accept more and more blindly that which is as right. . . . If we have gotten into the way of taxing the many for the benefit of the few, we gradually get to think that it is inherently right to do so: simply because to undo the wrong would involve loss to somebody, and a rearrangement of economic forces which the timid view with apprehension. If we have gotten into the habit of stealing the works of foreign authors, the dollars and cents involved in this nefarious business stimulates our ingenuity, and we profess to see an essential moral difference between stealing from a foreigner and stealing from a native, or between the stealing of brain products and the stealing of material products. . . .

"There are, indeed, a few authors among us who make a living by their pen, but the majority of them make a scanty living, and only two or three have, under particularly favoring circumstances, achieved financial independence. All the rest, among whom there are some conspicuously endowed, have to devote the best of their energies to extraneous pursuits, and can in moments of stolen leisure never give a full and ade-

---

[21] *Century*, 31:628 (February, 1886).

A Bolder Champion

quate utterance to the thoughts and feelings which most deeply agitate their souls. . . .

"Why do our young men and women among the wealthy and leisured classes betray such an inordinate admiration for the aristocratic institutions and the rigid system of caste, which prevail in England? Is it not, in a great measure, because they have during the most impressionable years of their lives depended for their entertainment upon English fiction?"

No doubt this last argument had a double appeal to Boyesen, whether he believed it or not: It was good propaganda, and it allowed him to attack the romantic fiction which enticed readers away from more serious realistic novels. He insisted on many occasions that Walter Scott and other English romantics turned the heads of American girls. Pirated reprints of English novels sold very cheaply. It seemed logical to Boyesen that aristocratic young ladies would buy these books. He explained: "The young lady who wants a novel to wile away an idle hour takes, naturally, the cheapest; and she grows in the midst of democratic institutions a bitter aristocrat at heart, sighing for the picturesque splendor of feudalism and looking with ill-disguised contempt upon the unpleasant equality and dreary monotony which society presents under a republican government." [22]

The climax of the league's efforts was a march on Washington, March 17, 1888, led by R. W. Gilder. Gilder's letter to his wife reports on the contingent: "The trip was pleasant. Hutton and Boyesen brought along their wives and Hutton some other ladies. Stedman and his boy were along, and Palmer of the Madison Square, Clemens and Riley. Storytelling and all that." [23] Gilder took a small group to the White House to tea. The bill passed the Senate but was blocked in the House. Final passage of the international copyright act did not come until March 4, 1891.

---

[22] *Cosmopolitan*, 4:485–489 (February, 1888).

[23] Rosamond Gilder, ed., *Letters of Richard Watson Gilder*, 195 (Boston, 1916). Laurence Hutton (1843–1904) was a New York drama critic and author of some fifty books, mainly about the theater and his literary pilgrimages abroad. The league's Washington task force was obviously chosen for its oral and physical effectiveness. E. C. Stedman was a successful Wall Street broker; Mark Twain and James Whitcomb Riley (1849–1916) were highly successful as readers of their own works and were enormously popular entertainers; and Hutton and Albert M. Palmer (1838–1905), who was manager of the Madison Square Theatre, were urbane and impressive personalities of the theater.

Hjalmar Hjorth Boyesen

During the eighties Boyesen wrote half a dozen stories about Norwegian-American immigrants. "A Dangerous Virtue," the only impressive narrative that he produced early in the decade, was followed by several that were published in *Vagabond Tales* (1889). Like the stories written during the seventies, these offer little evidence that Boyesen was acquainted with the lives and problems of the Scandinavian-American immigrants. But if they are not genuinely realistic, they avoid the idealistic optimism and the easy, sentimental solutions of Boyesen's earlier fiction. In most of the stories there is a sharp note of disillusionment.[24]

This pessimism is even more apparent in Boyesen's topical writing. He was especially concerned about the problems facing immigrants, and he became more and more dubious about their chances in the New World. The darker tone of his fiction could be charged to his convictions about realism, but the arguments he put forth in three articles on immigration must be credited to the growth of his political consciousness, and, more specifically, to his transformation from an idealistic democrat to a reforming Democrat.

Like most other Norwegian Americans, Boyesen was a Republican during his first years in the United States. Later he was wont to ascribe this allegiance to irrational prejudice, and to say that he had preferred the Democratic platform in 1876 and 1880 even though he voted the opposite ticket and went so far as to write an elegy on President Garfield. In 1884, however, he came out for Grover Cleveland, and in later campaigns he actively supported Democratic candidates. He was an enthusiastic member of the Reform Club, but the chief factor in his political coming of age was probably his editorial connection with the *Nation*, the most important and distinguished reform journal of the post-Civil War era.[25]

Boyesen's knowledge of America and his right to voice criticism of his adopted country were challenged by those who disagreed with his social and political views. Among his friends, however, there were many

[24] "A Dangerous Virtue," in *Scribner's Monthly*, 21:745–759 (March, 1881), was reprinted in *Queen Titania*.

[25] Boyesen, "The Scandinavian in the United States," in *North American Review*, 155:527 (November, 1892); Boyesen, *Idyls of Norway*, 20–22; Austa Boyesen to Larson, April 19, 1936. The Boyesen obituary in the *Nation*, 61:257 (October 10, 1895) mentions that he was for many years a contributor to the *Nation*. Carl Schurz was an editor. Edwin L. Godkin, the founder, was a member of the Authors' Club. Boyesen "occasionally furnished leaders in the 80's and 90's" to the *New York Evening Post*, Godkin's other publication. See Allan Nevins, *The Evening Post: A Century of Journalism*, 527 (New York, 1922).

A Bolder Champion

who knew that this "Norwegian author" was an exemplary citizen who seized every opportunity to show his devotion to the nation. This aspect of Boyesen's career is reflected in the tribute, "A Citizen by Adoption," printed by the editors of the *Century* after his death: "Prof. Boyesen was one of the most devoted of American patriots. His love for the country of his adoption was not a pallid flame, devoid of heat and motive power. Whenever good citizenship required the urgent action of every decent member of the community, this scholar-citizen did not merely 'stand up and be counted' as a man: he could be counted as doing the work of a dozen men. His advice, his effort, his voice, were given quickly and effectively to the cause of good government. The country that he loved was not only dear to him for what it was, but for what it might be — for what, indeed, it yet must be, unless failure should be written upon its brow. He did not regulate his political action in America in reference to the condition of his native country. He stood in America for America. This citizen by adoption was an example to all citizens, whether native or adopted. Would there were more of his kind." [26]

Whether "The Dangers of Unrestricted Immigration" was the idea of the author or of the editor of the *Forum*, which printed the article, Boyesen claimed to speak on this subject with some authority. This essay, much expanded, became his speech on "Immigration," delivered before the National Evangelical Conference in Washington, D.C., on December 7, 1887. "I doubt if there is another man in a private position in New York who has come into closer contact with the miseries which unrestricted immigration entails, and who has been the repository of more tales of alien woe than I," he told his audience. The American system of unrestricted immigration had increased the nation's territory, wealth, and power, Boyesen conceded, but the cost had been a lowering of political morality. The danger was becoming even more grave, for "a large proportion of the foreigners who come to us now are hungry malcontents, who arrive with the avowed purpose to overthrow our institutions." The old free and easy American way of opening the nation's doors to all the world was no longer feasible; for with the supply of free land running out and the labor market glutted, even the best intentioned of the new immigrants would become disappointed, embittered, then desperate, and would inevitably "become enemies of the state." [27]

[26] *Century*, 51:314 (December, 1895).
[27] *Forum*, 3:533 (July, 1887). The speech, published with others delivered at the conference, is in *National Perils*, 55–76.

Hjalmar Hjorth Boyesen

Boyesen voiced the same fears about the flood of immigrants in "The Modern Migration of Nations," published in the *Chautauquan* in 1889. "I have stood and watched them by the hour in that modern Babel called Castle Garden," he said; and as the immigrant ships discharged their cargoes he considered that all these people brought "a small bit of Europe with them, within their craniums, and this bit of Europe will take shape, somehow or other, for good or for ill, in our social conditions, our laws, and our institutions." How much of this could America stand, he asked, without endangering her national character and democratic institutions?

But if Boyesen was worried about the nation, he was equally concerned about the immigrant. In "The Modern Migration of Nations" he tried to assess the effect a change of nationality had on an individual. Referring specifically to his own personal knowledge of Norwegian migration, he concluded that "the land-hungry Aryans" who flocked to America were not necessarily well advised to emigrate, even if they were assured of finding land and a reasonable prosperity in the New World. A man past thirty was not likely to find happiness if he pulled up his roots and sought a new homeland, Boyesen judged. He felt that such a man could never adjust to strange neighbors, customs, and physical conditions.[28]

His awareness that a discontented population could be dangerous also lay behind Boyesen's criticism of the American public schools. He began questioning these schools and their teachings almost as soon as he reached the United States. While he was in Ohio he observed an American phenomenon which impressed him strongly: He heard a principal tell a class of boys at commencement, "Every one of you, boys, has as good a chance of becoming President of the United States, some day, as Grant or Lincoln had when he was of your age." Boyesen said, "I marvelled at the lack of judgment the man displayed. But I could not find a person in that section of the country who agreed with me. They all told me that that was the American spirit." [29]

"What Shall the Public Schools Teach?" in the *Forum* was a plea for practical, "realistic" education. The average boy would become an industrial worker: Therefore the schools should prepare him for such a role. And since the average girl would become a wife and mother, she should

[28] *Chautauquan*, 9:281–283.
[29] *National Perils*, 63.

be taught how to raise children properly, how to manage a household, and how to cook.[30]

Boyesen's opinions on higher education were expressed in a number of articles. He thought Americans should learn to distinguish between a college, where boys from fourteen to eighteen years of age received from a faculty of "schoolmasters" the discipline and moral guidance such boys needed, and a university, intended for young men from eighteen to twenty-two, who needed "the strengthening discipline of life itself." He disapproved of President Eliot's "hazardous experiment" at Harvard, the attempt to transform an old American college into a German-type university. Much wiser was the course pursued at Columbia in "trying to restore the college to its proper function as an intermediate institution, preparatory to the higher study of the university; and . . . superimposing the university as a new structure upon the secure and well-grounded foundation of the college."[31]

Boyesen's most impressive and interesting writing appeared in a new series of essays on social and literary subjects: From 1886 to 1889 he wrote eight of the pieces that were later collected in *Literary and Social Silhouettes*. "The Meridian of Life," marking his fortieth birthday, September 23, 1888, is a familiar essay; and "The Ethics of Robert Browning" is as close to pure literary criticism as anything he wrote. The rest of the selections, however, are a composite of social and literary criticism, and a cross between the topical article and the chatty, discursive essay. The combination is a happy one, well suited to Boyesen's talents. In this new form he did his best work, and in these essays he explained why the fiction he himself wrote during this decade was so trivial.[32]

The new efforts include "The American Novelist and His Public," a well-known essay that to this day is frequently quoted by cultural and social historians; "Types of American Women"; and "America in European Literature." Other articles, like "The Hero in Fiction," "Mars vs. Apollo," and "Philistinism," are somewhat broader in scope. The tone of all is cosmopolitan, but they are obviously aimed at American

---

[30] *Forum*, 6:92–100 (September, 1888).

[31] See especially "Cornell University," "Columbia College," and "The University of Chicago," in *Cosmopolitan*, 8:59–66, 265–275, 14:665–673 (November, 1889, January, 1890, April, 1893). The quotations are from "Where Should a College Be Located?" in *Chautauquan*, 13:467 (July, 1891). Boyesen's argument was that a college should be in a country town, a university in a large city.

[32] Presumably the two essays, both of 1888, first appeared in periodicals that have not been identified; see *Literary Silhouettes*, 131–146, 205–218.

Hjalmar Hjorth Boyesen

readers or, more specifically, at the readers of popular American magazines. There is no single proposition unifying all eight of these articles, but in nearly all of them Boyesen manages to castigate frivolous fiction and to plead for modern realists who deal frankly and truthfully with the important problems of their day.[33]

All of these critical articles — whether they are concerned with Scandinavian and German literature, cultural phenomena, or the problems that confront artists in all lands — reveal Boyesen's maturing judgment. His ideas were taking permanent form, and he was less hesitant about expressing his opinions. He had become a belligerent champion of realism, insisting that novelists must deal with pressing social issues if they were to be considered serious writers. It may be that Boyesen was publicly compensating for his own pot-boiling fiction by his uncompromising critical stand, and by his emphasis on social, political, and economic questions.

The reader might well assume that Boyesen's preaching was much better than his literary practice during the late eighties. But even while he was turning out stories for boys and other commercial fiction, he was slowly and carefully writing his most serious, most ambitious, and most realistic novel. On March 3, 1888, in response to a questionnaire from *Critic* about methods of writing fiction, he said he was so deeply involved with a novel he had been writing for two years that he could not interrupt his thoughts to answer the queries.[34] Obviously the story was *The Mammon of Unrighteousness*. By the end of that year the book was completed.

Howells read the manuscript and approved it highly, and Boyesen set about finding a publisher. Writing to Howells January 5, 1889, he said he was sending the novel to Gilder of the *Century*. On February 6 he wrote Howells that he had taken the manuscript to Alden of *Harper's*. Both these men were friends of Howells and Boyesen, and their close associates in various ventures, but neither would undertake to publish

---

[33] "America in European Literature" and "Philistinism" have not been traced to any periodical publication; they are dated 1887 and 1888 in *Literary Silhouettes*; see p. 117–130, 163–177. "The American Novelist and His Public" appeared as "Why We Have No Great Novelists," in *Forum*, 2:615–622; "Mars vs. Apollo," in *Chautauquan*, 8:584–586 (July, 1888); "The Hero in Fiction," in *North American Review*, 148:594–601 (May, 1889); "Types of American Women," in *Forum*, 8:337–347 (November, 1889). In the collection, dates for the last four are, respectively, 1887, 1888, 1889, 1890.

[34] "On the Writing of Novels," in *Critic*, 12:136 (March 24, 1888).

the book. At the end of the decade Boyesen had found no one who would bring out his most serious and painstaking work.[35]

By 1890 Boyesen had no illusions about the financial rewards an American writer could count on, and he did not intend to repeat his mistake of ten years before, when he arrived in New York expecting to support his family as a free-lance writer. He knew now that Lillie Boyesen's style of living required the combined income he received from teaching, writing, and lecturing. By 1890 he himself had apparently forgotten his hope of living only for his writing, and had become concerned with a way of life that had a "stately appearance." He was quoted by the *Author*, a new publication founded in 1889: "I know but two American authors who could secure an income sufficient to live on, in comfort, from their writings — 'Mark Twain' and Howells. The latter, I fancy, does not live on his literary income. I suppose the majority of them could keep soul and body together, but it would be a cramped, skimpy, threadbare sort of a life. If you cannot live roomily, and with an existence near a somewhat stately appearance, what is the good of living at all? I am well paid for all the literary work I do; but I could not begin to support my family in any sort of comfort (according to my notion of comfort) on what my writings bring me." [36]

Boyesen prospered during the eighties; by 1889 he had acquired his own summer place at Southampton, Long Island. The property included twelve acres of land on the seashore, a house described by a literary columnist as "beautiful," and a stable of horses. Here his family lived from May until November. The professor had to take temporary quarters in the city in September and October, to be on hand for his Columbia classes. He worked very hard, but he kept himself in fine physical condition by taking long walks and by riding as often as possible. Edward Bok commented on the impression Boyesen made at the end of the decade: "The bridle paths of Central Park have not a more ardent devotee than a pleasant-faced man of about forty, who, upon almost any bright Sunday afternoon can be seen striding a horse as if he were born in the saddle. His short, thick-set form, smart coat, brown beard, and curly hair give him the air of a commercial man, rather than of a college professor and novelist, as is Hjalmar H. Boyesen, the Nor-

---

[35] Henry Mills Alden (1836–1919) edited *Harper's Monthly* from 1869 to 1919 and thus earned the title of "dean of American magazine editors." In 1908 he published *Magazine Writing and the New Literature*.

[36] *Author* (Boston), 2:36 (March 15, 1890).

wegian story-teller and poet. Professor Boyesen has but just reached the prime of life."[37]

In that decade, when Boyesen's literary activities seemed to be completely pointless and lacking in direction, two clearly discernible aims could nevertheless be detected in most of his work. He used every opportunity to increase his income by means of his pen, and he consistently fought for more realistic American fiction. His eagerness to see his efforts and activities properly publicized and his satisfaction in his role as a popular man of letters are perhaps related to the first purpose; and his concern with the social, political, and economic questions of the day have an obvious connection with the second. Thus, Boyesen wrote frothy short stories for the popular magazines, a young people's history of Norway, and a number of books for boys because these works cost him comparatively little effort and promised a sure return. But at the same time he advocated a more responsible American fiction. This was the age of realism, said Boyesen, and the world was moved by scientific thought and an industrial economy. Serious novelists must observe the life of their time and write about it honestly and faithfully. They must, of course, come to grips with real social problems in their novels. The romanticists, who refused to deal with such vital materials, were mere purveyors of amusement, and romanticism was really a throwback to feudal times.

But Boyesen was well aware that the romanticists had a formidable ally, one who made the task of the American realist very difficult, especially if he counted on the financial return from his fiction. This was the young American girl, the "Iron Madonna, who strangles in her fond embrace the American novelist." Because the editors of the paying magazines feared to offend the young girl, and because "American authorship scarcely could exist" without these monthly magazines, it was nearly impossible to discuss serious problems in American fiction, as the best of the European writers were doing.[38]

[37] See Arthur Stedman, "New York Topics," in *Dial*, 15:302 (November 16, 1893). Boyesen described his Southampton establishment in "My Rural Experiences," in *Lippincott's Magazine*, 58:122 (July, 1896); see also Austa Boyesen to Larson, April 19, 1936. Bok's statement is in *Author*, 3:39 (March 15, 1891). Edward W. Bok (1836–1930), Holland born, was just beginning his career. He edited the *Ladies' Home Journal*, 1889–1919, and was vice-president of the Curtis Publishing Company from 1891 until his death. His best-known book, *The Americanization of Edward Bok* (1920), won a Pulitzer prize.

[38] *Forum*, 2:619–621.

8

The Uneven Road to Realism

THE fiction produced by Boyesen's free-lancing experiment is disappointing. Scribner's published two collections in 1881, *Ilka on the Hill-Top and Other Stories* on January 14, and *Queen Titania* on October 8. The latter is a novelette; two tales were added to fill out the volume. "A Dangerous Virtue" is the only promising contribution in either collection. It is a somber, realistic narrative that contrasts sharply with the sentimentality of the others. Taken as a group, the nine pieces in the two volumes are trivial and highly romantic.

It is difficult to see why Boyesen, the disciple of Howells and Turgenev, should have written "Ilka on the Hill-Top," which tells of a pair of Tyrolese sweethearts who make love by yodeling at each other. After Hansel goes to war, Ilka is hired to sing in Berlin's finest beer garden; she is performing there when the German and Austrian troops return from their "glorious" victory over Denmark. She is at the mercy of her money-loving mother and of the owner of the beer garden until her Alpine lover appears among the Austrian soldiers. The sentimentality of the tale is only slightly offset by the author's cynical gibes at the arrogance and boastfulness of the Prussians, especially in his lampoon of the *Siegesfest* (victory celebration), with its "Germania" pageant and warlike songs.[1]

"Annunciata," second in the *Ilka* collection, is another product of Boyesen's year in Europe. The Italian heroine is "a living poem and

---
[1] *Scribner's Monthly*, 19:120–130 (November, 1879).

stately epic" to the Harvard-bred American hero, "not a shrill and nervous modern like himself, with a second-rate physique and a morbidly active intellect." But Boyesen loses interest in the Italian dream girl and focuses his attention on a scuffle between the aesthete and his wealthy, baseball-playing college roommate. "Under the Glacier" is the story of a Norwegian-American scientist who rescues his Norwegian relatives when a glacier sweeps their ancestral farm into the fjord. The piece owes much to Hawthorne's *The House of the Seven Gables*. "How Mr. Storm Met His Destiny" tells of a Norwegian-American misanthrope who finally marries his widowed childhood sweetheart after her baby daughter has softened his heart. "A Knight of Dannebrog" may be a picture of P. G. Müller, the Knight of Dannebrog who was a fellow editor of *Fremad* during Boyesen's first year in America. The plot follows the steadily declining career of Victor Julien St. Denis Dannevig, who won a Danish decoration in the war with Prussia. This profligate aristocrat is scornful of America's "detestable democratic cookery" and its "all pervading plebeian odor of republicanism," but he dies in a Chicago barroom brawl. The ending is reminiscent of Bret Harte: "Myself and two policemen followed him to the grave; and the cross of Dannebrog, with a much soiled red ribbon, was carried on a velvet cushion after his coffin." [2]

The most difficult story to assess in *Ilka on the Hill-Top* is "Mabel and I (A Philosophical Fairy Tale)." The narrator, a young tutor at a college (obviously Cornell), is fond of German philosophy, and he is also in love with his professor's daughter. The piece begins with the following dialogue:

" 'I want to see things as they are,' said I to Mabel. . . . 'I see men and things only as they seem. . . . Appearance is deceitful.'

" 'In case that was so, I shouldn't want to know it,' said Mabel. 'It would make me very unhappy.' "

When Mabel's interest in her lover lessens after he has made a trip to Germany, he explains what is wrong with Americans: "We are too prosy and practical and businesslike, and we don't believe in anything except what we can touch with our hands, and see with our eyes, and sell for money." With a pair of magic spectacles procured from a New World gnome, the young philosopher sees his professor as a parrot, the local

[2] *Scribner's Monthly*, 13:547–557, 18:911–923, 19:593–608, 21:234–245 (February, 1877, October, 1879, February, December, 1880).

The Uneven Road to Realism

minister as a fox, and a famous sportsman as a bulldog. But the hero returns the glasses, repudiates his disbelief, and decides to avoid "the dangerous tendencies of modern speculation," which the professor had warned him against. He finds it better to accept life — and Mabel — on faith.[3]

Contemporary critics were somewhat dissatisfied with these stories, particularly "Mabel and I." Some of them may have suspected that Boyesen was torn between realistic convictions and romantic inclinations in thus raising uncomfortable questions and then backing away from the answers. The reviews, however, were generally favorable. A paragraph in the first issue of the *Critic* indicates that public taste was partially responsible for the *Ilka* collection: "Mr. Boyesen's stories, whatever their defects may be, have a literary quality that places them above the ordinary magazine tale, and makes their appearance in book-form a natural sequence. Publishers say that volumes of short stories 'do not sell.' The writings of Bret Harte, Saxe Holme, Mrs. Burnett, Mr. Boyesen, and a very few others among American authors, are exceptions to this rule."[4]

It should not be forgotten that Boyesen, the immigrant author, was unusually impressionable, always eager to please, and determined to become successful in America. Judged by present standards, "Ilka on the Hill-Top" is one of the worst tales Boyesen ever wrote. Yet the author chose it as the title story of the collection; and since five of the pieces had appeared in magazines, he probably selected this one because it was the most popular. A second edition of the book was printed ten years later, in 1891. In 1883, as we have seen, Boyesen made "Ilka" into a successful play.[5]

"Queen Titania" appeared as a *Scribner's* serial in August, September, and October, 1881. Although the novelette is romantic and sentimental in plot and characterization, its setting is fashionable New York society, the milieu of Boyesen's later realistic novels. Quintus Bodill, a handsome and scholarly Norwegian, finds himself obliged, because he is "an absurdly tender-hearted fellow," to adopt a little English child, "Queen Titania," whose mother died on the steamer bringing them to New York.

[3] The story was first published in *St. Nicholas*, 4:206–214 (January, 1877). The quotations are from *Ilka on the Hill-Top*, 180, 183, 200.
[4] *Critic*, 1:7 (January 29, 1881).
[5] The play was *Alpine Roses*, which opened January 31, 1884, at the Madison Square Theatre, New York City.

Hjalmar Hjorth Boyesen

Working as an obscure clerk in a book firm, he gains the publisher's respect by pointing out evidence of "ignorance or very careless editing" in a new edition of Demosthenes. Thereafter his rise is rapid, until he becomes, "in a sort of half-acknowledged way, the most trusted and confidential adviser of the firm," and, incidentally, the favored suitor of the publisher's bluestocking daughter. When "Queen Titania" is sixteen, Bodill's fiancée introduces the child into New York society; but the ungrateful orphan rejects an eligible suitor, and that night runs back to Quintus in a sleet-storm. As a consequence of the exposure, she is ill for several months. Quintus nurses her back to health and makes his choice: A warm and loving heart has triumphed over the brilliant intellectual star of society. Boyesen does not explain what happened to the junior partnership in the publishing firm.[6]

"The Mountain's Face," a very slight tale printed with "Queen Titania" when it appeared in book form, was immediately recognized by critics as Hawthorne's "Great Stone Face" in a Norwegian setting. It is also the *Gunnar* idyl, ending in disillusionment.[7]

In 1889 Boyesen told an interviewer that Turgenev was directly responsible for the third story in the *Queen Titania* volume: "I wrote a short story called 'A Dangerous Virtue,' which was intended to be real rather than romantic, and sure enough it won his praise."[8] One could ask why Boyesen waited so long to write this realistic story, for it does differ from the other tales. Turgenev had advised his young friend to write what he knew best. The parallels that can be traced between many of Boyesen's stories and his personal experiences indicate that he had tried to do this earlier, but his sentimental nature always led him to contrive romantic endings.

"A Dangerous Virtue" opens with a scene Boyesen had observed in Norway: a group of boats ready to take their cargoes of emigrants to a steamer waiting in the middle of the fjord. Anders Gudmundson Rustad is a fine-looking young man, but, being a peasant, he is not so beautiful and dreamy-eyed as Boyesen's genteel heroes. He even appears rather obstinate. His reason for emigrating is one Boyesen had heard about while he was making a walking tour in Norway: As the youngest son, Anders goes to America with $1,500 instead of claiming his in-

[6] The quotations are from *Queen Titania*, 7, 29, 45.
[7] This story has not been found in any periodical.
[8] *Scribner's Monthly*, 21:745–759; for the interview, see "Professor Boyesen on Realism," in *New York Daily Tribune*, July 29, 1889.

heritance in land; thus there is no need to lessen family prestige by parceling the large farm into mere subsistence plots.[9]

Boyesen dwells at length on Anders Rustad's reaction to New York, with its deafening noise and swarms of people. The bewilderment of the simple and straightforward peasant becomes almost nightmarish. The imposing façade of the Immigrants' Savings Bank and Trust Company finally reassures him, and he entrusts his $1,500 in gold to the care of "Hon. Randolph Melville, Sr., President." When Anders finds, the next day, that the bank has closed, he nearly loses his senses. He remembers his Norwegian pastor's assurance that God will right all wrongs in the hereafter, but his old faith fails to comfort him. The Norwegian consul listens sympathetically to Rustad's story, but gives him some practical advice: "Have we not all daily to accept compromises where, for some reason or other, it is impossible to obtain absolute justice? In fact, isn't our whole political life and our whole civilized society made up of compromise between right and wrong? Prudence dictates it; religion recommends and sanctions it. You know the parable of the unjust steward, and Christ's counsel to his disciples to make friends with the mammon of unrighteousness." [10]

Later Boyesen, in his realistic novels, was to attack the rule of mammon in America, but these full-scale efforts do not match "A Dangerous Virtue" in impact. Anders Rustad invades a testimonial banquet given for Mr. Randolph Melville, the banker, and hears a guest say, "Really I can't see why the laboring classes should be so horrid and discontented. . . . They have not our fine sensibilities. . . . Why, then, should they not accept their lot in a Christian spirit of submission?" When the guest of honor rises to acknowledge the tributes paid him and suggests that the recent misfortunes "have been the chastening discipline of a just Providence," Anders Rustad springs for his throat. Melville magnanimously refuses to appear against his assailant, but Rustad won't be placated. Refusing the 10-per-cent settlement paid to the bank's depositors, he attacks Melville again. This time the banker is killed in the scuffle. Anders reads a prepared speech at his trial, but his imperfect English turns the procedure into a farce. The court finds him insane. Rustad's wife comes to seek him in the Tombs; she refuses to believe that the haggard man with the terrible eyes is her husband. As the man dies, the

---

[9] See Boyesen, in *Chautauquan*, 9:281.
[10] *Queen Titania*, 219.

Norwegian consul tells the doctor what destroyed him: "It was the over-development of a virtue. His sense of justice killed him."[11]

The *Critic's* review of *Queen Titania* praised this realistic tale: "The most powerful of the three stories is undoubtedly 'A Dangerous Virtue,' illustrating one of the most painful facts of American social and political life: that he who undertakes to see justice done will have not only his trouble for his pains, but considerable more trouble than he takes voluntarily. The story is admirably told, and although court trials have been the *pièce de résistance* of novelists from time immemorial, we cannot recall one which combines with such brevity an equal amount of pathos and just satire."[12]

If a single selection were to be made from Boyesen's considerable output of fiction to show his best style and subject matter, it should be "A Dangerous Virtue." By present-day standards it is too melodramatic in plot, characterization, and language, but the same criticism would apply to Stephen Crane's *Maggie* and to other realistic writings of the late nineteenth century. "A Dangerous Virtue" combines two of Boyesen's real assets as a writer of fiction: his understanding of Norwegian life and character, which gained him his earliest fictional successes, and his knowledge of the social and financial world of New York City, which furnished material for his realistic novels. The combination seems a little artificial; but if the result is theatrical, it is also effective, because each of the protagonists accentuates the qualities of the other. Anders Gudmundson Rustad and the Honorable Randolph Melville, Sr., both real persons whom Boyesen knew well, are also type characters. They represent the different worlds of Boyesen's experience. In bringing them into conflict, he violated Howells' "realism of the commonplace" and transgressed Turgenev's "logic of reality," but he produced a genuinely moving narrative that shocks anyone who reads Boyesen's other tales, or any American fiction written in 1881. If Boyesen had followed the course pursued in "A Dangerous Virtue," American naturalism might have become an established school before Stephen Crane or Frank Norris wrote their stories.

Boyesen's first completely American novel was *A Daughter of the Philistines*, published anonymously in 1883 in Roberts Brothers' *No Name Series*. In many ways it belongs with the three realistic works he

---
[11] *Queen Titania*, 226, 231, 254.
[12] *Critic*, 1:291 (October 22, 1881).

was to publish in the nineties: *The Mammon of Unrighteousness, The Golden Calf,* and *Social Strugglers.* All contain satirical gibes at American small towns, attacks on the frivolity and hypocrisy of New York society, and indictments of political and financial corruption. It may be argued that Boyesen concluded this earlier work on an optimistic note with the regeneration of his Philistine heroine, whereas *Mammon* and *The Golden Calf* end in disillusionment; it should be observed, however, that he turned again to a happy ending in his last book, *Social Strugglers.* In fact, *A Daughter of the Philistines* has much in common with Boyesen's final novel: Both tell of rich western girls who seek to break into New York society, and after their heroines marry the scions of old eastern families they are induced by their husbands to renounce the fashionable life. These two novels, moreover, were popular successes, whereas *Mammon* and *The Golden Calf* were not.

In *A Daughter of the Philistines,* Boyesen begins by filling in the background of the heroine, Alma Hampton. Her mother, the belle of Saundersville, a town in the Far West, accepts Zeke Hampton "because at first sight of him she cast his mental horoscope, and foresaw at once that he was destined to become a prosperous man." Once married, she "stimulated his ambition . . . now by flattery, now by pretended contempt . . . the moment he showed the faintest disposition to repose on his laurels." Zeke knows intervals "when a little peace seemed more precious than the wealth of California or the Presidency of the United States."[13] Instead, he is goaded into successful ventures in army contracts and undeveloped timberlands. When their son Walter is eighteen and their daughter Alma sixteen, Mrs. Hampton is ready for New York.

The daughter has been educated by the novels of Walter Scott and by a French governess, who is afraid of her. But Alma is exceedingly beautiful, and because a visiting prince dances with her three times, New York society accepts the Hamptons. She makes a great stir by declining the most eligible bachelor in New York, a phenomenally successful Wall Street speculator. The Hampton family is very roughly handled in Boyesen's novel: The father dies when his mining bubble collapses; the profligate son, Walter, who is fool enough to be greatly flattered when someone takes him for an Englishman, is obliged to sell his yachts and horses; but Mrs. Hampton salvages enough from Wall Street manipulations to live magnificently in Paris.

---

[13] *A Daughter of the Philistines,* 15 (Boston, 1883).

Hjalmar Hjorth Boyesen

The daughter of these Philistines undergoes a regeneration and becomes a good wife and mother: She has dropped out of society, but, more important, she has married Harold Wellingford, a Bostonian and a German-trained scientist. Young Wellingford is a very proper hero; he refuses to falsify an ore assay to promote a sale of mining stock, or to condone similar Wall Street manipulations. He proves his worth in another way by winning Alma Hampton from her most eligible suitor, the financial wizard. Subsequent Boyesen heroes were to become victims of the Alma Hamptons, turning into Philistines themselves to be able to afford such wives.

At the conclusion of *A Daughter of the Philistines*, Mr. and Mrs. Harold Wellingford speculate about the careers of their infant sons. The mother hopes her eldest will become ambassador to England (proving that she has not completely reformed, for she retains the fashionable New Yorker's admiration for everything English):

"You know, by the time Hugh will be ready to represent his country abroad, we shall have civil service reform and that sort of thing, so that a man may enter public life without drinking bad whisky and leaving his honor at home. Under such circumstances wouldn't it be nice to have it reported in the papers that yesterday the Queen gave an audience to the Hon. Hugh Wellingford?"

Her husband, a true visionary, expresses high hopes for science and the new century:

"As civilization progresses, the sphere of gambling, speculation, diplomacy and all the things that depend upon chance and intrigue will be gradually narrowed, and the sphere of all activities which depend upon orderly development, upon honest mental and physical labor, will be proportionately widened. I wish my sons to invest their energies, not with the waning forces of the past, but with the growing forces of the future. . . . But I must own I have great hopes of the twentieth century. Happiest of all I should be if my sons were endowed with a wide vision like Goethe, Darwin, or Newton, and could stand in the vanguard of knowledge, and discover some new, great principle which they should extend like a clear, calm lamp into the darkness which everywhere surrounds us. But if this be too daring a hope, I shall be satisfied to see them as honest and obscure workers and humble questioners of nature, as their father has been."[14]

[14] For the quotations, see *A Daughter of the Philistines,* 324, 325.

The Uneven Road to Realism

These statements accurately reflect Boyesen's own opinions, as they were in 1883. As a member of the Reform Club he was actively working for improvement of the civil service, and as a believer in Herbert Spencer's evolutionary philosophy, he had great confidence in the progress of the race. The conclusion of this novel may therefore be perfectly consistent with Boyesen's notions about realism, for he was still idealistic and optimistic in 1883. On the other hand, the happy ending may have been a concession to the reading public, since he was certainly interested in profits. In this novel Boyesen's own moral and philosophical attitudes are the attitudes of his hero. It may be that the hero's problems are also Boyesen's. The driving social ambition and the need for money that characterize the two Hampton women may reflect the demands that Lillie Boyesen was making on her husband.

Boyesen's anonymous novel caused no great critical stir.[15] The *Atlantic Monthly* did not consider it worthy of evaluation, but only mentioned it: "In the No Name Series (Roberts) a new volume is A Daughter of the Philistines, which deals with American life in some of its expansive activities." The *Dial* took the novel more seriously but found nothing good to say about it: "It aims to present a view of fashionable life in New York but lacks verisimilitude. There is not force enough in the outlines to give the characters definiteness and substance, nor is there sufficient consistency in their action to induce belief in them as exponents of society. In brief, the work is crude, and has no merit or promise in it which warrants commendation."[16]

A half dozen uncollected short stories, published in nearly as many different magazines from 1882 to 1886, are neither better nor worse than the average of those in the *Ilka* and *Titania* volumes. These tales have few characteristics in common. They are, in fact, surprisingly diverse. They indicate little about their author, except, perhaps, that he was trying to imitate a number of other writers. Five of the stories have European settings. The sixth is entirely American—the scene is laid in Brooklyn—and is noticeably more realistic than the others.[17]

The hero of "In the Wrong Niche," Halstead Swinger of Brooklyn, quits his job on the *Weekly Bassoon* to study law because he feels that his great talents are being wasted. To support him and their child, his

---

[15] There was, nevertheless, a conjecture that it might have been written by Henry James or Robert Grant; see *Critic*, 3:246 (May 26, 1883).
[16] *Atlantic Monthly*, 51:718 (May, 1883); *Dial*, 3:280 (April, 1883).
[17] *Harper's Weekly*, 29:330.

wife Rose does sewing and writes romantic tales, but when she finds out at last that her husband has been a pretentious fool, she dies. Boyesen is ironical about the heroine's efforts at authorship. First she writes a quiet story but the editors reject it, admitting its excellence but asking for something more spectacular. Although she is horrified at what she is doing, she churns out gory tales of seductions and murders. The author observes: "It was she who was in the wrong niche, being compelled to sacrifice her conscience for bread."[18]

"A Highly Respectable Family" is a gently ironic vignette of life in Christiania. A student outwits two proud but impoverished old maids and marries their lovely niece. This story has something in common with another short but artfully contrived tale, "Mr. Block's One Glorious Night," which deals with a poor but proud Swiss artist in Rome. When a wealthy self-made man finally buys several of Block's paintings for $2,500, the proud artist spends the entire amount on a sumptuous banquet to disprove the talk about his meanness and poverty.[19]

Boyesen's first contribution to the *Century*, published in April, 1883, was "Anastasia." It is worth examining for its promising beginning, an amusing attack on American business morality and small-town life. Frederick Houston was born the day his father went bankrupt, but this was neither a bad omen nor an indication of trouble ahead: "One or two failures . . . were in Clayville among the normal incidents of a well-regulated existence, and were not even remotely associated with dark visions of ruin and despair. The unfortunate merchant shut his shop with a jolly bang, sold out his old goods at auction prices, closed with his creditors at ten or fifteen cents on the dollar, and within a month or two was again started on the high road to prosperity." At this point Boyesen intrudes a Norwegian touch: Ole Bull plays a one-night stand in Clayville. The virtuoso is furious at the stolid silence of the fifty people who turn out to hear him, but "he had awakened the immortal spark in one youthful bosom, and lifted a humdrum life into a nobler and purer atmosphere." If fourteen-year-old Frederick Houston had not sneaked into that concert, he would have been doomed to prosper in the family mercantile business, Boyesen implies.[20]

Instead of suffering such a fate after his father's death, Frederick lets

[18] *Harper's Weekly*, 29:331.
[19] *Harper's New Monthly Magazine*, 64:571–576; *Harper's Weekly*, 29:154.
[20] *Century*, 25:839.

his mother and younger brother do the prospering while he goes first to Harvard and then to Italy. Here the story takes a new turn. While young Houston is writing an "immortal sonata" in Rome, he becomes involved in a plot which strongly suggests that of *The Marble Faun*, much simplified and robbed of all subtlety. He falls in love with the dovelike Anastasia and incurs the enmity of her evil brother, "Black Vittorio." This wretch drowns accidentally in the Tiber when Anastasia's timely warning thwarts his attempt on Houston's life. The hero marries Anastasia and takes her home to Clayville, but she pines away and dies of remorse over her part in her brother's death.[21]

"A Daring Fiction" is a silly, half-romantic tale about an American student in Leipzig, who, to escape the designs of his German landlady and her three marriageable daughters, invents an American fiancée, "Miss Jones." When, to complicate matters, a real Miss Jones appears, the tale becomes a sentimental farce.[22]

In "The Story of a Blue Vein," Boyesen borrows Friedrich Spielhagen's favorite character, the plebeian who is the natural son of a nobleman. Poor Rikka Bollmann, only a child herself, saves the life of her foster brother Richard after her parents die in a drunken brawl. A blue vein ("It looked like a lasso flung up in the air and traced itself with a bold curve under the transparent skin, vanishing under the curls about the right ear") proves that young Richard is the son of the Countess von Turgau and the late lamented Lieutenant von Peplitz. Richard, in spite of himself, is ashamed of the plebeian girl who has reared him and fallen in love with him. Rikka offers to go to America, leaving him to his mother, but the hero becomes embittered about the "sham of the favored few." The young pair then resolve to go together to "the great free land beyond the sea," where all barriers vanish. As the steamer pulls away, Richard sees his mother on the dock and nearly jumps overboard. He nobly "clasps Rikka in his arms instead," but Boyesen does not explain whether the girl continues to mother the young hero in America or becomes his wife. This sentimental tale reads like a throwback to

---

[21] Boyesen, while in Rome, was under the influence of Hawthorne; see *Scribner's Monthly*, 18:660. He undoubtedly referred to "Anastasia" when he wrote Cable, July 13, 1879: "I am struggling with a little Italian story which interests me greatly. . . . The story grew out of an incident which we happened to witness in Rome, & is my first venture in the sensational line, & may possibly be my last."

[22] This story, first published in the *New York Commercial Advertiser*, November, 1884, is included in *Stories by American Authors*, 10:112–153.

Boyesen's early period.[23] "The Story of a Blue Vein," "A Daring Fiction," and "Ilka on the Hill-Top" proved definitely that the use of German characters brought out the worst in his fiction.

"A Problematic Character," a serial published in the *Century* in August, September, and October, 1884, never appeared in book form. The story betrays its kinship to Henry James's work: The impressionable Boyesen could not have written about an American artist in Paris or a brilliant Parisienne in the New World without echoing James. But if James was concerned with his countrymen in Europe, Boyesen's interest centered on Europeans in America, or America as seen through a European's eyes. The chief importance of the novel lies in Boyesen's delineation of his ideal American hero, and in his solution to the problem of "the artist in America."

Boyesen's Norwegian-born hero was almost always handsome, talented, warmhearted, and usually a recent graduate of the university in Christiania. The qualities of his ideal American hero were crystallized by 1884: He was a scientist or an artist who had spent some years at a German university or in an artists' colony in Paris, Rome, or Munich. Fred Swart, Harold Wellingford, and Frederick Houston were such men, and Hannibal Tarleton, of "A Problematic Character," made a fourth.[24] Boyesen gives a good deal of attention to the peculiarly American characteristics of Tarleton, portraying the young man through his aggressive manner of speaking and the impression it makes on a cultured lady from France. A brief summary of the plot, with a few quotations, will reveal Boyesen's artist hero and his optimism about the future of American culture.

The problematic person in the novel is Madame Valerie de Salincourt, whose intrigues in Paris misfire and force her into exile in the United States. For most of one year she teaches French at the Young Ladies Seminary in Catoville, a western town. She spends the Christmas vacation with a favorite pupil, Alice Beach, who has a "pure and sequestered New England soul." Alice's father has made a fortune in paper and her Uncle Joel "had gained immortality as the producer of a popular soap." At the Beach home the French lady meets Alice's fiancé, Hannibal Tarleton, who is an aspiring painter. Quite naturally the discussion turns to

---

[23] *Cosmopolitan*, 1:3–11.

[24] For the first three, see "Swart among the Buckeyes," *A Daughter of the Philistines*, and "Anastasia."

The Uneven Road to Realism

art. The hero does not share the views of Hawthorne and Henry James: "I have no patience with those fellows who shake their heads lugubriously and say that we have no artistic atmosphere and that sort of twaddle. If we haven't got it, it is for them to make it. It makes me mad to hear people of common sense lament our youth, and say we can't do anything in the way of art because we are young and strong. We have a grand future before us, and we mean to produce things here which will take away the breath of the old monarchies on the other side. You just wait; our turn is coming, and it is coming soon."[25]

This "declaration of independence" draws approving nods from Madame. She is not annoyed by Hannibal's cocksureness, though "as a Parisienne and a flower of an old and ripe civilization, she felt a superior pity." Her reasoning about the rightness of Hannibal's character suggests that Hjalmar Boyesen was thinking about the restrictions he escaped by leaving Norway for America:

"It was so perfectly comprehensible that the typical youth of this huge continent who stood facing westward, with the vast fertile prairies and the slumbering wealth of the mountains spread out before him, should exult in his strength, and only feel eager to plunge headlong into the stress of action. He could never feel the sickening sense of limitation and impotence which is the uppermost emotion of him who, at the threshold of his career, finds himself part of a fixed and inflexible machinery, and doomed to revolve all his life long in one narrow little circle of social and official routine."[26]

When Hannibal Tarleton turns out to be a man of genius (something the cultivated Parisienne could instantly perceive, even though the paintings he showed her were ludicrously bad), he is instantly commanded to go to Europe:

"What is a man of your powers to do in this respectable little hole? God has equipped you splendidly, but He made a mistake in permitting you to be born in New England. You were made for a larger role than can be comfortably played in a community where no free soul has elbow-room. It is pathetic to see you with your irrepressible intelligence aspiring downward, longing from genius toward mediocrity. Ah! there blows a different breeze, a breeze laden with the perfumes of all the centuries, through the old lands of Europe, and one whiff of it will trans-

[25] *Century*, 28:613 (August, 1884).
[26] *Century*, 28:613.

form you into a different being. Your chief drawback now is that your culture is deficient, and you are ignorant of the thoughts which agitate the world. It is only when your mind shall have expanded in a congenial atmosphere, and your hand shall have acquired the skill which dances over technical difficulties as if they were mere child's play, — it is then, and not until then, that your genius will find its adequate expression. Other ties, though ever so dear, are of minor consequence and must not be allowed to interfere with this supreme destiny." [27]

The last part of "A Problematic Character" takes place in Paris and Rome. A sudden turn in Madame's fortunes recalls her from exile. Established in her Parisian salon, she rebuffs Hannibal, who has followed her to Europe. Nevertheless, the aspiring artist still heeds Madame's advice about his need for European training and goes on to Rome to study.

Four years later Madame de Salincourt suddenly remembers her little friend Alice Beach, and invites her to Paris. "Alice . . . was exported by Uncle Joel to the delightful city where all good Americans are said to go once, either before or after their demise." The girl is properly escorted, because "Uncle Joel had so far conquered his prejudices against monarchy as to consent to the introduction of his soap in Europe, and actually intended supervising this hazardous undertaking in person." Just at this moment Hannibal Tarleton reappears, or rather, bursts "upon the horizon of the American colony like an unheralded comet." In Paris "American art, and particularly the question whether there were any such thing as American art, were the problems of the hour, and excited much virulent discussion." Madame decides that she now wants to capture this ideal prototype of the hero in Henry James's *The American:* "He had none of the artificial elegance which characterizes the aristocrat of the Old World, but a frank and spirited straight-forwardness which was very winning." [28]

The aging Madame de Salincourt, now showing the sinister side that has been hinted at, feels that Alice can best be disposed of by marrying her off to a French aristocrat. Madame has already begun to instruct this daughter of the Puritans: "'All men are potential lovers. . . . At all events, it is only in that capacity that I find them interesting. I have had men of all civilized nationalities in love with me, and some barbarous

[27] *Century*, 28:616.
[28] *Century*, 28:750, 755 (September, 1884).

besides.'" This last reference is to a pasha who tried to buy Madame from her late husband. Failing, the smitten man had strangled himself. "'That is the kind of flattery to which I am keenly susceptible. If a man paid me such a compliment again, I think I could do anything for him in a moderate way, as, for instance, assuming his name, wearing weeds for him, and spending his money.'"[29]

The Frenchwoman's wicked machinations are thwarted. Alice Beach escapes from the clutches of the decadent, evil aristocrats, and Hannibal resists the charms of Madame de Salincourt, despite a carefully staged midnight scene at a villa outside Rome. He is suddenly attracted by Alice Beach's prejudices, even by her refusal to drink a toast to him:

"'You know I never drink anything,' she whispered. . . .

"'It is a queer thing, that New England conscience,' he thought. . . . 'It is the only constant thing in this inconstant world: the only absolute and uncompromising thing in a world of fleeting vanities and make-shifts.'"[30]

When the lady with the problematic character abandons the contest, she also gives the lie to Hawthorne and Henry James: "'You Americans are a queer people,' said Madame thoughtfully. . . . 'There is nothing under the sun which you respect. It may be because you are unhampered by tradition of any kind, that you are destined, for a couple of centuries to come, to lead the world. For we on this side of the water are engaged in getting rid of our traditions. You who have none to get rid of will advance the faster.'"[31]

Boyesen compared Europe and America in many of his stories and novels, from *A Norseman's Pilgrimage* (1875) to the end of his writing career. The emphasis was nearly always on the cultural advantages of the two continents, and America, of course, did not fare too well. But in "A Problematic Character," though the hero needs a period of training in Europe to transform him from an ambitious dauber into a great painter, America wins all the arguments. And even if Europe has the cultural advantages, the bold and free American spirit is a more valuable element, even in the making of an artist.

Boyesen's last book of short stories, *Vagabond Tales*, was published in 1889 by D. Lothrop Company of Boston. Unlike the collections in

---

[29] *Century*, 28:753.
[30] *Century*, 28:759.
[31] *Century*, 28:898 (October, 1884).

Hjalmar Hjorth Boyesen

the earlier volumes, this one is selective. The seven tales represent only a part of his total output. Four had appeared previously, two each in the *Century* and in *Scribner's Magazine*. Three others—"Monk Tellenbach's Exile," "Liberty's Victim," and "A Disastrous Partnership"— have not been traced to any periodical.

"A Child of the Age" begins as the serious study of a willful, wayward boy, a radical at the Norwegian university, who is unable to get along with his conservative father. After he has acquired a wife and child, he conforms outwardly, but a visit from Bjørnson to the home valley finally results in a violent quarrel between father and son. After this promising beginning, however, Boyesen's story ends like his early emigrant tales. The young man goes to America, makes a great fortune, and returns to a tender reconciliation with his family.[32]

"A Perilous Incognito" employs the same threadbare plot: the false accusations of a jealous mother-in-law drive Ewald Nordahl to America. With his fortune made in gold, cattle, and land, he returns to Norway to get revenge. But far more interesting than the narrative is the characterization of the hero. Boyesen, who wrote "The Hero in Fiction" a few months later, was self-conscious about using a hero at all. Fortunately he could make the young lady in the story responsible for this vestige of romanticism: "Here was a man who spoke of his experience in the lowliest positions without a shadow either of shame or of ostentation; who by the labor of his hands and his brain had accumulated a fortune and gained an insight into life in its more varied phases. There was a healthy, out-of-door atmosphere about his whole personality— his energetic, sunburnt face, his straightforward manners, and his unstudied talk. She had never met such a man before, and being a girl, could not well avoid making this one a hero."

Boyesen is even more self-conscious about his romantic story, for which he tries to avoid responsibility: "There was a dash of Bret Harte in the situation. . . . He might well have passed for one of those picturesque pioneers whom the California author has introduced to the favor of womankind." In the heroine's conversations with this hero, she reveals that she is well acquainted with the western writer: "She asked him about America, which she had been accustomed to view through

[32] *Century*, 31:177–192. This plot recalls the ideological and temperamental differences between Boyesen's father and his grandfather. Essentially the same story is outlined in *A Norseman's Pilgrimage*.

The Uneven Road to Realism

Bret Harte's haze of oaths, whiskey fumes, and pistol smoke. She was frankly astonished at everything he told her, and particularly at his patriotism. She had never imagined that anybody could have any sentiment for a mere geographical definition, she said."[33]

"Crooked John" is even more sentimental. Harold Von Graven is handsome and dashing, until a daring feat, breaking a log jam, leaves him a cripple for life. After everyone has forgotten the gallant deed, he becomes "Crooked John," a ridiculous figure; but blind Helen loves him because she hears the old Harold Von Graven in his voice. The cripple laboriously saves a hundred dollars so the girl's eyesight can be restored. His dilemma is solved sardonically. When Helen insists on seeing her noble lover, the resulting shock counteracts what has been accomplished by the operation and her eyesight fails once more. Harold dies from the overexertion caused by his efforts to finance the surgery.[34]

"Charity" tells of a cynical summer visitor from New York who falls in love with Charity Howland, a simple girl living on the island of Poltucket. Boyesen embellishes a thin plot with satirical gibes at New England primness, a little gentle ridicule aimed at an angular feminist from Vassar who serves as a foil to the warmhearted heroine, and some observations on old sea captains who deplore the passing of an old Poltucket industry:

"'Ef wrecks wasn't good for somethin', the Lord wouldn't send 'em. . . . I don't pray the Lord fer ships ter be wrecked; but I do pray the Lord that ef ships has ter be wrecked, they be wrecked on Poltucket. . . . I voted the Republican ticket every blessed year, but now I don't no more. Sence they put up the two life-savin' stations on the island and six light-houses, I am a Democrat.'"[35]

"Liberty's Victim," like a number of Boyesen's earlier stories, begins with scenes of university life in Christiania.[36] Albert Bonstetten, the handsomest man in his class, marries the most beautiful girl in the Norwegian capital. At graduation he makes a speech in which he likens liberty to the wild horse of the plains. Although he has been cautioned

---

[33] *Scribner's Magazine*, 2:120–128, 222–228; *North American Review*, 148:594–601. Boyesen's point is that the hero has outlived his usefulness, that modern fiction should have not heroes but "typical" men.

[34] *Century*, 34:405–412 (July, 1887).

[35] *Scribner's Magazine*, 4:490–500 (October, 1888).

[36] See "A Good-for-Nothing" and "The Man Who Lost His Name," in *Tales from Two Hemispheres*; and *Falconberg*. "Liberty's Victim" is in *Vagabond Tales* (Boston, 1889).

to guard against excessive idealism, Bonstetten finds his progress too slow in Norway. He decides to migrate to America, where his talents will be properly appreciated and success will come swiftly.

In contrast to "liberty's victim," Albert Bonstetten, Boysesen pictures the son of immigrant parents, Oscar Rood, who begins his career in America selling papers on the streets of Milwaukee. By living on boiled potatoes he manages to work his way through the University of Wisconsin. Oscar is proud of his dumpy wife and children and of his cheap house and furniture. He is enthusiastic about his job as agent of the Excelsior Plow Company, for the superior product he sells is to play an important role in the New World. Bonstetten scorns Oscar Rood's advice and help, for a job with a machine company does not spell success to him. Though he knows nothing of farming, he invests his capital in land in Dane County, Wisconsin. The venture fails, he becomes a barkeeper ("Swedish Al"), and finally dies in a hovel on Chicago's West Side.

Boyesen thought enough of this story to recommend it to a young friend who wanted to give up his teaching job and try free-lance writing. George Hyde of the *Dial* suspected that "Liberty's Victim" was a reflection of Boyesen's own feelings after he resigned from Cornell.[37]

"Monk Tellenbach's Exile" tells about a cultured but rebellious Norwegian who tires of his own respectability. When he "appeared in public in the company of agitators and other compromising personages," he became intolerable to his family:

"A Tellenbach who established schools for little ragamuffins and made inflammatory speeches in the Laborers' Union, could only be relegated to nonexistence, or, what amounts to the same thing, to the United States. There, it was said, a man could hold unauthorized opinions without loss of dignity." Boyesen stops to philosophize about the sin of nonconformity: "Society though it may forgive almost everything else, knows one unpardonable sin, and but one — radicalism. No excesses, so long as they are venerable and traditional, disqualify a man for office, but the slightest originality of conduct, especially in the line of philanthropy, stamps him as a suspicious character."[38]

---

[37] *Dial*, 19:323. Hyde, however, accepted John Barry's word that Boyesen wrote the *Vagabond Tales* while he was at Cornell. See Barry, in *New York Illustrated American*, 17:178–180. Barry made several questionable statements in this article, and the one about the *Vagabond Tales* may be rejected.

[38] *Vagabond Tales*, 99.

The Uneven Road to Realism

Monk is not a worker, and America has no more place for him than has tradition-bound Norway. Fortunately, he finds a humble friend in the New World. Very often in Boyesen's tales the Norwegian peasant immigrants, who do not really interest the author, give their more brilliant brethren a helping hand (and are very happy to be able to serve "the judge's son" or "the colonel's heir"). The prize example is Lars Klufterud, a small and ugly little ex-stableboy who "doubted if he had ever, in later life, experienced so keen a delight as when, fourteen years old, he strutted up the aisle in the church to be confirmed, in Monk's discarded trousers."[39] Lars has succeeded as a harness maker in Chicago, while Monk fails at a dozen jobs. The boy insists that his idol accompany him to a claim in Oregon, and there allows him to fish all day while his host clears the wilderness. At the end of the tale the two men become rivals in love. The girl prefers Monk, who, rather than betray his humble benefactor, disappears into the void.

Boyesen's best short story about Norwegians in America is "A Disastrous Partnership," but he betrays his uneasiness about his subject matter in the opening sentence: "A journeyman cabinet-maker is an unheroic figure, and two journeymen cabinet-makers are doubly unheroic; nevertheless, as it is the story of two journeymen cabinet-makers I am about to relate, they will have to do for heroes."[40] The two journeymen open a workshop in Chicago. Truls Bergerson builds solid chairs and tolerates no shoddy workmanship, even when he has fifty craftsmen to supervise. His partner, Jens (or "James K.") Moe, is talented at designing furniture and advertising it. But while these men team well in business, their social lives follow different paths, and here is Boyesen's plot.

"A Disastrous Partnership" seems the wrong title for this story, up to the point where Truls Bergerson gives a party. This situation offers Boyesen his chance to castigate his bourgeois compatriots for their slowness in becoming Americanized. Truls Bergerson and his friends sneer at Moe for his "Yankee" ways, baiting him about his American wife, his betrayal of his "race." They hope to get him thoroughly drunk, to see if his fine wife will take him home and put him to bed, as a proper Norwegian wife would. The game is carried too far, and Truls hurls a bottle at his partner's head, nearly killing him.

[39] *Vagabond Tales*, 102.
[40] *Vagabond Tales*, 142.

Hjalmar Hjorth Boyesen

The author's strongly didactic purpose is clear at the end of this tale, when a remorseful Truls Bergerson realizes that the aspirations he shares with his wife (a competent Norwegian cook) are still "of the Old World, groveling and uninspiring." He and his circle, who still cling to their old language and ways, hate Moe and his wife for their social ambition. At the end of the story Truls thinks, "Moe, in allying himself to the new civilization and the new land, had been wiser than he, and had reaped his reward. . . . Moe had assimilated himself to the New World, and plunged into the rushing current that bore mankind onward."[41]

Taken as a unit, Boyesen's last collection of short stories is a far better, more mature group than the earlier ones in *Tales from Two Hemispheres* (1876) or *Ilka on the Hill-Top* (1881). Stories like "The Child of Luck," "Life for Life," or "The Little Chap," which compare very favorably with tales in the earlier collections, were now consigned to books for boys, and even these stories seem more serious and certainly more realistic than the earlier ones.[42] But the critics were not enthusiastic about *Vagabond Tales*, and as the rest of Boyesen's later short stories never appeared in book form, the public evidently agreed.

"It is true that just now we are experiencing a temporary reaction from realism," Boyesen told a reporter in July, 1889.[43] It seems unlikely that the realism of the *Vagabond Tales* should have discouraged readers, but Boyesen's growing reputation as an antiromanticist perhaps affected the sales of the book. The sentiment and melodrama in these stories may have been a concession to the reading public: Boyesen was aware that many critics and readers objected to the realism of the commonplace, and he was eager for his books to sell. The return to Norwegian subject matter may have been another concession, for tales about Norway had brought his early popularity, and critics were still asking why he did not write more stories like *Gunnar*.

In 1889 *Scribner's Magazine* published two stories by Boyesen that are weaker than any of the *Vagabond Tales*. "The Two Mollies: A City Sketch" is a short piece in Irish dialect. One Molly is Jimmy O'Flaherty's

[41] *Vagabond Tales*, 180.
[42] "The Child of Luck" appeared in *Harper's Young People*, a children's magazine published in New York, and in Boyesen's *Boyhood in Norway*; "Life for Life" in *Lippincott's*, 40:277–289 (August, 1887), and in Boyesen's *Norseland Tales*; "The Little Chap" in *Harper's Weekly*, 35:94 (January 31, 1891), and in *Norseland Tales*.
[43] *New York Daily Tribune*, July 29, 1889.

wife, the other his horse, and between them they drive the drunken drayman off a Hoboken pier. This tale may be a by-product of Boyesen's realistic novels. His political hacks always speak in a heavy brogue. The hero of "A Pagan Incantation" discovers an old Norse spell by reading ancient runes. The incantation transfers a person's disease to someone else, and as the hero is ill, he tries it on a woman far away. The spell works, but he falls in love with the girl, and she dies in his arms.[44]

Boyesen wrote Howells on January 2, 1890: "I sent you today my last novel, 'The Light of Her Countenance.' I don't know whether you will like it, though you will find some good characterization in it. It may be there are some slight concessions to the American girl in it, though, if so, I regret them." Boyesen's new novel was a reworking of "The Old Adam," a novelette published anonymously in *Lippincott's Magazine* in May, 1888. The complete novel appeared in Appleton's *Town and Country Library* in 1889.

Boyesen may have regretted his concessions to the "Iron Madonna," but they are neither slight nor inconspicuous in *The Light of Her Countenance*. Although the action begins in the United States, with a promising conflict between a self-made millionaire and his dilettante son, it is moved to Italy for the last three quarters of the book, and the story becomes watered-down, sentimental Henry James. A favorite Boyesen hero, the American seasoned by Continental experiences, has degenerated in this novel. "A young girl once said of Julian Burroughs that he looked like a dissipated lion." At thirty, both disillusioned and dissipated, he is yet, Boyesen makes it clear, a refinement of an outstanding American type. As for the elder Burroughs, he has "a shrewd, hard-featured, Uncle Sam kind of a face, a certain rude dignity, a consciousness of distinction in the way he carried himself."

This man "had been sixteen years in Congress and for six years represented his country as minister to a foreign court," but his son is a superior specimen: "The ex-minister bore the ineradicable marks of early hardships and a rude rearing, while his son had enjoyed all the advantages which two continents could lavish upon him. And yet to a close observer the type was fundamentally the same, and the son appeared what he really was — an *edition de luxe* of his self-made father."

Since Julian's father, a Republican politician ("scarcely a gentleman in the strictest sense"), buys the Democratic congressional nomination

[44] *Scribner's Magazine*, 6:116–120, 200–215.

for him, Julian is prepared to make an attempt to be a useful citizen. When the Tammany boss makes another sale and throws the election to the Republican candidate, Julian leaves for Rome. He finally wins the love of Constance Douglas, an expatriate American of such surpassing beauty that men commit suicide for love of her. There is a temporary setback in this romance: Julian foolishly tells the lady of his early philanderings; she cannot forgive him, although, "I could have forgiven you for deceiving me," she says. Reconciliation comes on the last page.[45]

Boyesen may have considered this novel a realistic psychological study of the relations between the sexes and of the double standard. He had known Ibsen's treatment of such subjects long before this, as his articles on Ibsen were to show. The critics objected to the character, Delia, an atheistic suffragette, but Boyesen qualified as an authority on American and European women in a dozen articles published from 1889 to 1895. In his most serious fiction, however, he rejected both Delia and Constance and went back to Alma Hampton of *A Daughter of the Philistines* for his type heroine.

Boyesen knew that American gentlemen considered politics a dirty game, best avoided, but even if he sympathized with their squeamishness, he could scarcely expect readers of *The Light of Her Countenance* to admire Julian Burroughs for quitting after an initial defeat. Why did he include this topic at all, since he obviously intended to make Julian a sympathetic character who signalized his success by marrying Constance Douglas? One might guess that he wanted to make use of such "typical American" material as a political campaign, but since he would not have known how to work out a romantic plot if his hero had won, he provided a defeat which sent him to Europe.

The girls who bought the volumes in the *Town and Country Library* when they came out twice a month were doubtless pleased. If Boyesen regretted the concessions he made to them, sales of the book salved his feelings. *The Light of Her Countenance* was reprinted in 1891 and 1893.

This period was one of transition in Boyesen's fiction, from the romanticism and enthusiasm of the seventies to the realism and disillusionment of the nineties. In this decade many of his stories combine satiric thrusts at manners and customs with a sentimental handling of plot and

[45] *The Light of Her Countenance*, 9, 36, 309.

The Uneven Road to Realism

character. But if the melodrama has not been eliminated, there is a more serious note in the best of his fiction, and a steadily darkening tone.

Boyesen had not lost all his idealism and optimism in the eighties: Still evident was his hope that the future would bring a triumph of science and a better world; and America remained the land where anything could happen. Yet he wrote more pessimistic stories, and his happy endings, his regenerations and reconciliations, seem spurious and forced. His most notable fiction is both somber and serious, and even his frivolous tales show the effects of his conversion to realism.

Boyesen himself realized that his work suffered because he published too much and wrote to please: His critical comments on the problems of American authors show that he was well aware of the pitfalls he had fallen into. And Howells, who had warned his friend repeatedly of the dangers of free-lancing, commented regretfully on Boyesen's experience: "He went to live in New York, a city where money counts for more and goes for less than in any other city of the world, and he could not resist the temptation to write more and more when he should have written less and less."[46] Howells was too loyal a friend to mention Lillie Boyesen's influence: It was she who had insisted on going to New York, and her style of living was not modest.

It should be remembered that Boyesen's fiction of the eighties does not represent his entire output: Even while he was turning out potboilers, he was at work on the novel that represents the culmination of his efforts toward realism.

[46] *Literary Friends*, 260.

9

Exit Poet, Enter Critic

BOYESEN'S only volume of verse, *Idyls of Norway and Other Poems*, was published by Scribner's late in 1882. Most of the poems had been printed in the seventies, chiefly in the *Atlantic* and *Scribner's*. But the longest in the collection, "Calpurnia," had come out in *Scribner's Monthly* for May, 1881; and "Marit and I" was printed in *Harper's Magazine* barely a month before it appeared in the book.

Only two or three of the poems had not been published previously. Boyesen could have filled another slim volume with the pieces he decided not to use. The selection was made to satisfy his own critical standards. He probably knew that some of the rejected ballads based on Nordic subjects would have been more popular with the public than the elegies he chose to include. As the title suggests, the collection does include a number of poems with Norse themes, but Boyesen seemed eager to prove that he had more than one medium.

Boyesen's verse does not deserve close and detailed study. Judged by any high standard, it is mediocre, and, by twentieth-century criteria, worse. Even the best poets of the tradition in which he wrote seem diffuse, sentimental, and spiritless now. And among them Boyesen was never held in high esteem.

The *Atlantic* review of *Idyls of Norway* was complete, judicious, and relatively favorable, though the critic thought the first six pieces might better have been omitted. These included the dedicatory sonnet "To

Exit Poet, Enter Critic

L.K.B." (Lillie Keen Boyesen), "The Lost Hellas" (which had been rejected by the *Atlantic*), "Elegy on A.G.L.," "Awake," "The Minstrel at Castle Garden," and "Elegy on President Garfield." The highest praise was reserved for "charming pastoral love-stories" like "Briar-Rose," "Hilda's Little Hood," and "Thora," all included in a second section entitled "Idyls of Norway." The reviewer quoted as "a good specimen of natural aptness," a line from "Earl Sigurd's Christmas Eve" that read, "And the scalds with nimble fingers o'er the sounding harpstrings swept." But he suggested that by substituting "their" for "with," Boyesen could avoid "the awkward spectacle of the bards sweeping their entire persons over the strings."

The *Atlantic* approved of the verse on Nordic themes that comprised the third and fourth sections of the book: "Earl Sigurd's Christmas Eve" and "Norse Staves." The reviewer said: "It is when we pass to the other pieces which the author has bound up with his Norse sheaf that we doubt his judgment of his own successes." Two groups of sonnets make up the fifth and sixth groups, the latter comprising ten inscribed "To Lillie." The concluding poem, "Calpurnia," indicated, according to the *Atlantic,* "a receptive mind, possessed of a true but not original poetic tendency, serving art with reverent hands and conscientiously." Of the sonnets, the *Atlantic* singled out the five on "Evolution" as praiseworthy: "He has gathered up and remoulded, with deep imaginative grasp the scientific views of the day, and given them a purely poetic and ideal scope."[1]

Other reviewers were less sympathetic. The *Dial* found the Norwegian idyls the most interesting in the collection, although "the sing-song measure in which they are written becomes rather tiresome." The critic believed that the chief interest in the volume would derive from Boyesen's reputation in other fields, and that he was a writer of delightful prose, who apparently attempted poetry as an experiment "rather than from an exalted inspiration." The *Literary World* found little to praise in any of the verse: The idyls were "very simple idyls indeed," and all of Boyesen's poems were deficient in "fundamental brainwork." The reviewer thought nothing could be less classic than "The Lost Hellas," with its "nebulous obscuration of Greek myths." Boyesen's inadequate knowledge of English versification was demonstrated in such rhymes as

[1] *Atlantic Monthly*, 51:421–423 (March, 1883).

Hjalmar Hjorth Boyesen

"flood" and "wood," "hare" and "near," "hood" and "blood," "valleys" and "chalice." [2]

When the *Critic*, usually favorable, damned Boyesen's poetry as prosaic, monotonous, and too hastily written, with at best nothing more than fair narrative power, Boyesen replied in a letter to the editor. The review indicated that the critic had not even read the book, Boyesen charged, but nevertheless it advised him to turn his Norwegian material into stories and novels, leaving poetry to the "exceedingly clever discoverers who bring taste, activity and learning to their work." The reviewer not only implied that the author of *Idyls of Norway* lacked these qualities, Boyesen said, but by remarking that "all" the poems had the stuff for novels in them, was deliberately misrepresenting the facts.[3]

Despite having thus defended his work, Boyesen published little verse after this one collection was printed. He occasionally contributed pieces to the *Independent* and the *Chautauquan*. He translated some of Ibsen's short poems, but these efforts were not well received. Even so, a second edition of *Idyls of Norway* was printed in 1893.

Boyesen's critical and topical writings of the eighties fall into three categories: reports on contemporary European writing, essays on the social aspects of literature, and articles on immigration and education. There is a closer connection between these various types than might seem likely. Boyesen was no purist in writing and seldom held strictly to the narrow limits of a topic: He attacked protective tariffs in an essay on the German novel and castigated the romanticists in an article on the need for an international copyright law. Furthermore, the strong convictions about realism which influenced nearly all his writing, no matter what the subject, effectively bridged the gap between literary and nonliterary matters.

Many of Boyesen's articles on European writers could be described as journalism, none as pure criticism. Because he believed that all serious fiction must be realistic and that novelists should come to grips with the problems of the day, his articles on literature tended to become sociological and political treatises. Two essays on Turgenev, written just after his death, are examples. Both mention Boyesen's friendship with the great Russian, and use the opportunity to emphasize the superiority of realistic writing. One of them, "Reminiscences of Tourguéncff," is de-

---

[2] *Dial*, 3:141 (November, 1882); *Literary World*, 13:489.
[3] *Critic*, 2:280, 299 (October 21, November 4, 1882).

voted largely to Russia, its despotism, corruption, and problems of reform. All this has some connection with realistic writing, but the new emphasis sounds strange coming from Boyesen, who had insisted some years earlier that Turgenev was an artist, not a reformer.[4]

In "The Modern German Novel," printed in the *Princeton Review* for March, 1884, Boyesen again draws on his personal contacts with the writers he discusses. Freytag and Spielhagen, whose novels he had reviewed ten years earlier, receive most of his attention, although some mention is made of Auerbach, Paul Heyse, Fritz Reuter, and Georg Ebers. This essay, slightly expanded and brought up to date, forms the chapter "Studies of the German Novel" in *Essays on German Literature*. "The Modern German Novel" is a fair example of Boyesen's method in writing such articles. He is always more popular than pedantic: Thus, he excuses himself from discussing Heyse's two long novels because they are "so remote from the horizon of American readers." Heyse is especially sympathetic to the matrimonial rebel, says Boyesen: "Madame Toutlemonde, the German Mrs. Grundy, has a great dread of Heyse, and it is said she keeps his books on the poison-shelf in her locked closet. Their pages are, however, dog's-eared and well fingered."

A discussion of Spielhagen as a chronicler of German life offers Boyesen a chance to voice his own socio-political views: "The militant spirit fostered by the late war [*the Franco–Prussian War of 1870–71*] has brought about a reaction toward autocracy, and a consequent decay of parliamentary institutions. The reaction, as every clear-sighted man must know, is of course temporary, but it is dangerous as long as it lasts, and retards the industrial development of the nation. A most oppressive system of protection (only rivalled in foolish severity by our own) increases the cost of living—makes the poor poorer and the rich richer. A vast military machinery is needed to keep the discontented in order, and only feeds the socialistic sentiment which it is intended to suppress. The whole force of evolution and the resistless logic of history are on the side of the oppressed masses, and in the end their cause must prevail."[5]

The last sentence is an indication of Boyesen's basic political phi-

[4] "Reminiscences of Tourguéneff," in *Harper's Weekly,* 27:615 (September 29, 1883); "Ivan Tourguéneff," in *Critic,* 3:365 (September 22, 1883). The earlier article was "Ivan Tourguéneff," in *Scribner's Monthly,* 14:200.

[5] Quotations in this and the preceding paragraph are from *Essays on German Literature,* 258, 259.

losophy, usually called social Darwinism; the reference to America's "severe" tariff is a clue to his tireless political activities in the Reform Club.[6]

The list of Boyesen's articles on Scandinavian literature is impressive and revealing: "Bjørnstjerne Bjørnson," "Bjørnson in the United States," "Kristofer Janson and the Norse Lutheran Synod," "A New Norwegian Novelist," "Social Problems in Norwegian Novels," "Hans Christian Andersen," "The New School in Norwegian Literature," "The New Literature of Norway and Denmark," and "Scandinavian Literature." The only book review of this period that has been identified as Boyesen's is an *Atlantic Monthly* article on Janson's *The Spell-bound Fiddler*. It is a full and thoughtful treatment that goes well beyond the work under consideration. In addition, the *Princeton Review* for March, 1886, printed a piece entitled "'John Sunde,' translated and adapted from the Norwegian of Jonas Lie by H. H. Boyesen." How much adapting was done is not readily apparent, but Boyesen prefaced his translation with a brief survey of Scandinavian fiction and an evaluation of Lie's work.[7]

Toward the end of his career Boyesen said that he "had been at work for nearly twenty years on a history of Scandinavian Literature."[8] This book never appeared. His *Essays on Scandinavian Literature*, published in New York in 1895, is basically a collection of magazine articles written during the eighties, including many of those cited in the preceding paragraph, some of them reprinted without revision. Like so much of his work, these essays were published with an eye toward their sales value. He knew most of the men he wrote about and corresponded with them. His lectures at Columbia on Scandinavian literature placed particular emphasis on contemporary fiction. It must be admitted, too, that most of these articles seem to have been written hastily, and that nearly all betray the sympathies and prejudices of the author. The haste was an

---

[6] The Reform Club was especially active on behalf of Grover Cleveland's attempts to lower the tariff. The members, who numbered 1,200 in 1888, prepared and sent out literature, recruited and trained speakers, and sponsored public gatherings. Boyesen took part in debates and discussions at the clubrooms with such men as Carl Schurz, E. L. Godkin, John De Witt Warner, G. W. Curtis, and Walter Hines Page.

[7] See *Scribner's Monthly*, 20:336–345 (July, 1880); *Critic*, 1:58, 2:8, 159, 7:133, 10:225 (March 12, 1881, January 14, June 17, 1882, September 19, 1885, March 7, 1887); *Dial*, 5:159–162 (November, 1884); *New Princeton Review*, sixty-first year, no. 2, p. 246–262, sixty-second year, no. 3, p. 370–385 (March, 1886, May, 1887); *Chautauquan*, 8:282–284, 335–337 (February, March, 1888); *Atlantic Monthly*, 47: 285–288 (February, 1881).

[8] *Scandinavian Literature*, preface.

unhappy result of Boyesen's way of life and crowded program of activities, but the bias was certainly deliberate.

"Bjørnson in the United States," not properly a literary article at all, illustrates this bias. "All the thought of the century is constantly seething in his strong and spacious brain," Boyesen writes. He immediately makes it clear how an author is to be judged: "Bjørnson is not a poet of the romantic order, even though he began his career as a writer of idyllic poems and novelettes. The romanticism of his youth he has long ago outgrown, and he stands now in the broad light of reality, grappling with the great questions of the time." [9] To Boyesen a writer was to be judged by his subject matter: If he boldly attacked large questions, propounded revolutionary ideas, and dealt seriously with controversial or unpopular topics, he was a realist, even though his treatment may have been melodramatic and sentimental. This explains Boyesen's persistent practice of extolling German writers like Freytag and Spielhagen, though they protested against and even violently attacked realism. He had better luck with his Scandinavian friends, who were becoming more didactic and more socially conscious.[10]

"Social Problems in Norwegian Novels" gave Boyesen an excellent chance to put in a word for fiction about vital questions. All the Norwegian writers were revolutionary in spirit, Boyesen said; they could best gain popularity through works that were displeasing to a Swedish, aristocratic, and conservative king. Bjørnson had become another Zola, though an optimistic one. He was currently emphasizing, in his novels, the need for more healthy mating through sex education. Other writers went even farther in their radicalism. "While Bjørnson primarily emphasizes the responsibility of the individual to society, Kielland chooses to emphasize the responsibility of society to the individual." Kielland and Ibsen had carried realism "to a point where no reviewer dares to follow." [11]

In the late eighties Boyesen wrote most of the essays that were collected and published in 1894 as *Literary and Social Silhouettes*. The first and probably the best of these appeared in the February, 1887, *Forum* under the challenging title, "Why We Have No Great Novelists"; but

---

[9] *Critic*, 1:58 (March 12, 1881).
[10] "Does not Spielhagen, in his last remarkable novel, 'The Sunday-Child' (Sontagskind), steer dangerously near to the theory of art which he so vigorously denounces?"; Boyesen, "A German Novel," in *Cosmopolitan*, 15:378 (July, 1893).
[11] *Critic*, 7:133.

Hjalmar Hjorth Boyesen

when it was reprinted in the 1894 collection Boyesen gave it the more accurate heading, "The American Novelist and His Public," and dated it 1886. Although it is best known for the characterization of the American woman as the "Iron Madonna," whose frivolous taste in fiction forces the novelist to eschew serious subjects, this essay makes some other points worth noting and it evaluates, from a realistic position, the accomplishments of American writers. After a few preliminary remarks, Boyesen comes to his central contention: "The public makes its authors in its own image and likeness. It demands a certain article and it gets it." Though the "hunger for popularity" produces little cliques whose members advertise each other's output, there are "other forces at work, in our literature, which are more permanently injurious." [12]

"Chief among these I hold to be the fact that the American public, as far as the novelist is concerned, is the female half of it. . . . The average American has no time to read anything but newspapers, while his daughters have an abundance of time at their disposal, and a general disposition to employ it in anything that is amusing. The novelist . . . knows, in a general way, what ladies like, and as the success of his work depends upon his hitting their taste, he makes a series of small concessions to it, which, in the end, determines the character of his book. He feels that he is conversing with ladies and not with men. . . . He shuns large questions and problems because his audience is chiefly interested in small questions and problems. . . . Their education has not trained them for independent reflection. They are by nature conservative, and have been told by their pastors and teachers that the so-called modern ideas are dangerous and improper to discuss."

Boyesen believed that "this silence concerning all the vital things of life" was the most serious fault of the modern American novel. Deference to the ladies excluded politics: "In all the tales of Howells and James, which are typical of the tendencies of the time, I do not remember a single political incident." Boyesen also surveyed the efforts of the lesser novelists. F. Marion Crawford was misinformed and not serious in *An American Politician*. De Forest's *Honest John Vane* was excellent, but the author afterwards abandoned fiction. Edward Eggleston was another exception. "Of the anonymous [Henry Adams] novel, *Democracy*, I have not spoken, because it was not what it purported to be – a char-

---

[12] Quotations in this and the paragraphs to follow are from *Literary Silhouettes*, 43, 46, 48, 50–56, 89, 92–96, 137, 145, 155, 159, 167–169, 175, 211.

acterization of life at our national capital — but a distorting and malevolent satire on it." Albion Tourgée was too vindictively partisan.

Although "a temperamental aversion for polemics" keeps Howells from grappling with social problems, Boyesen praises his friend for leading the attack on "the worn-out romantic ideals" and "the crude devices of the sensationalist." But "every novelist who reaches his public through the medium of the monthly magazines" is forced "to chew the cud of old ideas, and avoid espousing any cause which lacks the element of popularity." A nonconformist, or a writer who is in advance of his time, has the choice "of suppressing his convictions or remaining silent." The situation is very different in Europe (except in England), Boyesen explains, and the reason for the difference is our "family" magazine, "without which American authorship scarcely could exist." Admitting that few good magazines exist in Europe, Boyesen says that the serious novelists "prefer to seek their first publicity in the *feuilletons* [literary supplements] of the daily papers, which impose no restraints upon them in the interest of tender readers." The results are heartening: "Everywhere there are vigor, originality, a fresh and contagious radicalism" (in Germany); and in France "Daudet, Zola, and Clarétie likewise revel in the liberty which the daily press allows them, and develop there, for good or for ill, to the full limit of their individualities." In Norway, where Bjørnson publishes directly, "without the intervention of any paper or periodical," Boyesen finds that "all the vital questions of the day, in religion, politics, and society, are being vigorously expounded and debated in works of fiction."

Boyesen self-consciously admitted that he was being ungrateful to his reading public, but entered a counterplea:

"I confess I have never written a book without helplessly deploring the fact that young ladies were to be the arbiters of its fate. . . . To be a purveyor of amusement (especially if one suspects that he has the stuff in him for something better) is not at all amusing. . . . Nothing less is demanded of him by that inexorable force called public taste, as embodied in the editors of the paying magazines, behind whom sits . . . his final judge, the young American girl. She is the Iron Madonna who strangles in her fond embrace the American novelist."

Three other articles — "Mars vs. Apollo," "The Hero in Fiction," and "Types of American Women" — are closely related to the Iron Madonna essay. All four are concerned with problems that are partly social, partly literary. In "Mars vs. Apollo," for example, Boyesen begins by deploring the martial spirit of German and French literature since 1870 and ends by asking: "How will industrialism, when consistently developed in all relations of life, affect the fine arts?" He decides that the quarrel between Mars and Apollo is meaningless, since the future belongs to Vulcan: "Ours is an industrial civilization." Similarly, "Types of American Women" begins with Herbert Spencer's contention that all feminine wiles are forms of hypocrisy, and that the duplicity of the gentler sex will continue as long as a woman's primary purpose is to please a man. This leads to a discussion of the American girl, the Daisy Miller type universally recognized in Europe but ignored in America. The essay ends with Boyesen's warning to American women not to ape the English; in so doing they will lose their individuality.

"The Hero in Fiction" is a determined attack on the romanticists and a plea for realism. The evolution of fiction closely parallels the evolution of mankind, Boyesen argues. Throughout its history the novel, or the story, has been dominated by a heroic figure who is always larger than life, but the time has come for a change. "The latest development of the novel breaks with this tradition. It really abolishes the hero." His place is taken by the typical character. "This is the great and radical change which the so-called realistic school of fiction has inaugurated," Boyesen says.

"The novel, as soon as it sets itself so serious an aim, is no longer an irresponsible play of fancy, however brilliant, but acquires an historical importance in relation to the age to which it belongs. The Germans are never weary of emphasizing what they call *die kulturgeschichtliche Bedeutung des Romans* [*the significance of the novel in cultural history*]; and it represents to me the final test by which a novelist is to be judged."

"As a further evidence of the evolution of fiction," says Boyesen, "any observant reader will have noticed . . . that the hero of the modern novel is no longer a gentleman of leisure, whose sole business in life is to make love and run into debt." Therefore, since "the American people has probably less leisure than any nation under the sun . . . its novelists, if they aim at realism, must acquire the art of converting the national industries into literary material." Howells had progressed the most in this direction with his Silas Lapham and his Bartley Hubbard (in *A Modern Instance*). "Mr. James," says Boyesen, "does not know the country well enough to achieve anything so vital in American portraiture. . . . While Mr. Howells appears to be getting a stronger grip on reality . . . Mr. James soars, like a high-bred and cynical eagle, in the upper air of British society, and looks down upon his former country with a sad critical disapproval." Yet to Boyesen these two men represent "the latest evolution of realistic fiction. Their unheroic heroes are, as a rule, social types." Granted "long lives and unimpaired vigor," he hopes that Howells and James "may leave behind them a national portrait-gallery which will repay the study of the future historian."

Boyesen's study of "America in European Literature" (1887) convinced him that accurate information about the United States had eliminated the fabulous American uncle from Continental fiction. Now, according to Boyesen, Americans, especially those portrayed in German and Scandinavian writing, are more often emancipated women or men of new ideas and practical wisdom. This, of course, is another example of the evolution of fiction, another triumph of realism over romanticism.

Apparently he did not apply his realistic criteria to poetry. Yet, in "The Ethics of Robert Browning" (1888), he was bold enough to offend many of Browning's admirers. This English poet, said Boyesen, "preaches frankly the rights of passion and derides in his heroes all pusillanimous regard for duty." Not only does Browning represent "individualism carried to its extreme limit," but, "being healthily robust in dealing with the passions, he leaves morality to take care of itself."

In "Philistinism" (1888), Boyesen attacked some of his favorite targets: England, medievalism, and the frivolous, novel-reading American girl. The first two were paid off together: "I believe Great Britain is the only land of an advanced civilization where the Philistine spirit is so dominant, even in the universities, as to be able to exclude the greatest scholars from the academic chairs on account of their religious nonconformism."

Because of this "theological medievalism," Oxford and Cambridge had "dispensed with the services of men like Darwin, Herbert Spencer, Tyndall, Huxley, Faraday, Sir Humphrey Davy . . . and gloried, in the meanwhile, in their Puseys and Newmans and Mannings — all most excellent men, but, at heart, medievalists and utterly out of sympathy with the nineteenth century, for which (whatever be its failings) it is the business of universities to educate its students." In this essay Boyesen, having loosed his wrath on the English Philistines, spoke of American girls more in pity than in anger:

Hjalmar Hjorth Boyesen

"They are, in fact, the only leisured class of the United States; and for want of better things to do, they fill the yawning vacuum of their days with novel-reading. The greater part of what they read is shockingly bad; but occasionally they stumble upon a good book, which makes a miniature revolution in their miniature brains. . . . Then comes a hunger for culture which is truly pathetic."

Even the occasion of Boyesen's fortieth birthday impelled him to say a good word for realism and deplore the immaturity of the American reading public. In "The Meridian of Life," an essay dated September 23, 1888, he referred to Howells' analysis (in *An Indian Summer*) of the symptoms that give the "impression of middle age in the hero":

"It is his whole attitude towards life, his humorous acceptance of reality as it is, and his utter incapacity for sentimental self-delusion. That is a fatal —in fact, the most fatal — defect in a lover. Love, without it, is robbed of its poetry. It becomes a sordid thing; a physical attraction, or mental compatibility; a mere prose prologue to matrimony. It is because youth constitutes nine-tenths of the public of the American author, that the American novel (if it aims at popularity) is obliged to pander to this self-delusion, and represent life as, according to youth's sanguine scheme, it ought to be. It must blink facts, or view them in a vague and general way through romantic spectacles. The author must play Providence, and with a Rhadamanthine justice reward lowly virtue and visit retribution upon prosperous wickedness. He must reconstruct the scheme of things in accordance with the ideal demands of his reader, or forfeit his popularity. Not that I blame youth for demanding a so-called poetic justice! No, I envy it. I wish I were myself capable of that charming delusion; or capable of pretending that I believed in it, even though my faith had departed."

Boyesen's topical writings on immigration, education, and related subjects must be passed over. The impetus that caused him to write them and the general viewpoint they reveal have been explained. These articles do not add to his literary reputation, although they emphasize once more his conviction that a literary man must take an active interest in the social and political questions of the day. He took a strong stand on immigration and education because he felt that he could speak with authority on these topics. But his opinions are neither revolutionary nor impressive: They reflect the prejudices of a cultured Columbia professor, who looked with horror on the immigrant masses from South and

Exit Poet, Enter Critic

Central Europe pouring into New York City, and who feared that the lower classes were forgetting their natural role of honest and faithful workmen and were being influenced by the wild statements of socialist agitators.

Boyesen was more acute in his analysis of the problems facing a serious American novelist and more sure of his ground in predicting the triumph of realism. In calling the romanticists throwbacks to feudalism, and their popular thrillers a threat to American democracy, he was in grave danger of becoming ridiculous, but he struck the right note in decrying the frivolity and emptiness of such writing. This argument, Boyesen maintained, would be effective in America if its citizens could be persuaded that literature was a serious matter. He thought there was some hope when thousands of plain people listened to his arguments at Lake Chautauqua. After his experiences there, he was more convinced than ever that the cause of realism would triumph if serious-minded people became interested in it. Meanwhile, however, there was still the problem of finding editors and publishers who would brave the displeasure of the young girl.

Although Boyesen was technically a Norwegian immigrant, he had not been prompted to emigrate by the same forces that influenced the majority of his countrymen, nor did he face the same problems as they in the United States. He had been a professor in two American colleges, but he had not taught in the public schools. In the field of modern literature, however, he knew what was happening in Europe and America, and he was aware that the serious young writers of both continents were turning toward realism. He also knew, before 1890, that it was more profitable to grind out romantic claptrap than to write serious fiction. On such matters, Hjalmar Boyesen could speak with authority backed by experience.

10

The Best and Last Fight

AT THE beginning of a new year—and a new decade—Boyesen's first thoughts were of his current novels. Writing to his literary mentor, William Dean Howells, on January 2, 1890, he betrayed some uneasiness over the quality of *The Light of Her Countenance*, and he hinted that it had been aimed at the novel-reading young lady. But, as if to justify himself, he also referred to *The Mammon of Unrighteousness*, which still had no publisher because it was realistic, not romantic:

"Your letter was the best thing the New Year brought me. It gave me a 'sense of comfort wh[ich] religion cannot give.'

"I have no friend in the deeper sense of the term on this side of the water; & therefore it is essential to my happiness to hear from you semi-occasionally, when you move to such remote localities as Boston. May your sojourn there be brief! New York cannot do without you—after your having written such a book as 'A Hazard of New Fortunes.' It comes up to 'Silas Lapham.' . . . I am lecturing incessantly—last summer at Chautauqua I had audiences varying from 4000–6000.

"I sent you today my last novel 'The Light of Her Countenance.' I don't know whether you will like it though you will find some good characterization in it. It may be there are some slight concessions to the young Am. girl in it, though, if so, I regret them.

"My 'Mammon of Unrighteousness' still finds no publisher, & I am almost discouraged. But some time or other it will see the light, even if I have to pay for the plates."

The Best and Last Fight

Boyesen's work as a lecturer and scholar gained him a new rank at the beginning of this decade: On January 6, 1890, he was appointed professor of German language and literature at Columbia. After his death he was called "one of Columbia's three best known professors" by *Munsey's Magazine*, a popular periodical that stoutly defended the romances of Stanley J. Weyman and S. R. Crockett against the "insolent" and "farcical" utterances of Howells and Boyesen. The commentator found nothing good to say about Boyesen's criticism or fiction, but rated him high as a teacher and scholar:

"In his lecture room, with a small audience of interested students, he appeared at his best. On the history of German literature he was one of the greatest contemporary authorities. His methods of lecturing were so eccentric that his words imprinted themselves indelibly upon the listeners' minds. After delivering some particularly impressive statement, he would frequently rush from his desk, and, grasping a student by the shoulder, peer into his face and ask, 'Do you understand that?' so loudly that the person thus assailed would probably never forget his words.

"Professor Boyesen's admiration for Goethe was unbounded. The mere name would cause him to tramp up and down the room sweeping the students' notebooks to the floor as he passed. Then he would throw himself into a chair and pour out a flood of poetry with his eyes fixed upon the ceiling, entirely oblivious of his surroundings. A moment afterwards some train of thought would suggest itself which would cause him to fall into a profound reverie, and he would remain silent for several minutes. On the whole, he was a pronounced success as a lecturer."[1]

Boyesen's successes at Lake Chautauqua in 1889 called for a return engagement in 1890, though he delivered only one address the second summer. The audiences who heard him there spread his fame as a speaker, and during the nineties he lectured in many parts of the country, traveling as far west as Minneapolis to fill engagements. He made his last Chautauqua appearances at Bay View, Michigan, in the summers of 1894 and 1895.[2]

Since January, 1889, Boyesen had been trying to interest magazine

---

[1] "Literary Chat," in *Munsey's Magazine*, 14:244, 370 (November, December, 1895); see also *Critic*, 27:237.

[2] See J. A. Peterson to Boyesen, dated Minneapolis, July 20, September 30, 1892, in the Boyesen Papers; Boyesen, "The Summer Assemblies of 1895," in *Chautauquan*, 22:249 (November, 1895), and "The Chautauquan Movement," in *Cosmopolitan*, 19:147–158 (June, 1895).

or book publishers in accepting *The Mammon of Unrighteousness.* He had pinned his chief hope on some of the more serious magazines, but Richard Watson Gilder of the *Century* and Henry Mills Alden of *Harper's* rejected the manuscript early in 1889. Apparently Scribner's, his regular outlet, also turned it down for both book and magazine publication, as did the *Cosmopolitan,* his chief periodical outlet at the time. There might have been more rejections, perhaps from Lippincott, Roberts Brothers, Appleton, and Lothrop; all of these companies brought out some of his fiction during this period.[3] Boyesen, nearly desperate, asked Howells to intercede for him with a new and untried firm. This failure to find a publisher was, however, only one of a number of misfortunes that beset the Boyesens in the summer of 1890. He wrote Howells from his new summer home at Southampton, Long Island, on August 8, 1890:

"You had the kindness to suggest the last time I saw you, that possibly you might contrive to get me a proposition of some kind from Lovell in regard to my novel 'The Mammon of Unrighteousness.' I need not assure you how greatly I should appreciate a little friendly diplomacy on your part, in this matter. I am quite positive that the book, if once brought out, will make its own way — for the very reason that it is a serious social study; & I am very averse to emasculating it (as has been proposed), by eliminating the political portion. . . . I should, of course, prefer a cash offer, which I understand would be in accordance with their present policy. But if that is unattainable, an agreement might be arrived at on another basis. . . .

"Am going to Chautauqua to deliver an address next week & return here about Aug. 20th. Please direct your reply to Columbia College.

"Mrs. Boyesen has been in poor health all this summer; but is now better. You may have heard that the whooping cough prevented our trip to Norway & wrecked all our plans. We have had a wretched time; & now to cap the climax, a week ago my oldest son Hjalmar ran barefooted into a smouldering fire on the beach & burned his foot terribly. The skin hung like a loose-wrinkled stocking. The poor boy has suffered horribly, & is yet in bed but is now slowly mending. You have an ardent admirer in my brother Ingolf who has been visiting me here recently. He

---

[3] Boyesen, writing Howells January 5 and February 6, 1889, mentioned that he was sending the novel to Gilder and Alden.

The Best and Last Fight

sends all sorts of affectionate greetings. He is insolently prosperous — but works like a plough-horse." [4]

On Boyesen's forty-second birthday, six weeks later, he wrote Howells again from Southampton, showing some of his old enthusiasm. He could even joke about his birthday and the new difficulties encountered in finding a publisher for his "unlucky novel." He added:

"Bjørnson who is kicking up a row as usual in Norway sends all manner of affectionate greetings to you. But his handwriting is getting so wild that it takes me an hour or more to decipher it. I usually read his letters in installments — I finish them in two or three days." [5]

Early in 1891, Boyesen finally found a publisher for *Mammon*. Charles Wolcott Balestier, editor for the United States Book Company (successors to John W. Lovell Company) agreed to bring it out in June, 1891.[6] With the novel safely on its way to publication, Boyesen made new plans for a European trip. He was obviously looking forward to seeing Norway again, and to showing its beauties to his wife and three young sons. He even hoped that he might persuade Howells to join the party; he sent him this invitation from Columbia College on January 14, 1891:

"Is there any possibility of your going to Europe next summer? In that case, couldn't you be induced to make the tour of Norway in our company? I expect to leave during the last week of May, spend two weeks in London & the next three months in my native land, wh[ich] I have not seen in eighteen years. Please think of it, & try if it is not feasible. Lovell & Co. accepted my novel 'The Mammon of Unrighteousness,' & will bring it out in June. Balestier wrote me a charming letter about it — a letter wh[ich] gave me much satisfaction after my discouraging experiences with the book. For this I owe you thanks — as in fact I do for most of the pleasant experiences wh[ich] have come to me in my literary career."

Although Boyesen had been confident, before he found a publisher for *Mammon*, that the novel would "make its way" once it got into print, he knew very well that his most serious and realistic work would be treated roughly by the reviewers. As the publication date neared, he once again appealed to Howells for help. Boyesen was to be in Europe when

---
[4] Ingolf Boyesen was a Chicago lawyer.
[5] Boyesen to Howells, September 23, 1890.
[6] Balestier's letters and telegrams are in the Boyesen Papers.

Hjalmar Hjorth Boyesen

the book appeared, and he wished to make certain that a champion of realism would be enlisted in its defense:

"I take the liberty to send you by express the advance sheets of my 'Mammon of Unrighteousness' which will be published by the U.S. Book Co. (Lovell's) June 5th. I have also sold the right of German translation to the N.Y. Staats Zeitung where the book will appear as *feuilleton* during May & June.

"Now, what I am bold to ask — or rather impose upon — you, most respectfully is, that you will kindly give me a notice in Harper's, at as early a date as possible after publication. It will then have weight with the reviewers — & not only with the public. Of course, you know I should not have the audacity to ask this if you had not made the suggestion when you read the MS. three years ago & made my heart leap by expressing an opinion which I have ever since cherished as one of the few things which have really added permanently to my happiness.

"I expect to sail for Europe May 28th (with my whole tribe) & shall hope to bring out an English edition early in June. Whenever Janvier & I meet we have a rejoicing symposium in the anticipation of your coming here next winter. I hope you will allow nothing to interfere with this delightful plan. . . . I am lecturing about you, all over the country, in a way to make your hair curl." [7]

Having done his best to insure a favorable reception for his book, Boyesen departed for Europe just before the publication date. There were seven in his party; the parents and their three boys, twelve, eleven, and nine, were accompanied by a young niece of seventeen. A "Teutonic handmaiden" who became one of the group probably did not join them until they reached the Continent. Following the schedule Boyesen had outlined in his letter to Howells, he took his entourage first to England for two weeks. In his own writings he does not mention this part of the trip, but Professor Barrett Wendell of Harvard left an account of a dinner with Andrew Lang that he and Boyesen attended in London on June 10, shortly after the family's arrival:

"Shubrick and I had to hurry off to dine with Andrew Lang, at the

---

[7] Boyesen to Howells, April 25, 1891. Howells conducted "The Editor's Study" in *Harper's Monthly*, 1886–92, and later wrote "The Editor's Easy Chair" for the same magazine. Thomas Janvier (1849–1913), like Boyesen, was a regular *Cosmopolitan* contributor. The reference to him may mean that Howells had already agreed to become an editor of *Cosmopolitan*. He took over the position in March, 1892, but left a few months later.

The Best and Last Fight

Oxford and Cambridge Club. He had Saintsbury, and Boyesen of New York, to meet us. And really we had a most funny time. Lang is a languid, thin person, with dapple-grey hair, thin whiskers, and slightly unkempt aspect. He has a single eyeglass attached to a cord that has been broken so often that it looks like a string of knots. Saintsbury is a conventional Englishman, with very red nose, steel spectacles, and a cravat — concealed by a large beard — which he had not taken the trouble to tie at all. Both of them seemed in disposition all that could be asked, but perfectly unable to talk of anything outside the ways of London so they talked incessantly to each other. Boyesen occasionally broke in with anecdotes of Turgenieff and other people he had met; but to no avail. Such a revelation of the insularity of England I never had before. What added to the fun was that both Lang and Saintsbury — but particularly Lang — spoke English with so curious an accent that we could not understand more than half they said." [8]

Although Boyesen conceded that he had some British friends, "both men and women whom I am very happy to count among the most delightful people it has ever been my privilege to meet," he did not like the English. He added, "The fact is, collectively and in their natural capacity they repel me." He charged that English romantic novels, in cheap American reprints, debased the publishing business and New World taste. More fundamentally, he resented the British reverence for their heritage, which in literature took the form of snobbish antipathy toward anything not of Anglo-Saxon origin. He saw this snobbery mirrored in Anglophile Americans; in a dozen instances he lashed out at it, but he refrained from launching a full-scale attack.[9]

The party moved rapidly after visiting England. They did not, as Boyesen had told Howells they would, spend all the remaining months in Norway: Before the summer holiday was over, the father and guide reported that they were "jaded travellers who knew Switzerland by heart and had done all Europe by bits." In Germany an incident occurred that must have seemed momentous at the time. Boyesen himself never mentioned it in print, but his younger sister, forty-five years later, recalled:

[8] Barrett Wendell's letter to his wife is quoted by M. A. De Wolfe Howe, *Barrett Wendell and His Letters*, 101 (Boston, 1924); see also Boyesen, in *Cosmopolitan*, 17:152.
[9] Boyesen, in *Cosmopolitan*, 17:158, and *German Literature*, chapter 3. For his

Hjalmar Hjorth Boyesen

"It was on this trip that the German Minister of Interior invited him to call & told him that if he would either 'correct' or omit several chapters of Goethe & Schiller, he would make him independent for life by introducing the book as a text-book into the colleges of Prussia and Austria-Hungary. H. H. refused because he thought, what he had written about Goethe's opinions was correct." [10]

If this is a faithful account of what actually happened, Boyesen's response is in keeping with his character and his published opinions. Nothing would have induced him to tamper with his considered pronouncements on Goethe, whom he revered as a thinker as well as an artist. And if he admired many things about modern Germany, notably its educational standards, scientific progress, and even the seriousness of its novelists, he was hostile to German nationalism and militarism. In keeping with his firm belief in democracy and in the philosophy of Herbert Spencer, Boyesen was convinced that the New Germany of Bismarck and Wilhelm II was running contrary to "the whole force of evolution and the resistless logic of history." [11]

The party tarried longest in Norway, but even there they moved rapidly from Christiania to Sognefjord to the mountain haunts of the Lapps. These weeks paid off in the more than twenty articles on Norwegian subjects that Boyesen published after the trip was over.

Three of them, which appeared in the *Cosmopolitan*, included family incidents. "Two Visits to the Lapps" told of Boyesen's effort to retrace the route of a journey he had made in 1873 to a Lapp camp. The added impedimenta of the present expedition — two guides and three small boys, with only three saddles available — slowed them down considerably. The party did not reach the camp, but they met a Lapp girl who was visiting a saeter. On Boyesen's original visit he had observed that a "deeply rooted belief in their own superiority" made the Lapps "uncivilizable," but this girl wanted to go to Chicago to see the Columbian Exposition in 1893. "A vision of being saddled with a Lapp family in New York rose before me; and the direful newspaper notoriety which might result made me doubly cautious." Boyesen did not tell the girl where he could be reached in America, and he gave her no encouragement about visiting Chicago: "She could never have been the same after

anti-British attitude, see especially *Literary Silhouettes,* 22; *Cosmopolitan,* 4:489; *Forum,* 6:94.

[10] Austa Boyesen to Larson, December 29, 1936.
[11] Boyesen, *German Literature,* 258; Boyesen, in *Cosmopolitan,* 17:151.

The Best and Last Fight

such an experience. She would have been equally unfit for savagery and for civilization." [12]

Boyesen revealed his resentment of the superior attitude of the British in one of his articles. No doubt it was doubly irritating for a Norwegian American, who was proud of Norway and of the United States and of his own earned distinction, to see English tourists act like a privileged breed:

"The British had taken full possession of Kvikne's [*a hotel at Balestrand in Sognefjord*], and kept a parson in broadcloth — a great, burly, second-rate man — reading the prayer-book in the parlor for their edification. On Sundays, they had early communion, service and sermon at eleven, and vespers at five. They did not seem to dream of the existence of other religions, or of other people who might have as much right as they to monopolize the only public gathering room which the place afforded."

Boyesen remarked that the inn at Balestrand was very near his boyhood home: "I spent the happiest years of my childhood . . . at a place called, in ancient times, Systrand, and now Lekanger. Every bit of scenery is here so intimately associated with my own life, and the lives of those whose memory is dear to me, that it borrows a profound interest which elsewhere is lacking." [13]

The last of the travel pieces to get into print described a near disaster which took place during the party's stay at Kvikne's Inn. Boyesen and his niece scaled a glacier without a mishap, but the glare from the ice fields nearly destroyed his eyesight. An immediate trip to a Bergen eye specialist and a week in a darkened hotel room repaired the damage. [14]

Once more, as in 1873, the high point of Boyesen's return to his native land was a visit to Bjørnstjerne Bjørnson. Boyesen, who liked to quote Georg Brandes' apothegm about Bjørnson, "To mention his name is like running up the flag of Norway," proudly recounted that Bjørnson hoisted the Stars and Stripes when his American friend approached the farm at Boe. For several days the two talked of Norway and America, of democracy and progress, and of the writer's obligation to fight for the betterment of his fellow men. The strenuous life of the household at Boe impressed Boyesen. When the aging poet and his stalwart sons

---
[12] *Cosmopolitan*, 13:15–25 (May, 1892).
[13] *Cosmopolitan*, 17:152–158.
[14] Boyesen, "A Glacier Excursion in Norway," in *Cosmopolitan*, 23:625–632 (October, 1897).

initiated their guest into their daily bathing ritual, the waterfall that served as their shower nearly felled Boyesen with its force.[15]

In spite of the adventurous and stimulating quality of the visit to Norway, Boyesen was assailed, when he was confronted with the scenes of his boyhood, with sobering thoughts about the price he had paid for his own success. An essay, "My Lost Self," published three years after he returned from Norway, is a graceful and attractive piece of writing, but it is one of several indications he gave in the nineties that he was entertaining a new and more critical view of immigration. In this nostalgic reverie he even, for a moment, rebelled against social evolution:

"I would contentedly return to that primitive condition if . . . I could slip back permanently into my lost self . . . and have all the experience that has transformed me drift and vanish like a dream that dissolves at waking. The world was not draped in gray then, but lay dewy and fragrant, flushed with the lovely colors of the dawn. . . . And what an exquisite set of senses I had, forsooth! How keen-edged, quiveringly alert, and vigilant they were! I could almost weep (if that too were not one of my lost accomplishments) at the thought of all the happiness that I have forfeited by the gradual blunting of those delicate instruments for apprehending reality. . . . I fancied, until this fatal visit to Norway, that I was greatly to be congratulated on having risen in the scale of civilization; but now I would willingly descend the scale again, step by step, or at one grand stride, if I could be sure of recovering what I have lost."[16]

This revelation was what Boyesen's critics had been waiting for, and they attacked at once. It seemed to prove their contention that Boyesen's work had deteriorated steadily since *Gunnar*, and that his mistake was in failing to follow up that romance with others of the same type. *Munsey's Magazine*, which catered to the popular taste for idealistic, romantic, semi- or pseudo-historical fiction, insisted that this was the only valid form of writing. Its literary columnist set out to castigate a renegade:

"Professor Boyesen who teaches Columbia College boys nine months in the year and writes books and articles in the summer time, is one of the men who promised, ten or fifteen years ago, to add something substantial to American literature. It is a promise he has not kept.

---

[15] Boyesen, "Conversations with Bjørnstjerne Bjørnson," in *Cosmopolitan*, 15: 413–432 (August, 1893). The Brandes quip is from Boyesen, *Essays on Scandinavian Literature*, 208.

[16] Boyesen, *Literary Silhouettes*, 200–203.

The Best and Last Fight

"He came to America from Norway when he was very young, when the quality of the Norwegian mind was entirely fresh to Americans, and in his vision of us there was a charm, a freshness, that was delightful."

This reviewer, after citing statements from "My Lost Self," turned the author's confessions into arguments against his realistic fiction and criticism: "Professor Boyesen's impressions . . . have become blurred instead of sharpened. Or at least that is the idea which his later work gives." The explanation offered by *Munsey's* writer is a surprising conjecture: "He married an American wife—a rich American wife." [17]

Lillie Keen Boyesen had "rich" tastes, but no fortune of her own. Trying to satisfy these tastes had impelled Boyesen to write far too voluminously, but he had not altered his views about literature. He probably could have written the kind of romantic fiction these magazines wanted, and then his income would have soared. But even while he was doing literary hack work to support a wife who liked good society, Boyesen wrote realistic fiction about dazzling, materialistic American girls all of whom threatened to destroy their husbands. Kate Van Schaak, the heroine of his new and most ambitious novel, *The Mammon of Unrighteousness*, had many of Lillie Boyesen's traits.[18]

This volume caused a considerable stir when it came out in the summer of 1891. Howells wrote a detailed and favorable review in *Harper's Monthly*, for he fully shared Boyesen's feeling about the novel. Ten years later he was still praising it for showing "masterly strength" in its handling of American life:

"I call *The Mammon of Unrighteousness* a great novel, and I am quite willing to say that I know few novels by born Americans that surpass it in dealing with American types and conditions. It has the vast horizon of the masterpieces of fiction; its meanings are not for its characters alone, but for every reader of it; when you close the book the story is not at an end." [19]

Boyesen had other defenders: The *New York Daily Tribune*, in its "Fiction Worth Reading" column, called *Mammon* "a decidedly strong novel" and gave it a full and fair appraisal. The review concluded:

"There is plenty of movement in Mr. Boyesen's story, and it is care-

---

[17] *Munsey's Magazine*, 11:549 (August, 1894).

[18] These opinions are Austa Boyesen's, revealed in her letters to Laurence M. Larson.

[19] "The Editor's Study," in *Harper's Monthly*, 83:317 (July, 1891); Howells, *Literary Friends*, 260.

Hjalmar Hjorth Boyesen

fully and well written throughout. It may be objected to it that it points a moral, but it does not do this with offensive distinctness, and moreover, the moral is one which the world has, from time immemorial, ignored in action as placidly as it has accepted it in theory." [20]

But aside from support from Howells and the *Tribune*, the critical reactions to *Mammon* were negative. The book was ignored by magazines such as the *Atlantic Monthly* and the *Century*, and it got only a contemptuous paragraph from periodicals that gave full reviews to Boyesen's stories for boys. Other magazines were so hostile to the realism of the commonplace that they damned *Mammon* as a failure for its lack of romantic appeal. The *Critic's* notice reveals this type of reaction:

"H. H. Boyesen has written a story called *The Mammon of Unrighteousness*, the scene of which he lays in a small town in New York, and into which he introduces innumerable characters who do nothing in particular and are of no particular interest. An old man who founds a university and makes himself unusually hateful to professors and students, two nephews, one good and the other bad, and an infinite variety of womankind, go to make up a book in which the author has endeavored to depict persons and conditions which are profoundly and typically American. It can be left to the reader to decide whether a certain amount of success in this endeavor will repay him for a corresponding lack of interest in the story as such. The author has disregarded all romantic traditions, and simply asked himself in each instance whether it was true to the logic of reality — true to American soil and character." [21]

Boyesen probably expected such reactions, for his sharp and unrelenting attacks on the popular fiction of the day made him a prime target for critics who took the "good new school of romance" seriously. The champions of "healthy, robust fiction" would ask Howells and Boyesen, "Why keep stirring all the time in the cesspools?" One reviewer remarked, "It is indeed a pleasure to turn . . . from the heartache and bitterness and unbelief of the day, and bury oneself in one of Mr. Weyman's books, where everything is light and impetuous and rioting with bravery and action and the stern joy of combat." [22]

[20] July 12, 1892. It is not clear why the novel was not reviewed until a year after it was published. A less favorable review appeared in the *Tribune* of December 18, 1892.
[21] *Critic*, 19:106 (August 29, 1891).
[22] *Munsey's Magazine*, 14:244 (November, 1895). Stanley J. Weyman (1855–1928)

The Best and Last Fight

The author must have been prepared, too, for attacks on the accuracy of his social and political satire in *Mammon*. One of the critics protested against the "over-colouring" in "a number of more or less exaggerated pictures of society, business, finance," but added that readers prefer their fiction "hot and strong and sweet." [23]

But Boyesen was not prepared for the violent reproofs that focused on the author and not on the book. Because it seemed an easy and crushing answer to criticism made by a naturalized citizen, he was told to go back to Norway if this nation was not good enough for him. This reaction hurt the idealistic, democratic, and patriotic Boyesen. He expressed the bitterness he felt in the preface to another novel:

"A year ago, when I published a semi-political novel, 'The Mammon of Unrighteousness,' I was taken severely to task by many critics for having told the unvarnished truth concerning American politics. Such criticism came with ill grace from an adopted citizen, these gentlemen affirmed. . . . Censure of this sort seems to me excessively shallow. Has not an adopted citizen, who has spent the better part of his life here, as much at stake in the country as a native? And is he the better patriot who shuts his eyes to all abuses, shouts himself hoarse for the candidates of his party, without reference to their character, and with foolish optimism declares that it is useless to worry, and that everything will be sure to come out right in the end? . . . Evils are not cured by ignoring them, but by a determined struggle against them. . . . Every great state has great and complex problems to face, and its honor and welfare demand that it should face them uncompromisingly, grapple with them, and, if possible, solve them. And to this end it is first of all necessary that public attention should be called to them and their nature and gravity exposed." [24]

Boyesen's disillusionment never quite overwhelmed his essentially optimistic and enthusiastic nature, but it did build up gradually over the years. The depression he felt in Norway, when he contrasted his boyhood self with the man he had become, emphasized his present unhappy state of mind. The discouraging critical reception of his most thoughtful and carefully written novel deepened his pessimism. A new note of depression, almost of bitterness, is sounded in "The Emigrant's Un-

---

was one of the popular English romanticists whom Boyesen attacked as mere purveyors of amusement. His fiction appeared in *Munsey's*.

[23] *New York Daily Tribune*, December 18, 1892.
[24] *The Golden Calf*, 1.

happy Predicament." There can be no doubt that the attacks on *The Mammon of Unrighteousness* are reflected in this article. Boyesen now considered that he had failed as an American novelist, and he was tormented by the thought that he might have become a major writer if he had stayed in Norway with Bjørnson and Kielland:

"It is this chilling sense of difference between him and the natives which dooms the immigrant to failure or to a success below the utmost reach of his powers. It constitutes a discount, and a heavy one, which is charged by the land of his adoption on his life's capital. Of that margin of superiority which determines survival and dominance, he is obliged to sacrifice much, if not all, in the mere effort at adaptation to new conditions.

"He is more or less at a disadvantage and is apt to have a tormenting sense of misrepresenting himself, of having fallen short of high achievement, even when he is most vociferously applauded. If he be a poet he can but murmur in broken syllables (like a musician playing upon an untuned instrument) the song that in his native tongue would have burst clear and melodious from his breast. If he be a novelist (even though he be imbued with a deep love for the country of his adoption) he is constantly reminded by his critics that his point of view is that of an alien. . . . If he be a merchant the process of adaptation, of commercial acclimatization, is so exhausting, so wasteful of vitality, that success is likely to be bought, if at all, by an expenditure of talent and energy, much in excess of what would be required of a native." [25]

Boyesen's output of the early nineties was tremendous. In the first six years of the decade he published eleven books and a staggering amount of magazine material. He produced three novels, four books for boys, three critical volumes, and a collection of essays. Another novel and two novelettes appeared in magazines, along with a half dozen short stories and four poems. But the great bulk of the magazine material consisted of topical articles on a great variety of subjects.

The time Boyesen gave to his magazine writing was taken away from more serious work. The expense of the summer in Europe had doubtless been high; and maintaining establishments in Southampton and New York City, schooling three boys, meeting medical bills, and supporting Lillie in the manner she demanded added up to a heavy financial burden.

[25] "The Emigrant's Unhappy Predicament," in *Chautauquan*, 15:607–610 (August, 1892).

The Best and Last Fight

Not surprisingly, he took the most efficient way of making money that he knew: turning his personal experiences into hastily written popular magazine articles.[26]

He was in great demand as a magazine contributor. When S. S. McClure launched his periodical, the opening article of the first issue was Boyesen's "Real Conversation" with Howells. The first two issues of the American *Bookman* carried Boyesen's survey, "German and Scandinavian Literature in 1894." His fame reached across the country to San Francisco. When readers of the *Overland Monthly* asked for "name" eastern authors, the editor gave them "Zee-Wee: A Story of the Indian Agencies," by H. H. Boyesen.[27]

Boyesen's closest association was with the *Cosmopolitan*. He contributed the first offering in its initial issue, as he had with *McClure's*, and he continued to publish extensively in its pages. He was one of the regular reviewers who wrote for the section, "In the World of Arts and Letters."[28] It was Boyesen who introduced William Dean Howells to *Cosmopolitan* readers in "Mr. Howells and His Work," just before Howells became editor of the magazine. His own close connection with the editorial direction of the publication is revealed in John Brisben Walker's retrospective article, "Making a Magazine":

"Among those who contributed to *The Cosmopolitan's* growth were the members of a council which assembled every Saturday afternoon about a long table in the editor's room. The name given to this assembly was 'The Damnation Society,' the supposed object of the meeting being to anticipate adverse criticism by the public. . . . Chief in criticism and practical advice was . . . Hjalmar Hjorth Boyesen — one of the truest friends and sincerest critics that it was possible for any editor to have — a liberal-minded, earnest man, who constantly had in view, not merely the literary success of the magazine, but its usefulness to the men and women for whom it was published."[29]

---

[26] "Lillie, who had been brought up as a millionaire's daughter, made big demands upon him. He sat up all hours of the night, writing partially to increase his income." Austa Boyesen to Larson, December 6, 1936.

[27] *McClure's Magazine*, 1:3–11; *Bookman*, 1:26, 99–101 (February, March, 1895); *Overland Monthly*, 24:229–248 (September, 1894).

[28] This feature began in July, 1893. Boyesen wrote nineteen articles for it, the final one appearing in November, 1895. Other reviewers included Andrew Lang, Agnes Repplier, Israel Zangwill, Francisque Sarcey, and Thomas Janvier.

[29] Boyesen, "Mr. Howells and His Work," in *Cosmopolitan*, 12:502 (February, 1892); J. B. Walker, "Making a Magazine," in *Cosmopolitan*, 23:475 (September, 1897).

Hjalmar Hjorth Boyesen

During the nineties Boyesen published three works intended to be scholarly: *Essays on German Literature, A Commentary on the Writings of Henrik Ibsen,* and *Essays on Scandinavian Literature.*[30] They appeared simultaneously in England and in the United States. These ventures had little in common with *Goethe and Schiller,* which was a product of Boyesen's scholarly reading and research, and a by-product of his college lecturing. The three new volumes consisted of magazine articles and prefaces, some written as far back as the seventies, most of them reprinted without revision. The financial pressure that forced Boyesen to publish so much material is all too apparent. The volumes were hastily put together, breezy and journalistic; they revealed Boyesen's enthusiasms and prejudices as clearly as did his lectures and magazine pieces.

The volumes of essays were well received by the American reviewers, but English critics were irritated by the anti-British sentiment in the sections on Goethe. Boyesen, as in his other writings of this period, manufactured opportunities to attack romantic novelists in general; and reviewers on both sides of the water took exception to his criticisms of Scott and Stevenson.[31]

Neither American nor British critics were ready to accept *A Commentary on the Writings of Henrik Ibsen.* Even though Boyesen was temperate in his endorsement of Ibsen's plays, he was included in the general hostility toward the Norwegian playwright. Boyesen had met Ibsen twenty years before, and he reviewed one of his plays for the *Atlantic Monthly* as early as 1874, but the great dramatist's pessimism and antidemocratic philosophy had repelled him. Now, however, when his own time of disillusionment had come, he saw that the naturalistic drama was the ally of the realistic novel, and he stepped forth as a champion of Ibsen. He made it clear that Ibsen's philosophy was still unattractive to him, but the didacticism of the great social dramas coincided with Boyesen's conception of realism:

"To judge Ibsen as a mere playwright is absurd. . . . Each of his plays — with the exception of the early historical ones — is a dramatized piece of philosophy. Each preaches more or less incisively a moral lesson, lays bare a social canker, diagnoses a social disease."[32]

---

[30] The Ibsen volume was published late in 1894 by Macmillan, and by Heinemann (London).

[31] See, for example, the review of *Essays on German Literature* in *Spectator* (London), 71:339 (September 9, 1893).

[32] The quotation is from Boyesen, "Henrik Ibsen," in *Century,* 39:794 (March,

The Best and Last Fight

Literary and Social Silhouettes, the fourth book of nonfiction Boyesen published during the nineties, is another collection of earlier magazine articles. This small volume of thirteen essays was put out by Harper's in its *American Essayists Series,* which also included Howells' *Criticism and Fiction* and Henry James's *Picture and Text.* After the book went to press Boyesen turned out a dozen additional articles in the same vein and of like quality. These twenty-five essays, discursive but often discerning commentaries on life and literature, include most of Boyesen's work that is of permanent interest.

In 1894 and 1895 Boyesen launched a many-sided attack on purveyors of amusement and their allies, the critics who failed to see the need for realistic fiction and the young girls who fed their starved minds on thrilling tales of chivalry and romance. This, of course, was only a continuation of the crusade he had begun in the eighties. The "Iron Madonna" essay, a heavy skirmish, was fought in 1887; and Boyesen's Chautauqua speeches of 1889, preceded by "The Romantic and Realistic Novel" in the November, 1888, *Chautauquan,* touched off a minor campaign at the end of the decade. But now Boyesen was ready for all-out warfare.[33]

In "The Hero in Fiction" he had argued mildly that the old-fashioned hero had outlived his usefulness, that modern fiction demanded a typical man, rather than a superman, as its central figure. In "The Evolution of the Heroine," he spoke out more boldly. The immature, artificial "snow-white" heroine was the bane of fiction, because the young unmarried girl, that obsession of the romantic novelists, was never a really interesting person. The "unreal and unwholesome" heroes and heroines of the popular English romanticists were responsible for worse evils than bad literature, Boyesen argued:

"It is the princess-heroine of flawless goodness, purity, and perfection, promulgated to this day by the school of Scott, who is in a measure responsible for the reckless rashness and foolhardy credulity with which nine men out of ten enter into matrimony; as it is the chivalrous lover of the Ivanhoe type — an embodiment of all masculine virtues — who is in

1890). See also *Galaxy,* 17:460, and "Ibsen's Kejser og Galilaer," in *Atlantic Monthly,* 34:368–370 (September, 1874).

[33] The "Iron Madonna," a characterization still remembered by literary historians, appeared in the article, "Why We Have No Great Novelists," in *Forum,* 2:615–622, and was included in *Literary Silhouettes* as "The American Novelist and His Public"; Boyesen's Chautauqua speeches of 1889 were reported at length in the *New York Daily Tribune,* July 22–29, 1889.

even greater measure responsible for the readiness of nine girls out of ten to take their chances in the matrimonial lottery on slight acquaintance and without sufficient guarantee as to character and ability." [34]

Boyesen returned to the same charge in "The Matrimonial Puzzle," though he phrased his argument differently. Modern women were immature, said Boyesen, because "reality is expurgated for their benefit. . . . It is undoubtedly true that they have lost rather than gained by being shielded and protected from all rude and painful contact with reality." There were similar articles: "The New Womanhood," "The Plague of Jocularity," and "Woman's Position in Pagan Times." [35]

Boyesen's most extensive and uncompromising assault on the enemy and his boldest statement of the case for realism came in "The Great Realists and the Empty Story-Tellers." The strategy of attack is clear enough. The realistic novel is "a powerful educational agency," an important factor in preparing its readers for life itself:

"The modern novel — which should not be confounded with the romance — has set itself the task of exploring reality, and gauging the relative strength of the forces that enter into our lives and determine our fates. . . . It does not act as an opiate dulling our interest in everyday affairs, but it sharpens our observation and enables us to detect the significance of common facts and events. . . .

"It is because the romantic novel tends to unfit you for this prose of life that I condemn it; and it is because the realistic novel opens your eyes to its beauty, its power and deeper significance that I commend it." [36]

This article provoked replies from all directions: the *Dial* in Chicago, the *Critic* in New York, and *Longman's Magazine* in London. When Andrew Lang condemned the essay without reading it, Boyesen, never one to shrink from combat, retaliated in "Novels of Romance and Stories of Real Life." Once again he attacked the romanticists, and the battle showed no sign of abating.[37]

---

[34] "The Evolution of the Heroine," in *Lippincott's Magazine*, 54:425–428 (September, 1894). "The Hero in Fiction" appeared in *North American Review*, 148: 594–601, and in *Literary Silhouettes*.

[35] "The Matrimonial Puzzle," in *North American Review*, 160:203–209 (February, 1895). The last three articles appeared, respectively, in *Lippincott's Magazine*, 56: 126–130 (July, 1895); *North American Review*, 161:528–535; *Forum*, 20:311–316 (November, 1895).

[36] *Forum*, 18:724–731.

[37] See G. M. Hyde, "The Allotropy of Realism," in *Dial*, 18:231 (April 16, 1895);

The Best and Last Fight

The reading public was aware that Boyesen had a beautiful American wife and three handsome sons, of whom he was very proud. Yet even his closest literary associates and his Columbia colleagues knew little of his home life. Lillie Boyesen did not entertain her husband's friends. Boyesen's sister, who visited the family in New York occasionally during the nineties, wrote later about them:

"Hjalmar loved his home; was devoted to his family and was capable of great sacrifice for those he loved. . . . His kindliness was expressed in many little, thoughtful ways. He sent magazines, newspapers and books to persons who could not afford to have them. He personally gathered up his children's outgrown clothes, toys, etc., packed them and sent them to children who were less fortunate than his own. . . .

"He was a man of regular and temperate habits. He rose early; after breakfast did the marketing and walked to College. After the college hours, he took a long walk. After dinner he spent some time with his family, often helping his boys with their lessons. Then, he retired to his study and wrote until mid-night." [38]

Boyesen spent the summer of 1895 at Southampton, making one trip to Bay View, Michigan, for a Chautauqua appearance. At home he turned out his regular quota of stories, poems, and essays, and a formidable array of topical articles.

He enjoyed working in his garden and riding through the Long Island countryside, taking great pleasure in the role of country squire, though his family feared he was acting too much like a farmer when he himself used the scythe in his hayfield and weeded his vegetable garden. He commented:

"There is at present an impression that all forms of exercise must be useless in order to be gentlemanly. My family therefore pretend that this horticultural enthusiasm of mine is of a purely aesthetic character and not in the least profitable. So also the eccentricity I have developed for mowing is a reminiscence of the famous mowing chapter in Tolstoi's 'Anna Karenina,' and has no economic aspect. Well, it may be that

Critic, 26:99 (February 9, 1895); Andrew Lang, "At the Sign of the Ship," in *Longman's Magazine*, 25:650–652 (April, 1895). Lang's remarks are quoted in *Critic*, 26: 385 (May 25, 1895). Boyesen's "Novels of Romance and Stories of Real Life" appeared in the section, "In the World of Arts and Letters," in *Cosmopolitan*, 19:689–693 (October, 1895).

[38] Austa Boyesen to Larson, April 19, May 3, 1936; the quotation is from the letter of April 19.

they are right, but I should be far prouder if they were not. It is true, two hours of swinging the scythe secure me the luxury of a profound, dreamless sleep, — which is worth more to me than the wages of a dozen mowers." [39]

He preferred horseback riding to cycling. On August 22, replying to a query from the *Critic* sent to leading American literary men, "Do you ride a bicycle?" he wrote:

"No. I am one of the exceptional ones who have not taken to the wheel. My chief reason, I fancy, is my fondness for that noble animal, the horse, which I cannot bear to see ousted from creation by a mere machine. Though I have never tried it, I cannot imagine that a wheel-ride can be half so exhilarating as a horseback ride. On horseback I can accomplish that difficult task which the Bible says no man can do, viz., add a cubit to my height — and two to my self-esteem. In the saddle I feel buoyant, light and free; then, for once, the world is at my feet; and the fine, sentient creature that is bearing me along seems by sympathy to feel my mood and to respond with beautiful promptitude to every hint I convey by hand or foot.

"Now, if in the struggle for existence between the horse and the bicycle, the latter is to be proven the fitter to survive, I shall probably be fighting a losing battle in favor of the former. . . . I hope I shall not live to see the day when the poets of America shall have discarded the winged Pegasus for the wingless wheel. . . . If, nevertheless, this day is upon us, I shall probably be the last in the procession."

As if to test his own arguments, Boyesen did try the bicycle late that summer, and, in his strenuous fashion, became a skillful and enthusiastic performer.[40]

Late in September he returned to New York City for the beginning of the fall term at Columbia. As usual, the family remained at Southampton, and the professor took temporary quarters for a few weeks. On October 2 he supervised entrance examinations at the college. He became ill during the night, suffering from a severe chill. A doctor, called the following morning, found that Boyesen had pneumonia. At noon of the day following, October 4, 1895, Hjalmar Hjorth Boyesen died of edema of the lungs.[41]

[39] *Lippincott's Magazine*, 58:126.

[40] "Authors on the Wheel," in *Critic*, 27:227 (October 12, 1895). An added note reported that Boyesen had mastered the bicycle.

[41] *Critic*, 27:237; Austa Boyesen to Larson, April 19, 1936. For obituaries, see

The Best and Last Fight

Boyesen's death was a great shock to his family and friends, and to the literary world. The funeral was almost an official Columbia function. Faculty and students attended the services at St. Bartholomew's Church.[42]

Pallbearers were President Seth Low of Columbia and Professors J. H. Van Amringe, Nicholas Murray Butler, Munroe Smith, Brander Matthews, and W. H. Carpenter of the faculty; William Dean Howells, Edmund Clarence Stedman, Richard Watson Gilder, Hamilton W. Mabie, Carl Schurz, Charles S. Fairchild, Salem H. Wales, John De Witt Warner, John Brisben Walker, and Dr. Gaillard Thomas. Boyesen was buried in Kensico Cemetery.[43]

Columbia University felt Boyesen's loss for many years.[44] It paid him a final honor in an action taken by the trustees shortly after the funeral. Children of a faculty member could attend Columbia without paying tuition, but this privilege usually expired on the death of the father. In Boyesen's case it was extended until the youngest of his three sons had completed his university work.[45]

Most newspaper and magazine commentators reacted alike to the news that Boyesen was dead: "Professor Boyesen's strong vitality and uniform good health made his sudden death almost impossible for his friends to realize."[46] Others, who expressed the same thought, added another note:

"I know of no man who, so far as appearances went, seemed less likely to die in his early prime than Prof. Boyesen. He was strong in build, and, although he was a student & a professor, his cheeks were not 'sicklied o'er with the pale cast of thought'; they were ruddy with the glow of health. Nevertheless, Prof. Boyesen worked too hard. Besides

---

"W.H.C." (W. H. Carpenter), in Columbia University, *Bulletin*, no. 12, p. 45–49 (New York, 1895); *Critic*, 27:237.

[42] "W.H.C.," in Columbia University, *Bulletin*, no. 12, p. 45–49; *Columbia Spectator*, October 23, 1895.

[43] "W.H.C.," in Columbia University, *Bulletin*, no. 12, p. 45–49.

[44] On November 4, 1912, Nicholas Murray Butler, president of Columbia, wrote, "We have lost too many of our so-called culture courses, which are remembered with delight and satisfaction by many of the older graduates of Columbia College." He referred specifically to Boyesen's course on Goethe, which was really "a critical survey of modern European literature." Quoted in Edward C. Elliott, *The Rise of a University*, 2:169 (New York, 1937).

[45] Columbia often extended this privilege to families of staff members; Lamb's *Biographical Dictionary of the United States*, 1:370, says that Boyesen's sons were made wards of Columbia University, but this is certainly an error. See also Larson, *The Changing West*, 115.

[46] "The Rambler," in *Book Buyer*, 12:557 (November, 1895).

his professional duties, he lectured during the winter and wrote continuously."[47]

Others observed that Boyesen had tried to do too much, even for a robust and virile man, and some recalled that he had confessed to increasing weariness and a loss of elasticity in the months before his death. No one, apparently, knew or remembered that Boyesen had worked himself to the point of exhaustion nearly twenty years before, at Cornell, but it must have been common knowledge among his friends and associates that his efforts to "live roomily . . . to support [his] family in any sort of comfort" required a tremendous expenditure of energy. His varied activities had not gone unrewarded, for he left an estate valued at $39,000.[48]

More than forty years after Boyesen's death, his younger sister Austa expressed a conviction that many of his friends must have shared at the time of his death. He was becoming despondent over his family's demands and the strain of providing for their many wants. During the weeks he spent in rented rooms and hotels while his family remained at Southampton, this young sister, who was in New York attending school, was a cheerful influence. She remembered that when her brother came in for the fall opening of Columbia in 1895 he seemed greatly depressed over domestic affairs. She added, "And he seemed not to have any resisting power when he was attacked by pneumonia." It appears, too, that Boyesen had suffered for some time from a heart condition that he had regarded lightly.[49]

A new side of Boyesen's nature is revealed in "My Rural Experiences," published in July, 1896, nine months after the author's death. He mentioned the great satisfaction he had derived from working on his twelve acres of land behind the sand dunes and salt marshes on the east side of Shinnecock Bay, at Southampton, Long Island. His experiences in battling the malignant blackweed, defending his cabbages and beans, convinced him that the simple life was best. He closed his essay with a paean to Mother Earth:

"When I consider the amazing power of production that lurks under

[47] "The Lounger," in *Critic*, 27:233.
[48] "W.H.C.," in Columbia University, *Bulletin*, no. 12, p. 47; Boyesen to Cable, January 20, 1878; *Author*, 2:36; "The Lounger," in *Critic*, 27:269 (October 26, 1895).
[49] Austa Boyesen to Larson, April 19, December 29, 1936; *Nordstjernan* (New York), October 10, 1895, cited in Larson, *The Changing West*, 114.

the sod of these few acres of mine, why should anyone ever go hungry in the United States? With a national area of millions and millions of acres, of which but a small fraction has been brought under cultivation, it would seem that there ought to be land and food in abundance for all who really go in search of it where it is to be found. Nothing can persuade me that this fever of industrial competition which is now consuming the heart and brain of humanity is wholesome, or is destined to be enduring. In order to become sane again and tranquilly contented we shall have to return to the soil, and like the Titan Antaeus, renew our strength by the vivifying touch of Mother Earth." [50]

[50] *Lippincott's Magazine*, 58:121–126.

11

Mammon and Its Aftermath

"FULL-BORN novels require a period of mental gestation; and if they follow in too rapid succession they are sure to betray some defect which time would have remedied."[1] When Hjalmar Hjorth Boyesen made this statement, he was disparaging the phenomenal output of a rival author, but he must have realized that the words could be turned against himself. Only one of Boyesen's own books had the requisite period of gestation: *The Mammon of Unrighteousness*. This, his major work of fiction, was the longest, most seriously planned, and most carefully worked out of his dozen novels. He began it in 1886, two or three years after finishing the previous one; he was still hard at work on the story two years later; and though he began offering the manuscript early in 1889, it was not finally published until midsummer, 1891. In the latter part of the five-year period that followed 1886, Boyesen turned out two novelettes and an ephemeral longer work, but these were written while he was trying to find a publisher for *Mammon*.

This most ambitious of Boyesen's novels was designed to conform with his creed of realism, which meant that the time had to be the present, the place, America, and the characters and events, persons and activities that he had observed carefully and thoughtfully over a long period. He explained his intent in the preface: "My one endeavor in this book has been to depict persons and conditions which are profoundly and

[1] Boyesen, "A Survey of the Year's Fiction," in *New York Illustrated American*, 17:19 (January 5, 1895). Boyesen was discussing the work of F. Marion Crawford.

Mammon and Its Aftermath

typically American. I have disregarded all romantic traditions, and simply asked myself in every instance, not whether it was amusing, but whether it was true to the logic of reality — true in color and tone to the American sky, the American soil, the American character." [2]

The remaining fiction of Boyesen's major phase is slight and secondary compared with this book. He used two settings in *The Mammon of Unrighteousness*, the only ones in America that he knew well: the small college town and the fashionable world of New York City.

Ithaca and Cornell University are the prototypes of Boyesen's Torryville and Larkin University. He wrote in his preface, "I have used a definite locality which many no doubt will recognize (it is impossible for me to write a novel without having a distinct and real topography in my mind)." His description of Torryville fits Ithaca so well that readers familiar with Cornell must have noticed the similarity. And anyone who compares the opening chapters with Boyesen's article on "Cornell University" in the November, 1889, *Cosmopolitan*, will see at once a strong resemblance between Ezra Cornell and the character of Obed Larkin, founder of the fictional university. So strong and pervasive is the personality of Ezra Cornell that, even disguised, he emerges as the most interesting and memorable figure in the novel, although his role is a minor one.[3]

The New York milieu exposed in *Mammon* had been described in Boyesen's fiction many times before. Thanks to his wife, he had a painfully intimate knowledge of the segment of New York society that he was constantly writing about. It was a world of brilliance and artificiality, materialism, crassness, and squandered energy. He also knew of the political maneuvering and financial speculation that lay beneath the surface, and he had earlier attacked them in his fiction. Realistic writing involved dealing with the environment that the writer knew best. This, for Boyesen, was New York City.[4]

The plot and the character conflict in *Mammon* are suggested in the following lines:

---

[2] *Mammon*, 4.
[3] *Mammon*, 3. A serious contemporary evaluation of Boyesen's work claimed that the novel was based on Urbana, Ohio, and Urbana University — a theory difficult to understand. See Wells, in *Sewanee Review*, 4:308. Boyesen's editor wanted him to "modify" Obed Larkin in the early chapters of *Mammon*, where his resemblance to Ezra Cornell "seemed very close"; see Balestier to Boyesen, November 29, 1890.
[4] See especially *A Daughter of the Philistines*.

Hjalmar Hjorth Boyesen

"'I mean to be true to myself—true to my convictions,' ejaculated Alexander Larkin. . . .

"'I mean to succeed,' said Horace, his brother."[5]

These male figures are types rather than individuals. They are presented to the reader full-blown: The plot merely brings out what happens to each as he follows the course stated in the lines above.

In this last realistic phase of Boyesen's career, he worked from a conviction that the idealist was bound to come to grief in America. Alexander has only a thin skin to cover his lofty principles. During a brief and discouraging experience in politics and journalism, he barely manages to eke out a living; finally he is taken in charge by his uncle, old Obed Larkin, who makes him a professor at Larkin University.

Horace Larkin, the real hero of the novel, vows allegiance to "the mammon of unrighteousness." He rises rapidly in business and politics, jilts his country cousin (who dies of heartbreak and consumption), and climaxes his career by marrying an heiress.

The heiress, Kate Van Schaak, is the epitome of Boyesen's glamorous society women. She had appeared under other names in Boyesen's earlier fiction, but never so sharply drawn as here. In the early stories she is a beautiful and desirable prize; later she is a still desirable but spoiled wife. In her final phase she is a brilliant emblem of success, but she is also a heartless and domineering force, and she defeats the hero who has won her. How close the fictional Kate and her predecessors are to the real-life Lillie Boyesen can only be guessed.[6]

Kate marries Horace because she sees in him a man who is destined to succeed, one through whom she can realize her own ambitions. Horace soon finds that his magnificent consort and her fortune are dominating his life; his wealthy connections ruin his political chances in Torryville. So he can only meekly acquiesce when the Van Schaak money buys him an ambassadorship, the goal of Kate's ambitions.

At the end of *Mammon*, Horace Larkin is brought to ask himself: "What had he been but a dupe and a marionette in his wife's hand? She pulled the wires; he performed the part and arrogated a semblance of independence. But in the midst of the bitterness of his resentment,

---
[5] *Mammon*, 5.
[6] For earlier heroines of this type, see Edith Van Kirk of "The Man Who Lost His Name," in *Tales from Two Hemispheres*, and Alma Hampton in *A Daughter of the Philistines*. Boyesen's sister thought Kate Van Schaak had many of Lillie Boyesen's traits; Austa Boyesen to Larson, December 6, 1936.

Mammon and Its Aftermath

there awoke a feeling of profound respect and admiration for this marvellously cool and daring woman, who conceived such long plans and carried them out so ruthlessly." [7]

When *The Mammon of Unrighteousness* appeared, some reviewers asked Boyesen why the idealistic young man must necessarily come to grief. They might also have asked him what made the brilliant young woman so hard and pitiless. Certainly both these questions occurred to the author after the novel was finished, for he supplied the answers in two stories published early in the decade. In "A Candidate for Divorce" (1890) he explored the education of a society girl. "A Platonic Affair," published in February, 1890, is a slight tale, but Boyesen makes his point clearly enough: An idealistic, warm-hearted young man with a classical education is doomed to failure when he is subjected to the standards of go-getting, materialistic America.

The hero of the second story, a college graduate, goes west to find success, because a beautiful girl in New York refuses to marry him until he has enough money to support her properly. The young man fails even to get a job, because his education has made him unfit to attain his goal: "He was snubbed and patronized as if he had never known a word of Greek, and he disliked the latter mode of treatment more than the former. He had to listen to long discourses from lumber dealers and railroad kings on the uselessness of his accomplishments and on the lack of practical sense characteristic of scholars." [8]

Successful self-made boors and barbarians of this type insult the hero throughout the West; then a strange tale told by a Hoosier farmer and a glimpse of golden hair under a sunbonnet impel the young man to leave his train in southern Indiana. The college boy finally settles down to educate the simple maiden, who speaks a backwoods dialect. Meanwhile, the girl's brother pays off the mortgage on the farm that his father, preoccupied with Plato, has nearly ruined. He then rises steadily from a job in a Cincinnati machine shop, invents a gadget, and goes to New York, where he marries Kate Remington. In the last scene of the story, the successful young man brings his bride back to Indiana for a visit. The episode is developed just enough to show that the wife will dominate the marriage.

[7] *Mammon*, 385.
[8] "A Platonic Affair," in *Harper's New Monthly Magazine*, 80:348 (February, 1890).

Hjalmar Hjorth Boyesen

Boyesen expressed his contempt for the kind of education that wealthy American parents gave their daughters in his novelette, "A Candidate for Divorce," published in *Cosmopolitan* in 1890 and illustrated by Charles Dana Gibson. The story opens at St. Stephen's Ladies Seminary, a fashionable finishing school remarkable chiefly for its genteel disregard for reality. Boyesen explores the effect this institution has on Amy Hurst, a young woman with brains and talent. He furnishes detailed descriptions of the school and its faculty. He discusses Miss Hammond, the English teacher, her qualifications and ideas:

"She had drifted half blindly through life, uncomprehending and uncomprehended. And for this reason she was peculiarly fitted to teach English literature. For literature, in her opinion, belonged in a higher sphere of beauty and goodness which had nothing to do with the sordid reality; and in this sphere she felt very much at home. She read Shakespeare with the girls, with a vapory admiration of everything (for it is very safe to admire Shakespeare), and with an innocent obtuseness which hid from her the real meaning. She studied 'Romeo and Juliet,' and 'The Merchant of Venice' (for these were her favorite plays), as I imagine an amiable middle-aged pussy-cat might, and got about as much out of them." [9]

The author also examines the circumstances of the founding of this seminary. Miss Van Pelt, the owner and operator, is a genteel lady whose fortune has been squandered by a profligate brother. At her bishop's suggestion, she starts a school for girls. The fashionable success of St. Stephen's is assured by the bishop's patronage and endorsement, and by testimonials from other clergymen who carefully echo his commendation.

Boyesen explores the school's educational practices, and incidentally expounds some of his own theories:

"That education, instead of resembling the filling of a bag, resembles, rather, the careful tending of a young plant, which is capable of assimilating certain substances in the ground and in the air, while it must reject others, no teacher in St. Stephen's Seminary suspected. That some knowledge, in a general way, was more valuable than other knowledge was, indeed, admitted; but that one pupil required for her intellectual development an entirely different pabulum from that required by another would have impressed Miss Van Pelt as a fantastic proposition. If it had

[9] *Cosmopolitan*, 8:590.

been suggested to this estimable spinster that the normal fate of girls was wifehood and motherhood, and that the school should recognize this fact and train them for the duties and responsibilities which this noble destiny involved, she would have opened her eyes in holy horror, and questioned the sanity (and probably also the morality) of the person who could entertain so preposterous a proposition. Girls should, above all, be innocent, she would have declared — ignorant of the rude and contaminating phases of life; and it was her sacred mission to guard them against all premature knowledge which was calculated to spoil their lily-like freshness and virginal modesty. If allusions which implied such knowledge occurred in the lessons in literature (and particularly in the Bible and in Shakespeare), Miss Hammond, if she herself comprehended them, slurred them over, and read on with blushful haste, lest the girls should take it into their heads to ask embarrassing questions." [10]

After the girl leaves school, her family conspires to insulate her even more. Her parents prevent her from developing her dramatic talent, for fear she will exceed the limits prescribed for a gentlewoman. Amy is forced to live sheltered from every responsibility, for pleasure alone.

Finally this intelligent girl, now married, allows her baby to die and abandons her husband, evidently with no loss to either her self-respect or her social position. The author's indictment of the dazzling young woman is as pointed as he can make it, although he indicates clearly that her indulgent parents, the circle she moves in, and St. Stephen's Ladies Seminary must share the blame for her failure.

In an article on Ibsen's *A Doll's House*, Boyesen summed up his opinion of education for women most succinctly: "Every child, whether male or female, that comes into the world, has, abstractly speaking, a full right to know the life into which it is born, to test its educational value, and by its rough and trying discipline to develop whatever powers there may be slumbering in it. You cannot artificially limit experience, without impairing growth, diminishing the chances of survival, and stunting the stature of manhood or womanhood." [11]

In 1892 Boyesen published *The Golden Calf*, a novel similar to *Mammon* in more than its title. As if to answer charges that he had not explained how Horace Larkin became a hardhearted, cynical worshiper of Mammon, Boyesen carefully traced the spiritual fall of a good man

[10] *Cosmopolitan*, 8:596.
[11] "A Doll-Home," in *Cosmopolitan*, 16:87 (November, 1893).

Hjalmar Hjorth Boyesen

in this novel. The hero, Oliver Tappan, is fifteen years old when the story begins, and his German immigrant tutor warns him against the American evil, the worship of the golden calf. "True and blessed satisfaction will come to you from your labor — if it is well done. It is absurd and futile to expect great ecstasies and high paroxysms of rapture in this earthly life. But many sweet and temperate delights you may expect, and they are more to be desired, because they are lasting. And these come from congenial labor — from the sense of having done well — from the constant exercise of high faculties — from the fulfillment of a duty, however burdensome, in every relation of life." [12]

Oliver Tappan dreams of attending Harvard, but instead goes to New York to seek his fortune in the employ of a large railway firm. He absorbs reform ideas from reading the *Evening Post*, and demonstrates his rectitude by attending church regularly. His piety is his undoing, however, for the railway president sees him in church, notes his manly bearing, and decides that Oliver will make a good Washington lobbyist for the railroad. After some soul searching, the hero decides to put aside his idealistic plans until he has made his way in the world. He accepts the position offered him; and here begins his material ascent and moral decline. His fall is accelerated by the railway president's niece; when she sneers at his rustic ways, he forgets the professor's daughter he left back home and determines to marry the haughty heiress. He accomplishes this, is elected to Congress, and becomes wealthy. At the end of the novel, he is forty years old, a powerful railway magnate, and a member of the President's cabinet, but he is only the aging, disappointed husk of the man Oliver Tappan had promised to be.

Boyesen is explicit throughout about the hero's twinges of remorse. At a meeting of financial leaders and Irish politicians, Tappan's backers buy a Congressional seat for their lobbyist, whereupon "a horrible disgust took possession of him. . . . He loathed himself, he loathed his smooth and oily father-in-law." He soon loathes his frigid wife, too. He is so superior to his associates that even the wife sees "that nature had had generous intentions with him and had designed him for something better than a bank president and a millionaire." [13]

In the midst of the story Boyesen stops to explain why Oliver Tappan cannot escape his subservience to the golden calf: If he tries to turn

---
[12] *The Golden Calf*, 31.
[13] *The Golden Calf*, 136, 163.

Mammon and Its Aftermath

back, to repudiate his evil financial and political confederates, they will turn on him and crush him:

"The world resents the practice of a higher morality than its own, and it has no scruples in sacrificing an individual whose professions imply a reproach of his fellow-men. In point of morals it is scarcely less dangerous to be in advance of your age than to be behind it. The insidious miasma which we call public opinion, the average judgment, the atmosphere of the age, creeps into the soul and pervades it and, like the air we breathe, slowly changes its substance." [14]

As these passages show, *The Golden Calf* is more didactic than *The Mammon of Unrighteousness*. In *Mammon* Boyesen was a literary artist producing a realistic masterwork that would embody his ideas about America. *The Golden Calf* springs from the same theories, but it is a more hastily written piece, with the social and political commentary superimposed on the story instead of fused with it. At least one contemporary reviewer recognized this fact. The *Critic*, always hostile to realism, disposed of *The Golden Calf* by saying that Mr. Boyesen's book might do very well as a political tract but should not be passed off as fiction.[15]

The circumstances of publication may explain the heavily didactic, moralistic tone of *The Golden Calf*. The first half of the book appeared as a *Chautauquan* novelette in 1890; this section ends with Oliver's realization that his material rise, assured by his marriage, has brought him no happiness. The complete novel was brought out by the Chautauqua-Century Press at Meadville, Pennsylvania, in the summer of 1892. A favorable review of *The Golden Calf* is worth noting: "It is one of the few strong novels which would be entirely in place in Sunday School libraries everywhere." [16]

Boyesen turned toward a new audience in the 1890's: the "plain people," the God-fearing, hard-working, serious-minded, lower-middle-class small-town Protestants who listened so attentively to his Chautauqua lectures. He showed a growing respect for these sincere, if uneducated, folk who listened sympathetically to his call for more realistic, serious fiction in America. In "American Literary Criticism and Its Value," he

---

[14] *The Golden Calf*, 217.
[15] *Critic*, 22:20 (January 14, 1893).
[16] *Chautauquan*, 11:385–421 (July, 1890). For the review, see John Habberton, "All the Books," in *Godey's Magazine*, 25:406 (October, 1892).

Hjalmar Hjorth Boyesen

spoke sympathetically of the writers who wrote specifically for this unsophisticated public—J. G. Holland and the Reverend E. P. Roe—although he did not actually defend the quality of their fiction. He thought that "it was not to be deplored that men like Dr. Holland who exerted so great a power for good were the favorites of the American public." He concluded his introduction to *The Golden Calf* by saying: "Certain tendencies of the time which I regard as disastrous, I have endeavored to illustrate in the characters of this story; knowing that through the Chautauqua Press I shall reach a large and influential public which has the true welfare of the public at heart." [17]

In Boyesen's final novel, *Social Strugglers*, he retreated from the uncompromising realism of *The Mammon of Unrighteousness* and the preoccupation with political and social themes that characterized *The Golden Calf*. This story begins and ends on the beach at Atterbury (obviously Boyesen's summer home, Southampton, Long Island), and is lighter and sunnier throughout than its predecessors. The emphasis is on fashionable society itself, rather than the financial speculation and political corruption allied with it. Evidently Boyesen had made some new concessions to the Iron Madonna in this novel, which first appeared as a *Cosmopolitan* serial, September through November, 1892. But, light though the texture of the story is, this is perhaps his most unified and convincing novel. It was brought out as a book by his old publisher, Scribner's, in 1893, and dedicated to Howells.

Social Strugglers is essentially a reworking of *A Daughter of the Philistines*. It tells of a new-rich western family that breaks into New York society, and of the regeneration of one of the daughters through the good works of the hero. This young man has renounced his father's wealth to make his own way in a chemical firm. He has no time for balls and parties, because he is doing social work on the lower East Side. When the heroine accidentally sees him there while she is part of a slumming party, she realizes that life can have a higher meaning. The hero puts the case succinctly, explaining why he objects to the fashionable set:

"The pervading tone is one of false and hypocritical show, of envious comment, uncharitable criticism, and vain emulation in dress, entertainment, distinction, and all sorts of foolish extravagance. The result is a

[17] Boyesen, "American Literary Criticism and Its Value," in *Forum*, 15:459–466 (June, 1893), reprinted in *Literary Silhouettes*; *The Golden Calf*, 2.

tremendous overrating of the material things of life, which are not its true realities, and the wasting of life's best energies in a wild chase for vain and hollow things which yield no lasting satisfaction. I have seen enough of it to conclude that the game is not worth the candle."[18]

In this novel Boyesen was content to omit the political material that had aroused antagonism to *The Mammon of Unrighteousness*. The hero merely explains to the heroine that the frivolous social life of New York and Atterbury is symptomatic of more fundamental evils: "The fault lies with the spirit of the age and the organization of society itself, which is a tremendous machine for the mutual advancement of its members. . . . There are often enormous interests, now financial, now political, at stake in the apparently gay and harmless displays of society."[19] The girl seems convinced, and the hero asks her to share his life, which means that she must renounce her trivial role and substitute social work as a leisure-time activity. When she accepts him, his faith in American womanhood is restored.

In a previous *Cosmopolitan* serial, "The Elixir of Pain" (May–July, 1891), Boyesen retreated to Europe and the world of art. The hero, the son of an Ohio druggist, is carried off to Munich by his German mother. There he becomes a great artist, marries an English girl, and develops into a true cosmopolite, seeing fellow countrymen only in the American colony at Rome.

"A Harvest of Tares," a novelette printed in the May, 1893, issue of *Godey's Magazine*, is the story of a strong-minded Norwegian girl who rejects her deserving suitor, a clergyman. She flees to America, seeks out the young artist whom she loves, and marries him. Thereafter she supports him and their family by giving voice lessons and singing in churches, while her husband enjoys his role as a misunderstood artist.

"A Norse Atlantis," Boyesen's last short story about Norwegian-American immigrants, appeared in the November, 1890, *Cosmopolitan*. The Reverend Thorvald Gramm, a fashionable Christiania clergyman and a widower, promotes a scheme for a utopian colony on the Dakota prairies so that he can marry a bakery maid without sacrificing his social standing and self-respect. The group comes to grief because Gramm and his party, who visualize a Rousseauist paradise, lack any real knowledge of American life. They become easy prey of real-estate men and con-

---

[18] *Social Strugglers*, 289 (New York, 1893).
[19] *Social Strugglers*, 288.

tractors, of storms, mosquitoes, and the vastness of the plains; but above all, they are victims of their own genteel ignorance and their social codes. The settlement does not collapse completely, but its subsequent history is merely summarized. The coming of a railroad transforms the struggling community into a flourishing city. The humble workers who accompanied Gramm find a natural leader in the pastor's scapegrace son, who marries the bakery maid and becomes a pioneer politician. Boyesen loses interest in the colony when the dreamers flee back to Norway.

This tale should lay the myth that Boyesen was a writer of immigrant stories. The truly pioneering aspect of the narrative is hastily summarized, because the author did not know this material at first hand. But he knew the pompous Norwegian clergyman very well indeed, and his tale is really an elaborate character sketch, with a few melodramatic episodes to serve as a plot. Of the actual Scandinavian migration to the western states, the reader gets no concept whatsoever.

The collections, *Boyhood in Norway* (1892) and *Norseland Tales* (1894), do not deserve serious attention. The judgment, promoted by romance-minded critics when Boyesen died, that he was at his best in his Norse stories for boys, is nonsense. The opinion, however, has been repeated by some later writers who have been eager to dismiss Boyesen without taking the trouble to examine his work for themselves. The tales for boys usually betray hasty writing and they rarely include really exciting narratives. Even at best they are highly sentimental.

A few of these stories first appeared in magazines for adults. The best and most realistic is "The Little Chap," which came out in *Harper's Weekly* on January 31, 1891. It tells of Amund Myra, a Norwegian immigrant carpenter who is swindled out of his savings by a Chicago real-estate agent. But Boyesen's emphasis is on the son, who, born following five sisters, "took instant possession of his father's heart." Little Chap looks after the hard-working father, and at the end of the tale saves Amund from despair: "And he rose with the Little Chap in his arms, and the two began bravely the battle of life anew." [20]

A search of the boys' stories yields parallels with the author's own life; some also show his tendency to follow various popular models of all kinds. The longest and most ambitious tale in *Boyhood in Norway* is "Lady Clare: The Story of A Horse," first published in the October, 1891, *Cosmopolitan*. It describes the theft and maltreatment of a beau-

---

[20] *Norseland Tales*, 193, 209.

tiful filly, who is finally rescued and allowed to live out her last years in a quiet pasture. The plot recalls *Black Beauty:* Anna Sewall's novel first appeared in England in 1877, but the excitement in America over "the *Uncle Tom's Cabin* of the horse" began with its republication in March, 1890, by the American Humane Society of Boston, which sold 226,000 copies of the book in two years.[21]

Four full-length short stories that appeared in as many magazines were Boyesen's last fiction: "Zee-Wee," in *Overland Magazine*, September, 1894; "The Nixy's Chord," in *Cosmopolitan*, September and October, 1895; "A Mother in Israel," in *Harper's Magazine*, February, 1896, and "In Collusion with Fate," in *Scribner's Magazine*, July, 1896. They vary in subject matter, but all display the familiar Boyesen style. The Norwegian tale, "The Nixy's Chord," is one of the author's best efforts. "Zee-Wee: A Story of the Indian Agencies" and "A Mother in Israel" (which begins in a Russian ghetto and ends with a commencement ceremony at Columbia) are less successful, but interesting because of their subject matter. The fourth story, "In Collusion with Fate," is so poorly done that one suspects it was found after Boyesen's death and then sold to *Scribner's Magazine*.

[21] Frank L. Mott, *Golden Multitudes*, 163 (New York, 1947).

12

The Final Salvo

BOYESEN'S nonfictional writing from 1890 to 1895 was so extensive and the subject matter so varied that an appraisal of it is best made by sampling the total output and summarizing his major ideas. Such a treatment will yield definite, if not always consistent, impressions of Boyesen, and the result is a fairly accurate key to his prejudices and mental processes. This nonfictional output, in four books and dozens of articles, can be grouped by subject matter under these headings: (1) women, particularly the young American girl; (2) Norway, including the problems of immigration and the position of the Scandinavian in the United States; (3) German and Scandinavian literature; and (4) the inexorable progress of realism, a phenomenon closely related to the evolution of mankind and the steady onward march of civilization.

Boyesen, in his writings on American women, dealt with three types: the dashing western girl, the heartless society girl, and the new, emancipated woman. All three were indulged by their parents and poorly educated; they were materialistic and spiritually undernourished; although they were more interesting than American men and outshone their European cousins in beauty, vivacity, and sheer intelligence, they made poorer wives.

His western girl was a beautiful, spoiled creature, spirited and patriotic, who specialized in shocking conventional Europeans. Americans had always denied that she existed, said Boyesen, and he conceded that she had disappeared from eastern social circles. But she had been replaced by a second, less likable figure, the heartless, ambitious young

The Final Salvo

lady who read English romances, aped the British, and aspired to marry a foreign nobleman — or, failing that, to snare an American male who would indulge her every whim and support her luxuriously. This was the real "Boyesen girl," the one he usually chose as a heroine, the target for his diatribes.

The ambitious woman engaged his attention late in his career, though he maintained that he had met her as early as 1869. She was young, usually beautiful. Boyesen admitted that women grew old, but he seldom wasted much time on them after they had. The ambitious type came to his attention chiefly through her suffragette activities, or through the feminist novels she wrote.

In nearly all of Boyesen's articles on women he concentrated on the same points. They can be briefly summarized: (1) American girls were frivolous and selfish because the "American system" allowed them to rule their parents and their husbands; (2) they would continue like this so long as they were shielded from reality, but they could be reclaimed through education, which should include the reading of serious fiction instead of "feudal" romances, and an emphasis on duties instead of privileges; (3) such reforms would make for happy marriages instead of wrecked homes and divorces; with this accomplished, then (4) women would once more emerge as real personalities and the companions of their men, as they had been in ancient times.

Boyesen met an interesting specimen of the first variety soon after he came to America:

"The first woman whose acquaintance I made in the United States (in 1869) was a very pretty Western girl, who took a peculiar pleasure in saying and doing things which she knew would shock my European notions of propriety. She was slangy in her speech, careless in her pronunciation, and bent upon 'having a good time' without reference to the prohibitions which are framed for the special purpose of annoying women. I was sometimes in danger of misinterpreting her conduct, but soon came to the conclusion that there was no harm in her. She ruled her father and her mother, who sometimes interposed feeble objections to her plans for her own and my amusement; but the end invariably was that a puzzled assent was yielded to all her proceedings. She had about as much idea of propriety (in the European sense) as a cat has of mathematics. She recognized no law except her own sovereign will, and her demands were usually so emphatic that no one could disagree with her

Hjalmar Hjorth Boyesen

without the risk of quarrelling. Patriotic she was — bristling with combativeness if a criticism was made which implied disrespect of American manners or institutions. She was good-natured, generous to a fault, and brimming with energy." [1]

This was the American girl as she was caricatured in European fiction. Even Henry James's mild portrayal of her in *Daisy Miller* had outraged American patriots, and Boyesen's own Delia Saunders in *The Light of Her Countenance* was damned as an alien's invention instead of a real American woman. Since so many European novelists pictured this particular American girl, Boyesen maintained that she certainly existed: "The independent young *Americaine* who pleases herself without reference to the tastes of others, is not a wholly agreeable phenomenon; but it is of no use to deny her existence. She is very prevalent in Europe; and though she rarely invades the so-called best society of our seaboard cities, you need only go abroad or sufficiently far west to find her in all her glory." [2]

But while these traits of the society girls actually were becoming less pronounced, the women Boyesen described were still selfish, frivolous, and badly educated. Once he led the outspoken Bjørnstjerne Bjørnson to the subject of American women. Boyesen, posing as the defender of the type he so often criticized, baited Bjørnson by remarking that American girls were more beautiful than their Norwegian cousins. Bjørnson replied:

"Beautiful? Well, now, what constitutes beauty? They have soft skin, well-cared-for persons, good clothes. But the soul, the soul, my boy, that gazes out through this transparent covering is vain, self-conscious . . . [nevertheless] they know how to assert themselves and get the most out of their husbands and fathers. But they have been woefully spoiled. They never can get away from their own dear, little, pretty selves; they cannot lose themselves in a great thought, a great idea, and learn the blessedness of living for something better than vanity and flirtation and social tittle-tattle." [3]

In essay after essay Boyesen reiterated his charges against the Iron Madonna and re-emphasized the factors that made her what she was. In his harshest attacks, he tried to be specific about her: "It is the system

---
[1] *Literary Silhouettes*, 7.
[2] *Literary Silhouettes*, 10.
[3] Boyesen, in *Cosmopolitan*, 15:417.

The Final Salvo

of education to which I have alluded, or rather the lack of system, which is responsible for the prevalence of this type. It is the combination of lax indulgence and neglect on the part of the parents — indulgence as regards spiritual guidance and the training of character — which produces these fair, heartless sirens, whom we meet at Newport, Bar Harbor, and Narragansett Pier."[4]

At the cost of being repetitious, Boyesen kept insisting that the real harm was in insulating these girls from reality. This was his conclusion in "The Matrimonial Puzzle" (1895): "Women of the upper class have been petted and deferred to almost from babyhood, and have been taught to regard themselves as privileged persons. Every stone is carefully removed from their path, reality is expurgated for their benefit."[5] And the girls themselves abetted this situation by the fiction they chose to read: The Iron Madonna supported the "purveyors of amusement" instead of the novelists who honestly recorded the life of their time.

Boyesen was confident that improved education and exposure to realistic fiction would change the frivolous girl, but the woman who was on the side of progress, "an agent of civilization and a most powerful one," was another problem. She was the "aspiring woman," a type he had encountered during his first year in America; "I met her for the first time in 1869, and have been meeting her daily ever since." In many ways this lady was the exact opposite of the first: She was not handsome, nor well-dressed, nor given to frivolous talk. She usually neglected the life of the flesh and overestimated the things of the spirit. He mentioned one specimen he had observed, a Cornell girl whom he once asked to dance. As they swung out on the floor, she inquired, "Now, won't you be kind enough to give me just in a few words, the gist of Spinoza's 'Ethics'?" Boyesen adds, "It did not surprise me afterwards to learn that she danced because it was good for the digestion."[6]

Suffragettes' activities of the early nineties sharpened Boyesen's pen against these aspiring women. He was particularly annoyed by women writers whose "feverish, over-wrought declarations of independence, pitched in a high hysterical soprano" made very poor arguments for their cause. He ridiculed the woman's-rights argument that men and women deserved the same privileges and opportunities because they were exactly

---
[4] *Literary Silhouettes*, 35.
[5] Boyesen, in *North American Review*, 160:207.
[6] *Literary Silhouettes*, 12, 14.

alike. He enjoyed telling the story of the woman who stated this thesis before a large audience, then said, "Pardon me, gentlemen!" and fainted.[7]

Boyesen always assumed that a woman's first ambition was to be a wife and mother. His sharpest attacks on the American woman were prompted by her shortcomings in filling this role. But while he criticized the frivolous girl for lacking a proper sense of duty, and the suffragette for not knowing her proper function, he argued eloquently for a better understanding of woman's position in the world, for a realistic appraisal of woman's real nature, and for an examination of the factors responsible for both the fanatical suffragettes and the frivolous Nora of *A Doll's House*. A properly educated young lady who had the opportunity to discover for herself what the world was like would be her husband's mental and spiritual equal, as well as a loving mate and mother.[8]

In "The Evolution of the Heroine" and "The Matrimonial Puzzle," as well as in "Woman's Position in Pagan Times," Boyesen surveyed the historical position of woman, or, more properly, her ascent as a literary subject. "The earliest fiction had no heroine," he explained, because the beautiful lady was merely a prize attained by the hero. Such a viewpoint, which eliminated any development of the heroine's real character, was revived in modern times by Sir Walter Scott. In Dickens and Thackeray, too, only the comic and the bad women were interesting, because the good ones had to resemble the snow-white princesses of fairy tales and feudal lore. Boyesen had hinted many times in his fiction and now asserted quite seriously in his essays that Scott was responsible for the blindness and ignorance about woman's real nature with which nine out of ten men entered matrimony. On the other hand, George Eliot, whose heroines were the best in fiction, could help both men and women avoid the mistake of judging by superficial qualities and marrying the idealized persons of their callow youth.[9]

Boyesen's last word on the subject was in "Woman's Position in Pagan Times," an article which appeared after his death in the November, 1895, *Forum*. He attacked the "myth" that women owed their social elevation to Christianity, charging that "the Catholic church not only adopted, but immensely exaggerated the disabilities under which the sex had labored in Semitic lands." He cited Tacitus and the Norse sagas to

---

[7] *Literary Silhouettes*, 19; *North American Review*, 160:207.
[8] *North American Review*, 160:206.
[9] *Lippincott's Magazine*, 54:425–427.

defend his contention that "Paganism in the North . . . evolved sturdier types of womanhood than Christianity," that Teutonic women "were not permitted to regard themselves as standing outside the world belonging to the men," and that "primarily they were human beings; secondarily, women." He said, "St. Paul's injunction that women should not speak in meeting" produced characters like Madame de Maintenon and Madame de Pompadour, who exerted a new influence in public life. They were ashamed of this role, but it had been forced upon them by the precepts of the age of feudalism and chivalry. Boyesen continued:

"The frank and unsentimental comradeship of pagan antiquity was superseded by an exaggerated, mawkish, and artificial homage which implied a lessened respect under the mask of a heightened one. Only two feminine virtues came to be regarded as important, viz., chastity and piety; and so far as the Germans are concerned there is no disguising the fact that beyond this point they have never since advanced. . . . It is against the worn-out ideals of the age of chivalry that the women are now beginning to revolt; and although I am aesthetically shocked at their rebellion, my intelligence justifies and approves it." [10]

Thus he came to sympathize with the suffragettes, to see that the "few daring pioneers . . . have been apt to develop their pugnacity at the expense of their charm." In the conclusion of his final article, he trained his guns once more on the real villains:

"It may perhaps be impertinent to ask to what extent European and American women of today have emancipated themselves from this feudal ideal. The novelists, who not unfairly reflect public opinion, are tolerably unanimous in representing love as the one dominant and overshadowing concern in a woman's life. Most of them are also inclined to ridicule any member of the sex who aspires to wider spheres of activity. We fill the brains of our daughters with current conventional catchwords, as we fill their pockets with the current coin of the Republic, and it would no more occur to most of us to furnish them with the materials for forming independent opinions than it would to supply them with the tools for coining their own money. So long as this system remains in vogue, the happy comradeship between men and women which prevailed in pagan times is out of the question. For you cannot make a comrade of a cackling flirt, or a simpering fashion-plate, or an amiable echo. Until we cease to teach our girls the pernicious folly that they are to live only

[10] *Forum*, 20:311–315.

to love, they will in my opinion, not be worth loving,—besides being extremely trying to live with."[11]

In his essay on "Why We Have No Great Novelists" (1886), Boyesen had blamed the Iron Madonna for the triviality of American fiction. He was now blaming the fiction for the frivolity of the girl.

It is difficult to guess how much Lillie Boyesen had to do with his attitude. In "Types of American Women," her husband used her as a shield. Boyesen said he had "furnished the most incontestable proof possible" that he was not, like the hostile novelists of Europe, deliberately lampooning the American girl: "If I had been a party to such a dastardly plot, I dare say I should have forfeited my domestic peace long ago." On another occasion he referred to "my domestic critic." Boyesen's sister said of Lillie: "We considered her unusually beautiful, bright and intellectual. At times she was quite a help to my brother in his literary work." But Austa Boyesen also conceded that her sister-in-law was sometimes guilty of "caprices and tart speeches. . . . She was unfortunately the victim of false standards and education."[12]

The spate of articles on Norway that Boyesen produced in the nineties resulted from opportunism and was the product of his last visit to his native land, but even this journalistic writing contains points of interest. Thus, in an essay on Norway's struggle for independence, he warned his mother country against forming any tie with Russia; and in a survey, "Norwegian Painters," he described the real-life prototype of his earliest hero, Gunnar.[13] The twenty-odd articles on Scandinavia can be classified roughly: (1) reports on the political situation in Norway, which stressed the democratic nature of the Norwegians and the iniquity of the autocratic Swedes; (2) various essays on cultural and social matters, some describing Norway and his recent experiences there, others recalling his boyhood in Sogn; (3) literary and artistic criticism; (4) articles on Norwegian immigration and the Scandinavians in the United States. These groupings are not rigid: Boyesen could touch on all these topics in a single essay.

The most significant, though not the best, of these articles were those containing his observations on immigration and its results. "The Scandinavian in the United States," in the November, 1892, *North American*

---

[11] *Forum*, 20:314–316.
[12] *Literary Silhouettes*, 10, 39; Austa Boyesen to Larson, December 6, 1936.
[13] *Harper's Weekly*, 39:391; Boyesen, "Norwegian Painters," in *Scribner's Magazine*, 12:757 (December, 1892).

Review, was Boyesen's final evaluation of his fellow immigrants. These people were frugal, self-reliant, hard-working, democratic, and easily assimilated into their adopted nation, he said. One of their worst faults, drunkenness, was decreasing, and their clannishness was less their own fault than that of the native Americans, who were quick to exploit but slow to accept the immigrant citizen. He noted with satisfaction that the descendants of Cleng Peerson's colonists, the earliest Norwegians here, had been so completely absorbed into American life that only their names betrayed their origin.[14]

But while Boyesen still favored rapid assimilation, once the Norwegians came to America, he thought that they were better advised to stay in Norway. He admitted that those who emigrated improved their lot materially nine times out of ten, but by 1892 he was convinced that this prosperity was bought too dearly. "Wealth . . . rarely brings contentment," he argued, and quoted a successful Norwegian-American farmer: "'I don't think people in this country leave themselves time to be happy.'" Other considerations were more important to Boyesen:

"How much simpler and more unperplexed, how much more richly colored, for weal or for woe, is the life of the Norwegian peasant than that of the American farmer! . . . And if he migrates, it is a fatally detached and incomplete self he transfers to the western prairies. All the finest tendrils of the torn roots of his being remain in the old soil; and though he may thrive, in a crude fashion, after the transplantation, he loses in an indefinable way his distinctness of physiognomy; his individuality pales and flattens out, and he becomes frequently incredibly vulgarized."

The Norwegian immigrants, Boyesen said, "upon transplanting into the glaring American daylight, become, as it were, bleached and fade into a dire uniformity. They become like the prairie — blank, level, tedious, basking in a dreary featureless prosperity."[15]

In 1892, while Boyesen was most deeply involved with the realistic novel, he completed *Essays on German Literature*, his first scholarly book since *Goethe and Schiller*, which had appeared in 1879. The three essays on the German romantic school, published in the *Atlantic Monthly* in 1875 and 1876, were included without revision and made nearly a quarter of the whole. In a prefatory note Boyesen acknowledged that he

[14] *North American Review*, 55:527.
[15] Boyesen, in *Chautauquan*, 15:608–610.

was also reissuing, "in a revised and amplified form," introductions he had written to new editions of the works of Schiller and Goethe.[16]

The thirty-three-page section on Schiller is almost identical with the introduction of 1883, and the fifty-five pages on Goethe are nearly the same as the 1885 introduction. But the latter is followed by five more chapters on Goethe: "Goethe and Carlyle," "The English Estimate of Goethe," "Some English Translations of Goethe," "Sermons from Goethe," and "Goethe's Relations to Women." The whole last subject takes up nearly half of the book; for, as Boyesen said, he had "a wealth of information on Goethe." Three other chapters completed the volume: "The Evolution of the German Novel," "Studies in the German Novel," and "Carmen Sylva." These essays, too, were taken from magazine articles published earlier, expanded only slightly and brought up to date. The titles were changed somewhat.[17]

Parts of the book are scholarly, others are journalistic; but if Boyesen was guilty of uneven emphasis in his essays, his judgments were intelligent, pertinent, and positive. He did not hesitate to express opinions: "There is, to my mind, no doubt that Spinoza is the greatest philosopher of modern times"; and, speaking of Goethe, "Taking him all in all, he is the most complete man in modern history." Boyesen's essays were never pedantic or parochial. His discussion of German literature was aimed at American readers: "Spielhagen would probably be disinclined to subscribe to Mr. Charles Dudley Warner's proposition, that the prime requisite of the novel is that it should entertain; nor do I suppose that he would be entirely satisfied with Mr. James's emendation, that its object should be to represent life"; and "Berlin is now the only city in Germany which, in the American sense of the word, is alive." [18]

If the modern reader is tempted to censure Boyesen for bowing to the popular taste of his time, he should first examine the contemporary reviews of the book. The *Critic* gave *Essays on German Literature* a full appraisal, a much more complete and respectful examination than that given to any of Boyesen's novels, and it offered some advice: "The

---

[16] *Schiller's Works, Illustrated by the Greatest German Artists*, and *Goethe's Works, Illustrated by the Best German Artists* (Philadelphia, 1883, 1885).

[17] I have been unable to trace the first of these three chapters to its magazine source, but the second, under the title "The Modern German Novel," appeared in *Princeton Review*, 13:154–168 (March, 1884). "Carmen Sylva" was the pseudonym used by Queen Elizabeth of Romania, who produced numerous volumes in verse and prose, mostly in her native German.

[18] *German Literature*, 86, 250, 253, 255.

The Final Salvo

rather coarse chapter on Goethe's 'Relations to Women' needs a little pruning, we fancy, here and there." [19]

A slightly closer inspection of the essays would have revealed a really subversive statement in the objectionable chapter on women. Boyesen, explaining the Hellenic view of life which Goethe accepted in preference to the Christian, argued that the great poet was anticipating the American rugged individualist, and was being honest instead of sanctimonious:

"Taking the whole tendency of Hellenic civilization, you find that it strove to develop the individual to the highest perfection and recognized his right to subjugate the world to his uses, as far as his powers permitted — make it tributary to his own existence. Though we exercise this right (with slight legal restraints) at the present day, and abjectly admire the man who does it most successfully, we hypocritically profess a philosophy which teaches the beauty of self-abnegation and altruistic devotion to the cause of humanity." [20]

Boyesen was not an uncritical admirer of the fatherland or its literature. Two years after *German Literature* appeared, he had an opportunity to assess the German writing that had since come from the presses. "German and Scandinavian Literature in 1894," in the first two issues of the American *Bookman*, begins with an appraisal of the colossal blonde woman of the public monuments, Germania:

"Her defiance of creation is perceptible enough to any foreigner who may venture to linger in the shadow of her shield. Her magnificent self-assertion, which contrasts so glaringly with the modest self-depreciation of the eighteenth century, is certainly the most pervasive note in contemporary German literature. And yet the last quarter of the eighteenth century was a period of great literary achievements, compared to which the last quarter of the nineteenth sinks into insignificance." [21]

Saber rattling then pervaded German writing, even that of the pessimists. Hermann Grimm maintained that Goethe and Schiller were "the indispensable forerunners of the Franco-Prussian War of 1870–1." This statement incensed Boyesen: "Writers whose themes are of a purely scholarly or scientific character rarely neglect the chance to blow a little patriotic fanfaronade every now and then for the edification of their readers." Even aside from this flaw, Boyesen thought such scholarship

---
[19] *Critic*, 20:336 (June 18, 1892).
[20] *German Literature*, 150.
[21] *Bookman*, 1:26.

bad. He was caustic about a new study of *Faust* "which learnedly and elaborately explains what is in no need of explanation, but leaves the dark places as dark as they were before." Worse yet was the "deplorable revival of inquiry regarding Goethe's relation to Frederica Brion," daughter of the parson at Sesenheim: "Only a German who had a depression in his cranium as a substitute for the bump of humour could possibly perpetrate with a serious face anything so appalling. . . . Think of *Urkundliche Forschungen* [*documentary researches*] into the question — not to put too fine a point upon it, as Captain Cuttle would say — of the virginity of a young girl who died eighty years ago." [22]

From 1890 to 1893 Boyesen wrote articles on six of Henrik Ibsen's plays, which appeared in the *Dial*, the *Chautauquan*, and the *Cosmopolitan*. They formed the nucleus of his book, *A Commentary on the Writings of Henrik Ibsen* (1894). To what extent he was taking advantage of a growing interest in Ibsen and to what degree he was creating that interest cannot be definitely assessed, but Ibsen's prestige gave support to Boyesen's strong defense of realism. By July, 1895, he was hailing the growing naturalism of the European stage, largely the result of Ibsen's work and influence.[23]

A Commentary on the Writings of Henrik Ibsen begins with a sixty-page introductory chapter that includes an evaluation of Ibsen's basic philosophy, brief mention of the early historical plays, and a biographical sketch. Of the fifteen chapters that follow, one is devoted to Ibsen's poems and each of the others is given to a play, from *The Comedy of Love* (1862) to *The Master Builder* (1892).

Boyesen implied that he had a personal advantage in writing on Ibsen. In discussing Ibsen's five years as an apothecary's apprentice (1844–49), when he had managed "to get on a war-footing with the worthy Philistines of Grimstad," Boyesen said: "I may as well add that I speak from personal knowledge in this matter; as during my many visits to the town between 1860 and 1869, I had frequent occasion to hear the opinions which were entertained of the poet by his former fellow-townsmen. And to put it mildly, they were not complimentary."

Boyesen sounded envious when he spoke of the Ibsen who wrote *Rosmersholm* and *The Lady from the Sea*: "There is to me something

[22] *Bookman*, 1:26, 99. Captain Cuttle is a character in Dickens' *Dombey and Son* (1846–48).

[23] See Boyesen, "The Drama of Revolt," in *Bookman*, 1:384–388 (July, 1895). George Bernard Shaw published *The Quintessence of Ibsenism* in London in 1891.

The Final Salvo

almost imposing in Ibsen's imperturbable serenity and his utter renunciation of the weak desire to please or flatter his public. At a time when nine-tenths of the books published have the air of having been written to order, it is refreshing to encounter works which, resting upon a broad under-structure, are but the visible summits of fog-enshrouded mountains of thought."

"Ibsen's peculiar mission," said Boyesen, was to question "accepted truisms." Society would be saved from stagnation so long as men probed deeply into "the problems of human existence." Permanent solutions to many of these problems were neither possible nor necessarily desirable, but the evolution of mankind would continue so long as each new generation was willing to seek solutions. Thus Ibsen was not so negative as he seemed: "His is the wholesomely stimulating 'spirit that denies.'" But though Boyesen professed a "profound admiration" for Ibsen, he found a disturbing quality in him: "I fancy that I detect in Ibsen a certain cynical satisfaction in discovering the worm in the apple, the flaw in the diamond, the rift in the lute."

On the last pages of *A Commentary on the Writings of Henrik Ibsen,* Boyesen explained why he had become an Ibsen advocate:

"There is a fatal optimism which professes to believe that evils can be cured by ignoring them,—professing not to see them. It is the good, nice, religious people who are most prone to this delusion; and it is these, too, who, *a propos* of Ibsen, declare that no good can come of dragging moral ugliness into the light of day. I confess there was a time when I was myself of that opinion. But an ampler and deeper experience has convinced me that such a view is not only foolish, but exceedingly harmful. . . . Though not always agreeing with Ibsen, I am greatly indebted to him for having kindled in my mind many sparks of vital thought, and aroused my interest in subjects of vast concern which formerly I passed by with the Pharisee, and the Levite, and the rest of the respectable herd. He has the courage to look the ugliest truths in the face without flinching, and to record what he sees and feels with a relentless disregard of revered conventionalities. What he offers is not food for babes; but to a mature mind it is wholesome and stimulating reading." [24]

If Boyesen was still cautious in the *Commentary,* his later appraisal of Ibsen's influence, in *Bookman* for July, 1895, was an almost unqualified endorsement. His article, "The Drama of Revolt," began with a quota-

[24] *A Commentary on Ibsen,* 1–3, 16, 58, 316.

tion from Zola's essay, "Naturalism on the Stage," and ended with an estimate of the future of the new drama. Ibsen had now acquired major defenders in August Strindberg and Bernard Shaw, while in Germany naturalism commanded the stage. Boyesen praised the new plays of Sudermann, Hauptmann, Halbe, and Hartleben. In Berlin even the jingoistic Wildenbruch had succumbed to naturalism. France was not far behind: The old stage machinery and the clichés of Sardou and Scribe were being replaced by fresh and thoughtful dramas. Now the battle was being won in London; this meant that New York would soon fall in line, despite the reactionary influence of William Winter. In such matters America still aped England, said Boyesen.[25]

In his preface to *Essays on Scandinavian Literature* (1895) Boyesen wrote, "Some twenty years ago the ambition seized me to write a History of Scandinavian Literature. I scarcely realized then what an enormous amount of reading would be required to equip me for this task. My studies naturally led me much beyond the scope of my original intention." Boyesen explained that his chapter on Ibsen grew into a book and only "heroic condensation" saved the section on Bjørnson from reaching similar proportions. As it was, Bjørnson required over a hundred pages and Bishop Tegnér nearly that many. Other writers had to be omitted: "The Swedish authors John Ludvig Runeberg, Mrs. Edgren, and August Strindberg, and the Dane Oehlenschlaeger, necessity has compelled me to reserve for a future volume."

After Boyesen's death some critics said his major omission had been his failure to write this promised history, and they bewailed the resultant loss to literature. Writers like Charles Dudley Warner were convinced that Boyesen had wasted his time on realistic novels and on essays attacking the popular romantic fiction of the day. For more than twenty years Boyesen had been writing critical articles on German and Scandinavian literature, and they had made an impact in American literary and academic circles. Serious Scandinavian writing had won prestige in the United States by 1895, largely because of Boyesen's efforts.[26]

The *Critic*, commenting on a new library edition of Bjørnson's works that was being brought out by Macmillan in 1895, said the poet was easily the most popular Scandinavian writer in the United States, thanks

---

[25] *Bookman*, 1:384–388. See Emile Zola, *The Experimental Novel and Other Essays* (New York, 1894), for the discussion on naturalism in the theater.

[26] See Warner, *Library of the World's Best Literature*, 5:2273 (New York, 1896).

to Boyesen: "Bjørnson, it may be remembered, visited this country not so long ago, and was the guest of his countryman, the late Prof. Boyesen, who admired him greatly and really introduced him."[27]

To Boyesen, Bjørnson fulfilled "the concept of a poet which was prevalent in Norway in the olden time." The scalds, being warriors as well as poets, were bold and blunt in speech; in the softer modern age their dual role was not generally understood, even in Norway. "Bjørnson's increasing Radicalism and his outspoken Socialistic sympathies had by this time alienated a large portion of the Scandinavian public," Boyesen acknowledged. But he relished Bjørnson's reply to the charge that he had ceased to be a poet and had become a politician:

"'Oh, yes,' he cried, with a wrathful laugh, 'don't I know it? You must be a poet! You must not mingle in the world's harsh and jarring tumult. They have a notion that a poet is a long-haired man who sits on the top of a tower and plays upon a harp while his hair streams in the wind. Yes, a fine kind of poet is that! No, my boy, I am a poet, not primarily because I can write verse (there are lots of people who can do that) but by virtue of seeing more clearly, and feeling more deeply, and speaking more truly than the majority of men. All that concerns humanity concerns me. If by my song or my speech I can contribute ever so little toward the amelioration of the lot of the millions of my poorer fellow-creatures, I shall be prouder of that than of the combined laurels of Shakespeare, Milton, and Goethe.'"[28]

Bjørnson, who had influenced Boyesen's early romanticism, began to veer toward realism and naturalism as early as 1874, according to Boyesen. After that year, his novels, tales, and dramas moved farther and farther away from conventional, romantic fiction: "Here is a man who has resolutely aroused himself from the old romantic doze, cleared his eyes of the film of dreams, and with a sharp, wide-awake intensity focused them to the actual aspect of the actual world. He has sat down with his windows wide open, and allowed the sounds and sights and smells of reality to pour in upon him."[29]

A story of Bjørnson's published in 1894 reached "far toward the high-water mark of modern realism," but what impressed Boyesen most was the author's "scientific view of life":

[27] *Critic*, 27:349 (November 23, 1895).
[28] *Scandinavian Literature*, 61.
[29] *Scandinavian Literature*, 100.

Hjalmar Hjorth Boyesen

"I verily believe it to be a type of what the fiction of the future will be, when scientific education shall have been largely substituted for the classical; and even the novelists will be expected to know something about the world in which they live and the sublime and inexorable laws which govern it. At present the majority of them spin irresponsible yarns, and play Providence *ad libitum* to their characters. Man's vital coherence with his environment is but loosely indicated. Chance reigns supreme. They have observed carefully enough the external phenomena of life — and chiefly for their picturesque or dramatic interest — but of the causes which underlie them they rarely give us a glimpse." [30]

In his long chapter on Tegnér, Boyesen tried to forgive "a certain charming juvenility" in the author he had once admired. Tegnér's "scorn of all metaphysical subtleties" was characteristic of the Scandinavians, but they had no monopoly on this type of "intellectual immaturity":

"The love of brave words and brave deeds, the exaltation of the man of action above the man of thought, the pleasure in reckless gallantry and foolhardy adventure, are, however, not confined to Swedes and Norwegians, but are characteristic of the boyhood of every nation. In the Scotchman, Robert Louis Stevenson, this jaunty juvenility, this rich enjoyment of bloody buccaneers and profane sea-dogs, is carried to far greater lengths, and the great juvenile public of England and America, both young and old, rises up and calls him blessed." [31]

The gibe did not go unnoticed. At the end of the *Critic's* eulogistic review of *Essays on Scandinavian Literature*, a petulant note was added: "He *will* vent his occasional spleen on Sir Walter Scott and Robert Louis Stevenson, but is this not because he is a worshipper of Howells?" [32]

On the final page of the Tegnér essay Boyesen revealed why he paid less attention to Swedish literature than to Danish and Norwegian: "The academic tendency which 'idealizes' life and shuns earth-scented facts, had, through the decisive influence of Tegnér, been victorious in Swedish literature." [33]

As early as 1882, Boyesen had hailed his old classmate, Alexander Kielland, as a promising realist, but later he expressed the fear that this new novelist overstepped the bounds of art: "It is the pathology of vice rather than its psychology which occupies Kielland, and pathology lies

---

[30] *Scandinavian Literature*, 99.
[31] *Scandinavian Literature*, 219.
[32] *Critic*, 27:85 (August 10, 1895).
[33] *Scandinavian Literature*, 288.

outside of the domain of art." In 1891, however, Boyesen wrote a preface for the American edition of Kielland's *Tales of Two Countries*. In this foreword, which was reprinted as the Kielland chapter in *Essays on Scandinavian Literature*, Boyesen indicated that he had changed his mind about the boundaries of art. Granting that Kielland's novel *Jacob* was often rated "an immoral book," Boyesen thought "the question of its morality is of less consequence than the question of its truth." It was time we were shocked out of "our old idyllic faith in the goodness and wisdom of all mundane arrangements," because "our attitude toward the universe" must change "with the change of its attitude toward us." Kielland was a benefactor of mankind because he was helping to explain the modern world: "Success is but adaptation to environment, and success is the supreme aim of the modern man."[34]

There were still limits to Boyesen's radicalism in 1895, as his essay on Georg Brandes revealed. Brandes, because of his brilliant analytical ability, was clearly the foremost critic of the day, Boyesen said, but added that in recent essays, not yet translated into English, Brandes had indicated such "open sympathy with anarchism," such "a singular confusion of moral values," that even his earlier opinions were questionable: "Can a man ever have been a solid thinker who at fifty practically hoists the flag of anarchy?" The endorsement of "an obscure German iconoclast named Friedrich Nietzsche" was Brandes' undoing: "It is difficult to understand how a man of well-balanced brain and a logical equipment second to none, can take *au serieux* a mere philosophical savage who dances a war dance amid what he conceives to be the ruins of civilization, swings a reckless tomahawk and knocks down everybody and everything that comes in his way."[35]

Although the *Commentary on Ibsen* and the two volumes of *Essays* were called scholarly by Boyesen's contemporaries, the three books are largely journalistic in style and intent. Their contents differ only slightly from the other articles Boyesen turned out in the nineties: "An Acquaintance with Hans Christian Andersen," "The Mother of Ivan Tourguéneff," and "Conversations with Bjørnstjerne Bjørnson." A sketch of Boyesen in *Scribner's Monthly*, published in 1877, had mentioned that "even his criticism tends to take a biographical form." The accuracy of this observation is attested by the series of "Visits" and "Reminiscences"

[34] *Critic*, 7:133; *Scandinavian Literature*, 116.
[35] *Scandinavian Literature*, 214.

that he turned out. The articles Boysen wrote in the nineties, including the "Conversations," were similar, the lively and useful work of a literary liaison man and not real criticism.[36]

Under the heading "An International Boswell," the *Critic* discussed Boyesen's skill as an interviewer. His "Conversations" were more insidious than interviews: A friend could bait you and draw you out, but you would be on your guard against an interviewer. "If you wish an illustration of the art boswellian, you can find nothing finer of its kind than the work of Prof. H. H. Boyesen. . . . When the dictionaries add the verb 'to boswell' to their pages, they must also add the equally useful verb 'to boyesen' which means not only to boswell but to boswell internationally." [37]

Despite Boyesen's insistent and far-reaching propaganda during the nineties for the cause of realism—in lectures, fiction, criticism, and incidental writing—he offered few new arguments to bolster his cause. Instead, he propounded the same points in a variety of guises, and tried to persuade by repetition. At the same time he broadened the base of his platform, so that he designated as realists many writers whom Howells rejected. Boyesen showed little concern about form and style, and he forgave the use of sensational incidents when he considered the author's treatment and intent to be realistic. He was deeply concerned, however, about subject matter; a novelist had to deal with the present time and with typical characters, not with the age of chivalry and of superhuman heroes. Finally, he wanted a novel to be a "wholesome moral tonic," to help its readers to understand the world they lived in. He was not narrow on this point. The most moral of books, he said, was *Anna Karenina*.[38]

Although Boyesen acknowledged his debt to Howells and Turgenev (the two writers chiefly responsible for his own convictions on realism), by 1889 he realized that he differed from both of them on specific points. He did not agree with Turgenev about the use of imagination, and he took issue with Howells' insistence on the commonplace. These divergent opinions were brought out in an interview with Boyesen:

"I don't believe that realism means a mere photographic record of all the trivial things of life. I think the realist, as well as the romanticist,

---
[36] Heath, in *Scribner's Monthly*, 14:780.
[37] *Critic*, 23:131 (August 19, 1893).
[38] *Forum*, 18:727.

The Final Salvo

must select typical characters and typical incidents, and if he understands his art he will study the relation of values and arrange them to the best advantage on his canvas. I think, moreover, that it is a mistake to exclude the great passions of life from the realistic novel, since no novel can be truly realistic which is not a faithful transcript of reality. A realistic writer, in short, needs imagination as much as anybody. Mere perception alone, or acuteness of observation, will never make a novelist." [39]

"The Romantic and Realistic Novel" (1888) is chiefly interesting for the vehemence with which Boyesen attacked the currently popular romantic writers. Of Stevenson's new novel he wrote: " 'The Black Arrow' . . . is nothing but a clever dime novel of a very juvenile order. . . . If he produces more such stuff he will forfeit his rank as a writer of serious fiction." And of Rider Haggard: "He is simply debauching the public taste. . . . I fail to discover a single redeeming trait in his pernicious activity." [40]

In this essay Boyesen's praise for the realists was as fervent as his condemnation of the romanticists. Thinking perhaps of his own struggles with *Mammon*, he emphasized that writing entertaining novels of normal and typical life required much greater skill than did spinning out fantastic tales. As writers successful in producing realistic fiction he singled out Howells, Tolstoy, Thackeray, Turgenev, Balzac, Daudet, and George Eliot, who could "delve into the depths of the human heart." The predominant tone of Boyesen's article was optimistic. Despite the resurgence of romance, he was confident: "The tendency of the age is toward a more and more unflinching realism." [41]

"The Progressive Realism of American Fiction" (1892) traced the evolution of the novel in the United States. Boyesen began by quoting Goethe's poetic hope that America might be spared the horrors of romanticism. After a brief mention of the writers who belied that hope — Charles Brockden Brown, James Fenimore Cooper, and Edgar Allan Poe — he discussed the beginnings of American realism. As forerunners of the school he singled out Nathaniel Hawthorne and Harriet Beecher Stowe. He found in Hawthorne's fiction and notebooks a deep concern with reality, especially in getting the right "atmospheric tone and color" in his settings. And, after *Uncle Tom's Cabin*, "Mrs. Stowe . . . aban-

---

[39] *New York Daily Tribune*, July 29, 1889.
[40] *Chautauquan*, 9:96 (November, 1888).
[41] *Chautauquan*, 9:98.

doned much of her early extravagance, which was defensible enough in the cause of reform, and has steered closer and closer to the shores of reality. In *Oldtown Folks*, and particularly in the Sam Lawson sketches, she betrays a power of minute observation and an appreciation of local color which might almost entitle her to the name of a realist." [42]

The growth of interest in local color was the main point of Boyesen's essay: "Nothing could testify with more force to the fact that we have outgrown romanticism than this almost unanimous desire, on the part of our authors, to chronicle the widely divergent phases of our American civilization. There are scarcely a dozen conspicuous States now which have not their own local novelist." [43]

He admitted that by including the local colorists as a group he enrolled many doubtful candidates among his realists: Thomas Bailey Aldrich, H. C. Bunner, Thomas Nelson Page, and James Whitcomb Riley, to mention only a few; but he felt safer about some others. He was confident that Mark Twain's *Life on the Mississippi* and *Roughing It*, "in spite of their occasional grotesqueness, are important documents of social history." He hailed "that remarkable novel, *The Story of a Country Town*, by E. W. Howe," and called Hamlin Garland "the most vigorous realist in America." Summing up, Boyesen offered his definition: "Broadly speaking, a realist is a writer who adheres strictly to the logic of reality, as he sees it; who, aiming to portray the manners of his time, deals by preference with the normal rather than the exceptional phases of life, and, to use Henry James's felicitous phrase, arouses not the pleasure of surprise, but that of recognition." [44]

"The Great Realists and the Empty Story-Tellers" and "Novels of Romance and Stories of Real Life" contributed no new ideas, for all their combative, uncompromising tone. There was, Boyesen said, an increasing emphasis on the moral value of realism: The reading public that he had first become aware of at Chautauqua convinced him that he could best defend realism and condemn romanticism on moral grounds. "I know more than one young man in whom the seeds of corruption were sown by Dumas and Murger." George du Maurier's *Trilby* had the same effect; but *Nana* and *Sappho* were acceptable because Zola and Daudet were "unintentional if not unconscious moralists." His chief en-

---

[42] *Literary Silhouettes*, 63.
[43] *Literary Silhouettes*, 73.
[44] *Literary Silhouettes*, 71, 75, 77.

The Final Salvo

thusiasm was reserved for Thackeray, George Eliot, and especially Tolstoy.[45]

A roster of writers who are either acceptable or unacceptable according to Boyesen's realistic code could be drawn up from his articles of this period. The realists, as Boyesen might have listed them at the end of his career, would be headed by Tolstoy, George Eliot, Thackeray, Howells, Turgenev, Henry James, Flaubert, Balzac, Trollope, Hardy, and Mrs. Humphry Ward. High on the list of proscribed romanticists would be Scott, Dickens, Hugo, Wilkie Collins, Stevenson, Haggard, Conan Doyle, S. R. Crockett, and Stanley J. Weyman.

Boyesen's most complete statement of his creed, and the best clue to the reasoning behind it, is found on the last pages of his *Essays on German Literature:* "No art can reproduce life with absolute fidelity, nor is it desirable that it should. A vast deal must be omitted in the novel. . . . If a novelist . . . were to insist upon rendering everything . . . he would . . . be unfaithful because of over-fidelity. But to the laws of life, in so far as they are ascertainable — the logic of its sequence and development — he must adhere with the utmost fidelity that he can command."[46]

He tried to pin down the ideological basis for romanticism: "In modern times romanticism, typifying a permanent tendency of the human mind, has been placed in opposition to what is called realism, and has thereby undergone a fresh modification. If realism means insistence upon a life-like art, based upon experience, true to the logic and beating with the pulse-beat of reality, romanticism, in its latest combative attitude, has no choice but to mean sovereign art, dwelling in an ideal realm of fancy, scorning subserviency to the truth of life. Such a tendency we see exemplified in the brilliant caricature of Dickens, the lurid and unwholesome fictions of Wilkie Collins, and the medieval heroic juveniles of Robert Louis Stevenson."[47]

Finally Boyesen summed up his arguments and explained why, in accordance with his evolutionary philosophy, realism must prevail: "The intellectual progress of the world asserts itself in a progressive demand for verisimilitude in the arts. The childlike wonder-loving epics and legends of the Middle Ages reflected as truly the intellectual condition of

---

[45] *Forum*, 18:728.
[46] *German Literature*, 358.
[47] *German Literature*, 358.

the 'cultivated classes' of the twelfth and thirteenth centuries as Tolstoi, Howells, and James represent the vanguard of culture to-day. The romantic rear-guard is represented by the lovers of Dickens, Scott, Victor Hugo, and Stevenson. There will always be those who pander to the crude delight in marvels, and there will always be people ready to consume their wares. But let not these people fancy that their delight in these modified fairy tales is an intellectual enjoyment which argues 'literary tastes.' It was not suspected, even a hundred years ago, except in the most general way, how human fates were determined by heredity and environment; and the romances of that day were therefore excusable for a degree of arbitrariness which in a novelist of to-day would be unpardonable. A higher degree of fidelity, a deeper inward truth, as regards motives, impulses, causes, and effects, is demanded by realism; while romanticism (using nature as a painter does his colors, for purposes of mixture and arbitrary composition) gives yet a tolerably free rein to fancy and refuses allegiance to the logic of life." [48]

[48] *German Literature*, 359.

13

Boyesen in the Twentieth Century

THE objective of the foregoing chapters has been to see Boyesen whole, to examine his career and writings in the light of his life and times. Thus, organization has been chronological according to decades, with, at the end of each, an examination of the literary output of the preceding period. Such an approach is essential in attaining a clear perspective of the man and his work, because Boyesen began writing early and was very impressionable.

Few of Boyesen's writings, even those readily accessible today, are read except by students and scholars who are curious about the development of American thought and the emergence of a New World culture. Such researchers would do well to consider Boyesen's career and opinions; and, hopefully, the present study will be useful to them. Many critics have mentioned Boyesen's name, his connection with Howells and realism, or the "Iron Madonna" statement, but nothing more. He has remained too long a nebulous figure.

Boyesen's modest place in the development of American literature is closely linked with the trend toward realism. Words like "realism" and "romanticism" can be used safely in discussing his career, because he defined and described each of these often ambiguous terms as he himself understood and used them. He accepted naturalism as an extension of realism, and welcomed the naturalists as allies in a common battle against the literature of illusion, fantasy, and irresponsibility. The novelist's role was to write honestly and accurately, and through his art to interpret and explain the spirit of the age.

For Boyesen the question to be asked about literature, in assessing its worth, was a simple one: Was it true to the logic of reality, the logic of life? Modern realism could demand greater fidelity from the novelist because modern scholarship made it possible to identify motives and impulses, causes and effects. Boyesen knew that Darwin had revolutionized scientific thought, and he was convinced that Herbert Spencer had revolutionized social thinking. Society, like nature, would evolve and progress, transforming man and his world into a better, more productive place.

Boyesen was a thorough-going and optimistic social Darwinist. His whole view of life and literature, as it evolved during his years at Cornell, was predicated on his belief that in the inexorable and beneficial march of science man would shed his outworn shibboleths, customs, and institutions. It was the duty of every serious writer, and indeed of every good citizen, to become aware of progressive ideas and to fall into step with them. Marc Ratner, who has done a comprehensive study of Boyesen's ideas, is correct in maintaining that all of his opinions stem from this central conviction; Boyesen was not, however, born with such a philosophy. Mr. Ratner might have shown how Boyesen reached his point of view over a twenty-five-year period, from 1871 to 1895, when he did his writing. An analysis of Boyesen's ideas and convictions should also make allowance for the personal and social pressures that affected his thinking and his writings, especially the fiction. Boyesen's position on nearly all subjects can be explained by his views on social Darwinism and his notions about religion, education, women, politics, economics, and immigration. But another factor in his life probably did even more to shape his career and influence his writings, fiction and nonfiction.[1]

This factor was an all-consuming ambition to become a man of letters, to see his own thoughts and words and brain children in print. It could be called a creative urge; but, from the beginning, it was complicated by his dependence on the income from his publications. We should recall his schoolboy effusions in verse and the romantic and nostalgic outpourings of his first years in the United States. Writing was a natural and necessary outlet for him; his need for self-expression was unusually

---

[1] Marc Ratner's "Hjalmar Hjorth Boyesen: Critic of Literature and Society" is an unpublished doctoral dissertation submitted at New York University in 1959. A copy is in the library of New York University.

strong. His literary output was enough to fill thirty-five or forty volumes. This truly phenomenal feat included the mastery of a language not his own, to be used as his medium. Furthermore, except during one year, all his writing was done in leisure or vacation time while he was an active, highly successful college professor and a sought-after public lecturer.

Boyesen's change from a romanticist to a realist is an interesting one. It resulted from the maturing of his opinions under the impact of current ideas, especially those inspired by Darwin. Bjørnson, Howells, and Turgenev successively influenced his development. He was a natural romantic (by temperament and early tutelage) who was determined to produce serious, important fiction to match his acquired convictions. But equally important as a determining influence was his growing dependence on writing, from the very beginning, for a substantial portion of his income. When he no longer had to support his brothers and his father, he married a beautiful and socially ambitious American girl. He was devoted to his wife, Lillie Keen Boyesen, and his three handsome sons, but they cancelled any chance he might have had to become a major author. Their support required all the money he could earn by teaching, lecturing, and writing, and his writing had to pay as well as possible.

Boyesen became a magazinist of first rank in the heyday of the American magazine. The range of his subject matter was astounding. Between 1872 and 1895 few active writers were better known or more popular. Yet, almost immediately after his death, he was forgotten.

Boyesen repeatedly lamented his failure fully to realize his potentiality. He wrote Cable in 1878: "I have written nothing so far which I would wish to be judged by." In 1886 he remarked regretfully to Georg Brandes: "My books have unfortunately, up to now only given slight glimpses to [sic] that which actually is close to my heart." And in a letter to Howells of January 2, 1890, he looked back on his career with some misgivings, explaining that in the new novel he was sending Howells he had made some concessions to the American girl — his reading public.[2]

When he made apologies he also offered his excuses. He explained in some detail to Cable his incentive for producing so much: He had to support his two younger brothers, and when they finally finished college

---

[2] Boyesen to Cable, February 17, 1878; Boyesen to Brandes, September 27, 1886. The latter item, from the Brandes Archives, Royal Danish Library, Copenhagen, is quoted in Marc Ratner, "Georg Brandes and Hjalmar Hjorth Boyesen: An Exchange of Critical Views," in *Scandinavian Studies*, 33:221 (November, 1961).

Hjalmar Hjorth Boyesen

and attained independence, he became responsible for his father and his new family. No explanation was needed by Howells, who knew only too well what had happened to Boyesen after his marriage and his move to New York City: He wrote more and more when he should have written less and less.

There were other hindrances, almost as severe. He told Brandes: "My position as professor at one of our oldest and most orthodox universities places many a restraint on me. . . . Our large periodicals which pay good honorariums are, without exception, orthodox or so mildly liberal that they swagger with small, cautious steps of skepticism. Which they immediately hurry up to deny. Nearly all that I have written is published in these periodicals and they are returned to me in order to abridge and tone down an octave or so before they will be accepted for publication."[3] Boyesen's experience with *The Mammon of Unrighteousness* — finding a publisher, resisting emasculation of the story, and facing the bitter outcry that included personal attacks — convinced him, if he had had any doubts before, that it was a practical impossibility to write honestly in America on serious topics.

The famous Iron Madonna essay was, of course, unusually explicit about the tyranny of the young girl who must be protected against reality. To Brandes, Boyesen said: "No American writer can live by his pen unless he is a journalist. Cheap editions of English writers sell from ten to twenty cents and up, ruining the book market and superceding the native literature."[4]

It was precisely because Boyesen was so conscious of the literary market, so vitally concerned about the profits of authorship, that he was sensitive about the prevailing taste for genteel, sentimental, idealistic fiction. He made concessions to the young girl reader — consciously, as he admitted to Howells, and unconsciously in a way that he himself did not recognize. The cause of realism was an unpopular one in the late nineteenth century. When Boyesen mentioned that novels should be truthful and responsible about life, he was told that literature must be idealistic, in the Walter Scott tradition. American critics took their cue from the English, whose outcry against Thomas Hardy's frankness impelled him to end his novel-writing career in 1895. Until Hamlin Garland, Stephen Crane, and Frank Norris began writing in the 1890's,

---
[3] Boyesen to Brandes, September 27, 1886.
[4] Boyesen to Brandes, September 27, 1886.

In the Twentieth Century

Howells and Boyesen were almost the only realistic writers. They found little support and much opposition in such magazines as the *Atlantic, Century, Harper's, Scribner's,* and *Lippincott's,* or in journals like the *Critic, Dial, Literary World, Bookman,* and *Book Buyer.*

Boyesen, as a Columbia College professor and a popular writer, was in a favored but vulnerable position in the campaign for realism. He was an acknowledged scholar and teacher, but his attempts to introduce German and Scandinavian literature made slow headway against the intrenched position of English letters. His teaching field, modern languages and literatures, had none of the established prestige of Greek and Latin. Thus, though Boyesen was an innovator, he was a mild insurgent who tried to prove that his disciplines were both respectable and acceptable. As his position at Columbia became secure, his stand on matters of educational reform became bolder, but in the process he learned to please and placate. Early letters from his years in Urbana and at Cornell indicate that this attitude did not come naturally.

Like Howells, Boyesen was influenced and perhaps inhibited in the exercise of realism by his own way of life. A professor at Cornell and Columbia lived in a world no less sheltered and genteel than that of a magazine editor in Boston or New York. Boyesen was not, however, a typical professor. He had married a socialite and he spent his summer vacations at Nantucket, Newport, and Southampton. After seventy years, it is difficult to assess Lillie Boyesen's social life, but it was based on newly acquired wealth and superficial values. Boyesen often pictured a glittering New York society in his fiction of the 80's and 90's, evidence enough that he was familiar with the milieu and its shortcomings. Interestingly enough, he was often criticized for moving in such circles. It might be predicated that Boyesen lived in several distinct worlds: Lillie Keen Boyesen's, the academic, and a third realm of his clubs, the Authors', the Reform, and the Nineteenth Century. There he met his friends (who were not congenial to his wife), and there he threshed out his opinions and convictions with such men as Brander Matthews, Carl Schurz, and E. C. Stedman. Add to this his correspondence with European writers like Bjørnson, Kielland, Brandes, and Spielhagen. Boyesen's view of life and literature and his brand of realism were the product of these influences, mixed and shaped by his own personality.

Courageous though he was, his practice of realism was tainted by his personality and his era. He formed his fiction by grafting sharp social

Hjalmar Hjorth Boyesen

comment on the traditional domestic novel; his concept of character was sentimental and his plots were trite, no matter how vigorously he exposed corruption. But the new American literature of the twentieth century did not come into being full-blown. As a forerunner of the kind of fiction that eventually replaced the idealistic, romantic, and genteel, Hjalmar Boyesen has real importance; and it is in this light that recent critics have viewed him.

In 1915 Fred Lewis Pattee published *A History of American Literature since 1870*, asserting in the preface that this was the first study attempting to handle "as a unit . . . our first really national period." Fifty years later, Pattee's evaluations seem ludicrous and antediluvian, but at least one of his sentences is significant: "The Norwegian scholar and poet and novelist Boyesen, who did what Howells really did not do, take Tolstoy as his master, was thought for two decades to be of highest rank, but today his work, save for certain sections of his critical studies, is no longer read." Pattee was hostile to the new realism of the 1890's, and happy to report that it had been swept away by a new wave of romanticism.[5]

But he was accurate enough about the sudden eclipse of Boyesen's reputation. Only a few years later, when Pattee's appraisals were no longer accepted even in academic circles, other students of American literature and ideas began to re-examine Boyesen as a forerunner of twentieth-century realism and naturalism. In his *Main Currents of American Thought* (1927–30), Vernon Louis Parrington devoted a section to him entitled "The Beginnings of the Sociological Novel." He linked *The Mammon of Unrighteousness* with Robert Grant's *Unleavened Bread* and Edith Wharton's *The House of Mirth*—"studies that were symptomatic of a generation disturbed by the consciousness of a vulgar plutocracy rising in its midst, and yet ignorant of the nature of the disease."[6]

Such novels of social criticism had only a brief vogue, said Parrington. Economic unrest brought in the new school of naturalism, or "realism wedded to a deterministic sociology." Boyesen had anticipated this new school; in 1891 "he opened the new vein of realism which he worked industriously the remaining four years of his life." Parrington believed

---

[5] Pattee, *A History of American Literature since 1870*, 409 (New York, 1915).
[6] Parrington, *Main Currents in American Thought: The Beginnings of Critical Realism in America*, 3:180 (New York, 1930).

that *Mammon, The Golden Calf,* and *Social Strugglers* "were the nearest approach to the Tolstoyian type of realism that America had produced," and that they contained "in germ many of the ideas which the later city realists were to amplify and develop."[7]

Although Parrington conceded that today these three novels have only historical interest, he found several things in *Mammon* that characterize the new literature. "In the delineation of the character of Horace Larkin — the hero of a book that does not realize its promise — the note of the new realism is heard distinctly for the first time. The business man frankly breaks with the old ethics and erects a new ethics in conformity with his ambition; and it is the elaboration of the ethics of the Will to Power that justifies one in regarding *The Mammon of Unrighteousness* as a first study in the new city realism."[8]

Parrington considered Boyesen significant despite his failure to accomplish in *Mammon* what he had hoped. In one sense the novel was a vestige of the older "psychological realism" that focused on the individual; but in its "Nietzschean hero," Horace Larkin, a typical product of "the world of cutthroat business," Boyesen also heralded the new "realism of environment that conceived of the individual as a pawn on the chessboard of society," the new realism that "M. Zola had given the name *naturalism*."[9]

Granville Hicks, in his Marxist "interpretation of American literature since the Civil War," *The Great Tradition* (1933), found that Boyesen described a common phenomenon of the eighties and nineties, "the disintegration of idealism as a result of the desire for success." In his chapter entitled "Struggle and Flight," Hicks linked Boyesen with H. B. Fuller, Harold Frederic, and Stephen Crane. Though only the young Crane had any following, any appreciable influence on later writers, partly because "he defied taboos they held sacred," Hicks found the older trio more sensitive to social abuses and Boyesen the most earnest of the group. Boyesen's best quality was his "power of indignation," but he discovered "that an ethical theory is not necessarily the best clue to the understanding of a nation. His bad characters are stronger, more interesting, and more convincing than his good ones; they may deserve to be condemned, but to condemn is not to explain them. Obviously he had

---

[7] *Main Currents*, 3:180–182.
[8] *Main Currents*, 3:182.
[9] *Main Currents*, 3:180–183.

Hjalmar Hjorth Boyesen

understood part of the change that was going on, but not enough to make his characters fully representative. Earnestness and indignation had done what they could, but something more was needed." [10]

In Hicks's next chapter, "The Years of Hope," he turned from Frank Norris to liberal reform writers like Robert Herrick, Winston Churchill, and David Graham Phillips, whose works are usually labeled "muckraking" or problem books. These men "documented their novels more adequately," said Hicks, than Boyesen had, but: "They were rather more confused than he. At the same time that they condemned greed and materialism, they gloried in the material progress of the country." Furthermore, the liberal reform novelists who wrote in the first decade of the twentieth century "had little more to say than had been said by such men as Boyesen in the nineties." [11]

Alfred Kazin, in *On Native Grounds* (1942), also found Boyesen "a better realist in precept than in practice," perhaps because this "romantic academician" had "a wide knowledge of the traditions of European realism." Even his theoretical studies were mediocre, however, and "his mind was not that of a pioneer." Kazin concluded: "Boyesen's service to the emancipation and growth of American taste was to expound the work of the great Continental realists." Kazin called the *Essays on Scandinavian Literature* "valuable pioneer studies," and acknowledged that "[Boyesen] fought nobly for Ibsen at a time when it was dangerous even to expound the dramatist's ideas." [12]

But Kazin deplored Boyesen's "inveterate Victorianism." In his eagerness to adjust taste and belief to the Darwinian world view, Boyesen was no more daring than Tennyson and "not half so challenging as George Eliot." Not only was Boyesen "compromised by prudence"; he was "not happy in realism." Without explaining this judgment, which in any case cannot be proved or disproved, Kazin pointed to the real reason for Boyesen's failure: "He simply lacked the necessary skill" to cope successfully with the problems of characterization, dialogue, and style; in a word, "he lacked a necessary flair for the novel." [13]

This judgment is true enough and damning enough to dispose of Boyesen, but Kazin marred his evaluation with snide half-truths like "He had an alien's disposition to please." After quoting Boyesen's statement of

---

[10] *The Great Tradition*, 157–159 (New York, 1933).
[11] *The Great Tradition*, 182.
[12] *On Native Grounds*, 26 (New York, 1942).
[13] *On Native Grounds*, 28.

In the Twentieth Century

intention in the preface to *The Mammon of Unrighteousness* — devotion to reality — Kazin added, "In practice, however, he displayed a most tepid soul." Then, apparently echoing Boyesen's contemporary adversaries who found his realistic stories so pernicious, Kazin wrote: "The handsome, kindly, emotional academician did his best work in his romantic children's stories of Norwegian life. He never found himself in America, and he never found himself in realism."[14]

In spite of such statements, Kazin, like Hicks and Parrington, had obviously read Boyesen. The same cannot be said of some later critics. Boyesen is mentioned briefly in most books about the literature of the Gilded Age or the development of American naturalism; and he is treated with respect in some studies of even broader scope. In all of these books, however, he is a nebulous figure, "a vigorous Howellsian" whose novels are known to critics and historians only by title. They are more familiar with the critical essays, and one feels that most of them would have given him more attention if they had understood his career fully.[15]

Van Wyck Brooks, in *The Confident Years: 1885–1915*, treated Boyesen as a product of the immigration that transformed the Middle West after the Civil War. Brooks disposed of him quickly as a writer: "Boyesen himself became in time an American novelist, all but indistinguishable from other disciples of Howells, — in part because there was little to distinguish him at all." Other historians of ideas or literature, such as Henry Steele Commager in *The American Mind*, or Grant C. Knight in *The Critical Period in American Literature*, give passing mention to Boyesen's fight for realism, and to his introduction of Bjørnson, Ibsen, and other Scandinavian writers to American readers. And occasionally, as in Lars Åhnebrink's *The Beginnings of Naturalism in American Fiction*, there is a protest against the neglect of Boyesen's work and influence.[16]

It may be that the neglect of Boyesen has ended. In 1962 his essay

---

[14] *On Native Grounds*, 26–28.

[15] The phrase quoted is from Robert P. Falk, "The Literary Criticism of the Genteel Decades: 1870–1900," in Floyd Stovall, ed., *The Development of American Literary Criticism*, 141 (Chapel Hill, North Carolina, 1955). See also Charles C. Walcutt, *American Literary Naturalism: A Divided Stream*, 309 (Minneapolis, 1956).

[16] *The Confident Years: 1885–1915*, 78 (New York, 1952); *The American Mind*, 63 (New Haven, 1950); *The Critical Period in American Literature*, 66, 86, 153 (Chapel Hill, North Carolina, 1951); *The Beginnings of Naturalism in American Fiction, 1891–1903*, 42 (Uppsala, Sweden, 1950).

Hjalmar Hjorth Boyesen

"The Great Realists and the Empty Story-Tellers" was included in a collection of critical pieces on the novel, the first reprinting of a Boyesen article or story in more than sixty years. In the last dozen years, Boyesen's correspondence with G. W. Cable, Georg Brandes, and W. D. Howells (this only in brief) has appeared in print. Marc Ratner's work on Boyesen's ideas and opinions is as yet unpublished; two other scholars, one in the United States and the other in Norway, have projected studies of his career.[17]

A biography of Boyesen should have been written thirty-five years ago; then letters, now presumably lost, might have been recovered and used, and members of his immediate family and his close associates could have answered questions that now are a matter of conjecture. The present study of Boyesen has been put together from letters that survive, from references to him in contemporary periodicals, and from his own writings. There are regrettable omissions as well as unanswered questions, but a recognizable and convincing person nevertheless emerges from the sources.

[17] Boyesen's article was reprinted in Eugene Current-García and Walton R. Patrick, ed., *Realism and Romanticism in Fiction: An Approach to the Novel*, 161–169 (Chicago, 1962).

BIBLIOGRAPHY AND INDEX

A Selected Bibliography

I. BOYESEN'S PUBLISHED WORKS

A. Novels and Novelettes

Gunnar: A Tale of Norse Life. Boston, 1874. Reprinted, New York, 1880. Serialized in *Atlantic Monthly*, July–December, 1873.

A Norseman's Pilgrimage. New York, 1875. Serialized in *Galaxy*, December, 1874–May, 1875.

Falconberg. New York, 1879. Serialized in *Scribner's Monthly*, August–October, 1878.

A Daughter of the Philistines. Boston, 1883.

"A Problematic Character," in *Century*, August–October, 1884.

The Light of Her Countenance. New York, 1889. Adapted from "The Old Adam," published anonymously in *Lippincott's Magazine*, May, 1888.

"A Candidate for Divorce," in *Cosmopolitan*, March, 1890.

The Golden Calf. Meadville, Pennsylvania, 1892. The first half appeared in *Chautauquan*, July, 1890.

The Mammon of Unrighteousness. New York, 1891.

"The Elixir of Pain," in *Cosmopolitan*, May–June, 1891.

Social Strugglers. New York, 1893. Serialized in *Cosmopolitan*, September–November, 1892.

"A Harvest of Tares," in *Godey's Magazine*, May, 1893.

B. Short Stories

"The Norse Emigrant," in *Galaxy*, February, 1873.

"The Story of an Outcast," in *Scribner's Monthly*, November, 1874.

"Asathor's Vengeance," in *Atlantic Monthly*, March, 1875.

"Truls, the Nameless," in *Scribner's Monthly*, April, 1875.

"A Good-for-Nothing," in *Scribner's Monthly*, July, 1875.

"A Scientific Vagabond," in *Scribner's Monthly*, December, 1875.

"The Man Who Lost His Name," in *Scribner's Monthly*, October, 1876.

Hjalmar Hjorth Boyesen

Tales from Two Hemispheres. Boston, 1876. A collection of previously published stories.
"How Mr. Storm Met His Destiny," in *Scribner's Monthly*, February, 1877.
"Swart among the Buckeyes," in *Scribner's Monthly*, August, 1877.
"Annunciata," in *Scribner's Monthly*, October, 1879.
"Ilka on the Hill-Top," in *Scribner's Monthly*, November, 1879. *Alpine Roses*, a play based on this story, was first performed January 31, 1884, at Madison Square Theatre, New York City. It was privately printed in New York (undated) "for the exclusive use and control of Mr. M. H. Mallory," as *Alpine Roses: A Comedy in Four Acts.* Copies are in the Tulane University Library and the archives of the Norwegian-American Historical Association.
"A Knight of Dannebrog," in *Scribner's Monthly*, February, 1880.
"Under the Glacier," in *Scribner's Monthly*, December, 1880.
Ilka on the Hill-Top and Other Stories. New York, 1881. A collection of previously published stories.
"A Dangerous Virtue," in *Scribner's Monthly*, March, 1881.
Queen Titania. New York, 1881. The novelette, "Queen Titania," plus two short stories.
"A Highly Respectable Family," in *Harper's New Monthly Magazine*, March, 1882.
"Anastasia," in *Century*, April, 1883.
"The Horns of the Dilemma," in *Continent*, September 26, 1883.
"A Vicarious Poet," in *Independent*, September 11, 1884.
"A Daring Fiction," in *New York Commercial Advertiser*, November, 1884. Reprinted in *Stories by American Authors*, vol. 10. New York, 1885.
"Mr. Block's One Glorious Night," in *Harper's Weekly*, March 7, 1885.
"In the Wrong Niche," in *Harper's Weekly*, May 23, 1885.
"A Child of the Age," in *Century*, December, 1885.
"The Story of a Blue Vein," in *Cosmopolitan*, March, 1886.
"Crooked John," in *Century*, July, 1887.
"A Perilous Incognito," in *Scribner's Magazine*, July–August, 1887.
"Charity," in *Scribner's Magazine*, October, 1888.
Vagabond Tales. Boston, 1889. A collection of short stories, some previously published.
"The Two Mollies: A City Sketch," in *Scribner's Magazine*, July, 1889.
"A Pagan Incantation," in *Scribner's Magazine*, August, 1889.
"A Platonic Affair," in *Harper's New Monthly Magazine*, February, 1890.
"A Norse Atlantis," in *Cosmopolitan*, November, 1890.
"Zee-Wee: A Story of the Indian Agencies," in *Overland Monthly*, September, 1894.
"The Nixy's Chord," in *Cosmopolitan*, September–October, 1895.
"A Mother in Israel," in *Harper's New Monthly Magazine*, February, 1896.
"In Collusion with Fate," in *Scribner's Magazine*, July, 1896.

C. Juvenile Fiction

"The Runaway's Thanksgiving," in *Independent*, November 27, 1884.
The Modern Vikings: Stories of Life and Sport in the Norseland. New York, 1887.
"Life for Life," in *Lippincott's Magazine*, August, 1887.
Against Heavy Odds: A Tale of Norse Heroism. New York, 1890. *Against Heavy Odds and A Fearless Trio.* New York, 1894.

Bibliography

"The Little Chap," in *Harper's Weekly*, January 31, 1891.
"Lady Clare: The Story of a Horse," in *Cosmopolitan*, October, 1891.
Boyhood in Norway: Stories of Boy-Life in the Land of the Midnight Sun. New York, 1892.
Norseland Tales. New York, 1894.
[Many stories in the collections were first published in *St. Nicholas, Youth's Companion, Harper's Young People,* and perhaps other magazines of the same type.]

D. Poetry

Idyls of Norway and Other Poems. New York, 1882.
In *Atlantic Monthly*: "A Norse Stev," February, 1872; "Thoralf and Synnøv," October, 1872; "The Bride of Torrisdell," February, 1873; "St. Olaf's Fountain," April, 1873; "The Ravens of Odin," June, 1874; "Evolution," May, 1878; "Juno Ludovisi," July, 1879; "If I Should Lose Thee," February, 1880.
In *Century*: "The Fisher-Maiden's Song," February, 1896.
In *Chautauquan*: "The Poet's Vocation," January, 1889; "Nirvana the Blest," November, 1889; "The Church Bells," September, 1893.
In *Cosmopolitan*: "The Parley of the Kings," July, 1893.
In *Critic*: "To James Russell Lowell, on His Seventieth Birthday," February 23, 1889.
In *Galaxy*: "Norway," February, 1873; "Necken," May, 1874; "Birting the Strong," January, 1876.
In *Harper's New Monthly Magazine*: "Marit and I: A Norse Idyl," September, 1882.
In *Independent*: "Ode," May 31, 1883; "The Unknown God," March 8, 1888; "Canst Thou Hear Me?" October 25, 1888.
In *Lippincott's Magazine*: "The Glaciers of Paradise," April, 1873; "Two Sonnets," November, 1881; "The Lapp Maiden's Song," November, 1893.
In *New York Daily Tribune*: "The Brother-Feud," May 11, 1877.
In *Our Continent*: "Thora," October 18, 1882.
In *Outlook*: "The Midnight Sun," July 13, 1895.
In *Scribner's Monthly*: "Awake," November, 1875; "Hilda's Little Hood," January, 1876; "Elegy on A.G.L.," March, 1877; "Jarl Sigurd's Christmas Eve," January, 1878; "Little Sigrid: A Ballad," February, 1878; "Four Sonnets," March, 1878; "Calpurnia," May, 1881.

E. Literary Criticism, Articles on European Writers, and Translations

BOOKS:

Goethe and Schiller: Their Lives and Works, Including a Commentary on Goethe's Faust. New York, 1879.
Syllabus of Lectures on "English Poets." Philadelphia, 1890.
Syllabus of Lectures on the Old Norse Saga Literature. Philadelphia, 1891.
Essays on German Literature. New York, 1892.
Ten Lectures on German Literature. Albany, 1892-93. [A syllabus.]
Medieval German Literature. Albany, 1893. [A syllabus.]
A Commentary on the Writings of Henrik Ibsen. New York, 1894.
Literary and Social Silhouettes. New York, 1894.
Essays on Scandinavian Literature. New York, 1895.

Hjalmar Hjorth Boyesen

ESSAYS AND TRANSLATIONS:

"Kristofer Janson and the Reform of the Norwegian Language," in *North American Review*, October, 1872.
"Bjørnstjerne Bjørnson as a Dramatist," in *North American Review*, January, 1873.
"A Visit to Tourguéneff," in *Galaxy*, April, 1874.
"Social Aspects of the German Romantic School," in *Atlantic Monthly*, July, 1875.
"Novalis and the Blue Flower," in *Atlantic Monthly*, December, 1875.
"Literary Aspects of the Romantic School," in *Atlantic Monthly*, May, 1876.
"Two Norse Sagas," in *International Review*, March, 1877.
"Ivan Tourguéneff," in *Scribner's Monthly*, June, 1877.
Translation, Ivan Tourguéneff's "A Nobleman of the Steppes," in *Scribner's Monthly*, July, 1877.
"Reminiscences of Bayard Taylor," in *Lippincott's Magazine*, August, 1879.
"Two Visits to Victor Hugo," in *Scribner's Monthly*, December, 1879.
"Bjørnstjerne Bjørnson," in *Scribner's Monthly*, July, 1880.
"Tourguéneff and the Nihilists," in *Critic*, March 26, 1881.
"A New Norwegian Novelist," in *Critic*, June 17, 1882.
"The Life of Schiller," in *Schiller's Works*, 4:345–363 (Philadelphia, 1883).
"Ivan Tourguéneff," in *Critic*, September 22, 1883.
"Reminiscences of Tourguéneff," in *Harper's Weekly*, September 29, 1883.
"The Modern German Novel," in *Princeton Review*, March, 1884.
"Hans Christian Andersen," in *Dial*, November, 1884.
"The Life of Goethe," in *Goethe's Works*, 1:v–xxiv (Philadelphia, 1885).
"The French Academy," in *Independent*, January 1, 1885.
"Social Problems in Norwegian Novels," in *Critic*, September 19, 1885.
Translation, Jonas Lie's "John Sunde," in *New Princeton Review*, March, 1886.
"Why We Have No Great Novelists," in *Forum*, February, 1887.
"The New School in Norwegian Literature," in *Critic*, March 7, 1887.
"The New Literature of Norway and Denmark," in *New Princeton Review*, May, 1887.
"Scandinavian Literature," in *Chautauquan*, February–March, 1888.
Translation, "Complications," from a poem by Henrik Ibsen, in *Independent*, April 5, 1888.
"Mars vs. Apollo," in *Chautauquan*, July, 1888.
"Philistinism," in *Independent*, September 27, 1888.
"The Romantic and the Realistic Novel," in *Chautauquan*, November, 1888.
"The Ethics of Robert Browning," in *Independent*, December 13, 1888.
"The Hero in Fiction," in *North American Review*, May, 1889.
"Henrik Ibsen," in *Century*, March, 1890.
"Henrik Ibsen's Greatest Work," in *Chautauquan*, November, 1890.
"Mr. Howells and His Work," in *Cosmopolitan*, February, 1892.
"An Acquaintance with Hans Christian Andersen," in *Century*, March, 1892.
"Ibsen's 'Comedy of Love,'" in *Dial*, March 1, 1893.
"Henrik Ibsen's Poems," in *Cosmopolitan*, May, 1893.
"American Literary Criticism and Its Value," in *Forum*, June, 1893.
"Ibsen's Peer Gynt," in *Chautauquan*, June, 1893.
"Real Conversations. I., A Dialogue between William Dean Howells and Hjalmar Hjorth Boyesen," in *McClure's Magazine*, June, 1893.
"Ten Books to Be Read," in *Outlook*, July 15, 1893.

Bibliography

"Conversations with Bjørnstjerne Bjørnson," in *Cosmopolitan*, August, 1893.
"Lappish Fairy Tales, Truly Retold by Hjalmar Hjorth Boyesen," in *Outlook*, August 26, 1893.
"Ibsen's Treatment of Self-Illusion," in *Dial*, September 16, 1893.
"Writing My First Book," in *Philadelphia Inquirer*, October 1, 1893. A syndicated article that also appeared as "Boyesen's First Book," in *Indianapolis News*, September 30, 1893.
"A Doll-Home," in *Cosmopolitan*, November, 1893.
"The Saga of Eric the Red," in *Cosmopolitan*, February, 1894.
"The Mother of Ivan Tourguéneff," in *Century*, June, 1894.
"The Evolution of the Heroine," in *Lippincott's Magazine*, September, 1894.
"A Survey of the Year's Fiction," in *Illustrated American*, January 5, 1895.
"The Great Realists and the Empty Story-Tellers," in *Forum*, February, 1895. Reprinted in Eugene Current-García and Walton R. Patrick, *Realism and Romanticism in Fiction*, Chicago, 1962.
"German and Scandinavian Literature in 1894," in *Bookman*, February–March, 1895.
"The Drama of Revolt," in *Bookman*, July, 1895.
"Novels of Romance and Stories of Real Life," in *Cosmopolitan*, October, 1895.
"The Plague of Jocularity," in *North American Review*, November, 1895.

F. History and Social Comment

"Norway and the Norsemen," in *Scribner's Monthly*, January, 1877.
Boyesen's role at Urbana, in *New York Daily Tribune*, June 25, 1878.
"The University of Berlin," in *Scribner's Monthly*, June, 1879.
"The University of Rome," in *Scribner's Monthly*, September, 1879.
"George Sand's Lavinia and Owen Meredith's Lucile," in *Atlantic Monthly*, January, 1881. [An unsigned item in "Contributor's Club."]
"Bjørnson in the United States," in *Critic*, March 12, 1881. [A letter to the editor.]
"Kristofer Janson and the Norse Lutheran Synod," in *Critic*, January 14, 1882. [A letter to the editor.]
"The Flags of Sweden and Norway," in *Nation*, November 2, 1882. [Unsigned.]
"Cash Down or a Percentage?" in *Critic*, February 9, 1884.
"Janus-faced Candidates," in *Independent*, October 2, 1884.
"The Dangers of Immigration," in *Independent*, November 6, 1884.
The Story of Norway. New York, 1886. Reprinted, with a new chapter on the recent history of Norway by C. F. Keary, under the title *A History of Norway from the Earliest Times.* New York and London, 1900.
"Authors' Statements on International Copyright," in *Century*, February, 1886.
"The Dangers of Unrestricted Immigration," in *Forum*, July, 1887.
"Norwegian Politics," in *Nation*, September 1, 1887. [Unsigned.]
"Immigration," in *National Perils and Opportunities.* New York, 1888. [An address.]
"The Hope of the Nations," in *Independent*, January 19, 1888.
"A Defense of the Eighth Commandment," in *Cosmopolitan*, February, 1888.
"On the Writing of Novels," in *Critic*, March 24, 1888.
"The Victims of Progress," in *Independent*, May 17, 1888.
"What Shall the Public Schools Teach?" in *Forum*, September, 1888.
"The Problem of Happiness," in *Independent*, November 15, 1888.
"The Modern Migration of Nations," in *Chautauquan*, February, 1889.

Hjalmar Hjorth Boyesen

"New Reasons for Restricting Immigration," in *Our Day*, February, 1889. [Identified as an address by Boyesen.]
"Cornell University," in *Cosmopolitan*, November, 1889.
"Types of American Women," in *Forum*, November, 1889.
How to Choose a School. New York, 1890. [A Teachers College education leaflet.]
"Columbia College," in *Cosmopolitan*, January, 1890.
"How Can Criminals and Paupers Be Best Eliminated from among Proposed Emigrants to the United States?" in *Our Day*, July, 1890.
"German Student Life," in *Cosmopolitan*, January, 1891.
"Where Should a College Be Located? A Symposium," in *Chautauquan*, July, 1891.
"Two Visits to the Lapps," in *Cosmopolitan*, May, 1892.
"The Emigrant's Unhappy Predicament," in *Chautauquan*, August, 1892.
"The Scandinavian in the United States," in *North American Review*, November, 1892.
"Norwegian Painters," in *Scribner's Magazine*, December, 1892.
"Saunterings in Norway," in *Godey's Magazine*, March, 1893.
"The University of Chicago," in *Cosmopolitan*, April, 1893.
"Norway's Political Crisis," in *North American Review*, July, 1893.
"Village Life in Norway," in *Chautauquan*, October, 1893.
"A New World Fable," in *Cosmopolitan*, December, 1893.
"The Voyage of 'The Viking,'" in *Chautauquan*, January, 1894.
"Norwegian Hospitality," in *Lippincott's Magazine*, February, 1894.
"The Fjords of Norway," in *Cosmopolitan*, June, 1894.
"The Matrimonial Puzzle," in *North American Review*, February, 1895.
"The Crisis in Norway," in *Harper's Weekly*, February 23, 1895.
"A Youthful Reminiscence," in *Lippincott's Magazine*, March, 1895.
"Norway's Struggle for Independence," in *Harper's Weekly*, April 27, 1895.
"The Chautauquan Movement," in *Cosmopolitan*, June, 1895.
"The New Womanhood," in *Lippincott's Magazine*, July, 1895.
"The Scandinavian Wife," in *North American Review*, October, 1895.
"Woman's Position in Pagan Times," in *Forum*, November, 1895.
"Scandinavian Customs and Character," in *Monthly Illustrator and Town and Country*, May, 1896.
"My Rural Experiences," in *Lippincott's Magazine*, July, 1896.
"Another Day in Norway," in *Century*, August, 1897.
"A Glacier Excursion in Norway," in *Cosmopolitan*, October, 1897.

G. Reviews

In *Atlantic Monthly*: October, 1871, September, 1874, September, October, 1875, April, 1877, February, 1881.
In *Cosmopolitan*: July, August, September, October, 1893, January, May, July, August, December, 1894, January, February, March, April, May, June, August, September, November, 1895.
In *Nation*: September 2, 1875, January 4, 1877, February 12, May 6, October 28, 1880, January 13, March 31, 1881.
In *North American Review*: October, 1874, January, April, 1875.
In *Scribner's Monthly*: November, 1880.
[Some of these reviews were unsigned.]

Bibliography

II. SECONDARY SOURCES

A. Contemporary Discussions of Boyesen

Frank E. Heath, "Hjalmar Hjorth Boyesen," in *Scribner's Monthly*, October, 1877.

Frank Sewall, "Mr. Boyesen and Urbana University," in *New York Daily Tribune*, July 1, 1878.

Erik L. Petersen, in *Budstikken* (Minneapolis), December 21, 28, 1880. [Evaluations of Boyesen and his work by a Norwegian-American critic.]

Ole O. Lien, in *Budstikken*, February 1, 1881. [Reply to Petersen.]

Boston Evening Transcript, February 20, 21, 24, 28, March 3, 7, 1882. [Notices and reviews of Boyesen's lectures on the Norse sagas at Lowell Institute.]

"H.H.B.," in *Book Buyer*, October, 1886. [A biographical sketch, largely in Boyesen's own words.]

"The Lounger," in *Critic*, October 23, 1886.

"The Lounger," in *Critic*, June 11, 1887.

"Busy Day at Chautauqua: Prof. Boyesen's Popularity," in *New York Daily News*, July 25, 1889.

"Professor Boyesen on Realism," in *New York Daily Tribune*, July 29, 1889.

Edward Bok, "Personal Gossip about Writers," in *Author*, March 15, 1891.

"Mental Photograph: H. H. Boyesen," in *Book Buyer*, February, 1893.

Brander Matthews, "Literature at Columbia College," in *Dial*, April 1, 1893.

"An International Boswell," in *Critic*, August 19, 1893.

Arthur Stedman, "Boyesen's Boyhood," in *Detroit Sunday News-Tribune*, April 8, 1894.

"A Norwegian American," in *Munsey's Magazine*, August, 1894.

John D. Barry, "A Talk with Professor Boyesen," in *New York Illustrated American*, February 9, 1895.

Critic, February 9, 1895. [An editorial reply to Boyesen's "The Great Realists and the Empty Story-Tellers," in *Forum*, February, 1895.]

Andrew Lang, "At the Sign of the Ship," in *Longman's Magazine*, April, 1895. [Reprinted in *Critic*, May 25, 1895; an answer to Boyesen's "The Great Realists and the Empty Story-Tellers."]

George Merriam Hyde, "The Allotropy of Realism," in *Dial*, April 16, 1895. [An answer to Boyesen's "The Great Realists and the Empty Story-Tellers."]

"Authors on the Wheel," in *Critic*, October 12, 1895.

Theodore Stanton, "Professor Boyesen at Cornell University," in *Open Court*, February 13, 1896.

Daniel Kilham Dodge, "Hjalmar Hjorth Boyesen, the Teacher," in *Bachelor of Arts*, May, 1896.

Benjamin W. Wells, "Hjalmar Hjorth Boyesen," in *Sewanee* (Tennessee) *Review*, May, 1896.

"Making a Magazine," in *Cosmopolitan*, September, 1897.

William Dean Howells, *Literary Friends and Acquaintance*. New York, 1900.

Michael A. Mikkelsen, "Norsk-amerikanske forfattere: Hjalmar Hjorth Boyesen," in *Symra*, 2:60–76 (Decorah, Iowa, 1906).

For obituaries, see *Critic*, October 12, 26, December 14, 1895; *Dial*, October 16, December 1, 1895; *Harper's Weekly*, October 19, 1895; *Columbia Spectator*, October 7, 23, 1895; *Review of Reviews*, November, 1895; *Century*, December, 1895; *Munsey's Magazine*, December, 1895.

Hjalmar Hjorth Boyesen

For reviews of Boyesen's books, see, for example, *Critic, Atlantic Monthly, Nation, Dial*, for the years 1874–95.

B. Recent Studies of Boyesen

Ernest H. Wright, "Hjalmar Hjorth Boyesen," in *Dictionary of American Biography*, 2:530–532.

Aagot D. Hoidahl, "Norwegian-American Fiction, 1880–1928," in Norwegian-American Historical Association, *Studies and Records*, 1930.

Laurence M. Larson, "Hjalmar Hjorth Boyesen," in *The Changing West and Other Essays*. Northfield, 1937.

George Leroy White, Jr., *Scandinavian Themes in American Fiction*. Philadelphia, 1937.

George Leroy White, Jr., "H. H. Boyesen: A Note on Immigration," in *American Literature*, January, 1942.

Thomas Houghton, "Hjalmar Hjorth Boyesen: A Critical Biography." An unpublished master's thesis submitted at Columbia University in 1947. A copy is in the Columbia University Library.

Arlin Turner, "A Novelist Discovers a Novelist: The Correspondence of H. H. Boyesen and George W. Cable," in *Western Humanities Review*, Autumn, 1951.

Gerald H. Thorson, "First Sagas in a New World: A Study of the Beginnings of Norwegian-American Literature," in *Norwegian-American Studies and Records*, 1952.

Clarence A. Glasrud, "Hjalmar Hjorth Boyesen: A Critical Biography." An unpublished doctoral dissertation submitted at Harvard University in 1952. A copy is in the Widener Library.

Clarence A. Glasrud, "Boyesen and the Norwegian Immigration," in *Norwegian-American Studies and Records*, 1956.

Marc Ratner, "Hjalmar Hjorth Boyesen: Critic of Literature and Society." An unpublished doctoral dissertation submitted at New York University in 1959. A copy is in the library of New York University.

Marc Ratner, "Georg Brandes and Hjalmar Hjorth Boyesen," in *Scandinavian Studies*, November, 1961.

Marc Ratner, "Howells and Boyesen: Two Views of Realism," in *New England Quarterly*, September, 1962.

III. MANUSCRIPT SOURCES

Hjalmar Hjorth Boyesen's letters are filed as follows:

To Rasmus B. Anderson, Anderson Papers, State Historical Society of Wisconsin, Madison.

To George W. Cable, Cable Collection, Howard-Tilton Memorial Library, Tulane University, New Orleans.

To Willard Fiske, Fiske Collection, Cornell University Library, Ithaca.

To William Dean Howells, Howells Collection, Houghton Library, Harvard University, Cambridge.

To Horace Scudder, Houghton Library.

To Georg Brandes, Brandes Archives, Royal Danish Library, Copenhagen.

To Seth Low, Columbiana Collection, Low Memorial Library, Columbia University. Other letters and some Boyesen lecture notes are in this collection.

Hjalmar Hjorth Boyesen

Austa Boyesen's letters to Laurence M. Larson are in the Larson Collection, University of Illinois Library, Urbana. Austa Boyesen received some information from Thor H. Schoyen in a letter of October 30, 1936. Her papers are in the possession of a niece, Mrs. Louise F. Tompkins of Arbor Place, Mukwonago, Wisconsin.

An extensive collection of Boyesen material is in the possession of Hjalmar Hjorth Boyesen III, grandson of the novelist. It includes clippings, lecture notes, naturalization papers, personal notes, and memoranda, besides sixty letters from William Dean Howells, and letters from George W. Cable, Richard W. Gilder, Mark Twain, Henry Wadsworth Longfellow, Henry Adams, Alexander Kielland, Georg Brandes, Friedrich Spielhagen, and many others. Microfilm copies were made of these papers by the Columbia University Libraries. The originals are not now generally available, but the author has microfilms of the whole collection. Hjalmar Hjorth Boyesen III now lives in Leicester, England.

The archives of the Norwegian-American Historical Association at St. Olaf College, Northfield, Minnesota, have a collection of bound and unbound magazines and periodicals containing stories by Boyesen and articles by and about him. It also has copies of several poems in Boyesen's handwriting and a photostatic reproduction of his privately printed play, *Alpine Roses: A Comedy in Four Acts*.

Index

For a list of Boyesen's works, see the bibliography, pages 229–237.

Aasen, Ivar, 78
Abbott, Ezra, 24
Abolitionists, 21, 86
Adams, Henry, 156
Against Heavy Odds, juvenile novel, 13
Åhnebrink, Lars, 225
Alden, Henry M., 117, 124, 125n, 164
Aldrich, Thomas B., 37, 52n, 102, 104, 117, 214
Alpine Roses, play, 105, 129n
"America fever," 14, 64, 65
America letters, 13, 14
American (Philadelphia), 96
American Copyright League, 117
American Humane Society (Boston), 195
Americanization, of Boyesen and other Scandinavians, 3, 20n, 21, 26, 38, 54, 56, 58, 59, 62, 64, 66, 68, 72, 73, 90, 120, 121, 144, 145, 173, 203
Andersen, Hans C., 30, 32, 41, 55, 78, 154, 211
Anderson, Otto, 94
Anderson, Rasmus B., 57, 58, 80
Anti-Slavery League, 22n
Appleton, Thomas G., 32
Arnold, Matthew, 113
Atlantic Monthly, 25n, 26, 28, 28n, 31n, 81, 95, 102, 104, 117
Auerbach, Berthold, 51n, 153
Author, 125
Authors' Club, 221; program, 116–119, 120n

Baird, H. M., 116
Balestier, Charles W., 165
Balestrand (Norway), 169
Balzac, Honoré de, 208, 215
Barnard, F.A.P., 98
Barnes, A.S., 80
Bay View (Mich.), Chautauqua lectures, 163, 179
Beder, Sophus, publisher, 21n
Bellamy, Edward, 102n
Bergsøe, Vilhelm, 32, 33n
Berlin (Germany), 204; university, 88, 100
Bjarnason, Jon, 80
Bjørnson, Bjørnstjerne, 108, 142, 225; friendship with Boyesen, 30, 31, 34, 40, 41, 165, 169, 198, 211, 221; visit to United States, 32n, 109, 209; influence on Boyesen's writings, 55, 56, 58, 60, 78n, 81, 89, 154, 219; writings, 80, 82, 111, 155, 157, 208, 209
Boe (Gudbrandsdal, Norway), Bjørnson estate, 31, 32n, 169
Bok, Edward, 125, 126n
Bors, Christian, 106, 107
Bowles, Samuel, 38n
Boyesen, Alf, 22, 43, 111, 219
Boyesen, Algernon, 96, 98, 107, 166, 179, 181, 219
Boyesen, Austa, 5n, 44n, 167, 171n, 179, 182, 202
Boyesen, Bayard, 97, 98, 107, 111, 166, 179, 181, 219

238

Index

Boyesen, Hjalmar Hjorth, birth, 5; background and boyhood, 3–19; use of English, 3, 22, 46, 56, 90, 99, 106, 151; ambitions, 3, 4, 6, 8, 16, 17–19, 21, 22, 23, 27, 34, 36, 46, 53, 55, 87, 113, 126, 218; name, 3, 12, 113; travels in America, 6, 19, 20, 76, 113, 163, 179; education, 11, 12, 19, 21, 22, 41, 88; class consciousness, 11, 67, 70, 75, 111, 138, 145; trips to Europe, 12n, 30–35, 47, 50–52, 86, 165, 166–170; linguist, 12n, 23, 34, 87, 99, 113, 116, 221; in Urbana (Ohio), 21, 22, 26–30, 55, 69, 71n, 185n, 221; editor, 21, 120, 175; attitude toward immigrants and immigration, 21, 58, 64–66, 67, 72–76, 111, 120, 121, 130, 145, 152, 160, 170, 174, 193, 194, 196, 202, 203; appearance, 25, 49, 116, 125, 181; finances, 29, 38n, 43, 44, 45, 47, 52, 53, 55, 93, 94, 95, 97, 101, 103, 104, 106, 118, 125, 126, 135, 149, 154, 174, 176, 182, 218, 219, 220; German scholar, 30, 33, 34, 38, 41, 44, 46, 77, 81, 82–85, 91, 98, 99, 100, 101, 153, 163, 168, 175, 176, 196, 203–206, 208, 221; at Cornell University, 36–53, 95, 96, 97, 100, 182, 218, 221; lecturer, 42, 95, 99, 100, 101, 115, 116, 154, 163, 177, 191; health, 44, 47, 48, 181, 182; characterized, 46, 87, 179; marriage, 48, 49; attitude toward religion, 73, 109, 110, 114; political attitudes, 73–75, 76, 119, 120, 121, 147, 148, 153, 190, 191; moves to New York City, 95; at Columbia College, 95n, 97, 98, 100, 101, 111, 114, 115, 116, 125, 154, 160, 163, 179, 181n, 182, 220, 221; summer residences, 111, 112, 114, 125, 164, 174, 179, 180, 182, 192, 221; clubs, 116–119, 120, 135, 154, 221; censured, 120, 173; death, 180

WRITINGS: autobiographical, 3, 7, 8, 9, 10, 16, 17, 18, 20, 21, 23, 24, 29, 37, 39, 59–63; influence of Norway, 3, 11, 12, 13, 14, 15, 54–69, 72–76, 77–82, 89, 95, 96, 105, 107, 111, 120, 122, 130–132, 136, 142, 143–146, 150–152, 154, 161, 164, 168–170, 173, 193, 194, 196, 202, 208, 209; fiction, 8, 11, 13, 14, 15, 18, 23, 24, 26, 27, 28, 36, 37, 38, 41, 47, 54–76, 90, 93, 94, 96, 101–104, 108, 114, 120, 124, 127–149, 162, 165, 171–174, 184–191, 192–194, 195; juvenile fiction, 11, 101, 107, 124, 126, 146, 174, 194; verse, 16, 17, 18, 26, 27, 28, 38, 49, 79, 93, 95, 96, 101, 102, 107, 111, 150–152; reviews, 26, 38, 40, 77, 78, 79, 81, 82, 89, 97, 154; literary criticism, 28, 38, 50, 77–92, 108, 111, 123, 124, 152–161, 175, 176, 177, 191, 196, 203–208, 211–216; essays, 36, 38, 41, 77, 81, 83, 84, 89, 96, 155, 168–170, 174, 176, 177, 182, 202; output, 38, 126, 171, 173, 174, 176, 184, 219; use of American settings, 41, 64, 66, 67–76, 103, 129, 135, 137, 143, 171–174, 184, 185, 191, 192, 194, 195; criticisms of, 54, 56–59, 62, 63, 72, 75, 85, 87, 94, 96n, 103, 106, 129, 132, 135, 144, 146, 150–152, 165, 166, 170, 171–174, 175n, 176, 178, 187, 194, 204, 208, 210, 212, 220, 222–225; use of Continental settings, 60, 102, 103, 105, 127, 135, 137, 140, 141, 193; literary liaison man, 62, 77–92, 111, 208; social criticism, 87, 88, 109, 120–123, 124, 144, 152, 155, 160, 174, 178, 189, 196–203, 223; translated, 93, 94; play, 101, 104, 105, 111, 129; history of Norway, 101, 105–107, 126; modern interpretations, 217–226; bibliography, 229–237. *See also* individual published titles

Boyesen, Mrs. Hjalmar Hjorth (Elizabeth Keen—"Lillie"), 119, 135, 151; described, 48, 50, 179, 202; marriage, 49; wedding trip, 50–52; health, 52, 53, 93, 96, 97, 98, 149, 164; social circle, 53, 185, 221; tastes, 95, 97, 117, 125, 149, 174, 175n, 219

Boyesen, Hjalmar Hjorth, Jr., 52, 93n, 98, 107, 164, 166, 179, 181, 219

Boyesen, Ingolf, 19, 20, 21, 22, 43, 111, 164, 165n, 219

Boyesen, Peter, 5

Boyesen, Mrs. Peter (Helga Tullberg), 5

Boyesen, Capt. Sarolf, 17, 43; influence on Hjalmar Boyesen, 4, 5, 14, 20, 64n, 142n; family, 5, 6, 7, 44, 47n, 220; attitudes, 7, 8, 18, 21, 22, 73; death, 7n

Boyesen, Mrs. Sarolf Fredrik (Helga Helene Tveten), 5, 6, 7, 44

Boyesen, Mrs. Sarolf Fredrik (the second), 7, 44

Boyhood in Norway: Stories of Boy-Life in the Land of the Midnight Sun, 194

Brandes, Georg, 169, 211; correspondence with Boyesen, 219, 220, 221, 226

Brentano, Clemens, 84

Brion, Frederica, 206

Brooks, Noah, 116

Brooks, Van Wyck, 225
Brown, Charles B., 213
Browning, Robert, 115, 123, 159
Budstikken (Minneapolis), 109
Bull, Ole, 31, 32n, 136
Bull, Mrs. Ole, 109
Bunner, Henry C., 102n, 214
Burnett, Frances H., 104, 129
Burroughs, John, 117
Butler, Nicholas M., 181n

Cable, George W., 104; sketch, 7n; friendship with Boyesen, 39, 40, 44, 45, 47, 49, 50, 61, 69, 72, 91, 112, 137n, 219, 226
Caen, Just M., publisher, 21n
Cammermeyer, Alb., Christiania publisher, 94
Carlyle, Thomas, 79, 204
Carpenter, W. H., 100, 181
Castle Garden, 72, 122
Catholic Church, 200
Century, 39n, 103
Charles Scribner's Sons, *see* Scribner's
Chautauqua lectures, New York State, 116, 161, 162, 163, 164, 177, 191, 214; Bay View (Mich.), 163, 179
Chautauqua-Century Press, 191, 192
Child, Francis James, 24, 25
Christie, Hartvig C., 12
Churchill, Winston, 224
Civil service reform, 135
Clarke, James F., 109n
Clemens, Samuel, 51, 52, 117, 119n, 125, 214
Clemens, Mrs. Samuel, 52
Cleveland, Grover, 120, 154n
Collins, Wilkie, 215
Columbia College, 108, 123; Boyesen at, 95n, 97, 98, 100, 101, 111, 114, 115, 116, 125, 154, 160, 163, 179, 181n, 182, 220, 221
Columbia University, 97n, 181
Commager, Henry S., 225
Commentary on the Writings of Henrik Ibsen, 176, 206, 211
Congress, 118, 119
Cooper, James F., 213
Copyright laws, 93, 117–119, 152
Cornell, Ezra, 41, 185
Cornell University, 108, 128, 185; Boyesen at, 29n, 30, 33, 36, 37, 40, 45, 47, 50, 52, 95, 96, 97, 100, 182, 218, 221; students, 41; described, 42

Corson, Hiram, 43
Cosmopolitan, 102, 164, 166n, 175
Crane, Stephen, 132, 220, 223
Crane, Thomas F., 43
Crawford, F. Marion, 156, 184n
Critic, 94, 104, 113, 124, 180, 191
Critics, treatment of Boyesen: American, 54, 56–59, 62, 63, 72, 75, 85, 87, 94, 96n, 103, 106, 129, 132, 135, 144, 146, 150–152, 165, 166, 170, 171–174, 176, 178, 187, 194, 204, 208, 210, 212, 220, 222–225; English, 175n, 176, 178, 220
Crockett, S. R., 163, 215
Curtis, G. W., 117, 154

Danish immigrants, 30
Danish language, 78n, 94, 99
Darwin, Charles, 41, 134, 154, 159, 218, 219, 224
Dasent, G. W., 80
Daudet, Alphonse, 51, 52n, 87, 157, 213, 214
Daughter of the Philistines, novel, 103, 104, 132–135, 192
DeForest, John W., 102n, 156
DeGoncourt, Edmond, 51, 52n
DeGoncourt, Jules, 51, 52n
DeKay, Charles, 116
Democratic party, 73, 74, 76, 120, 147
Denmark, literature, 154, 210
Dickens, Charles, 200, 215, 216
Dickinson, Mrs. Lydia, 28n
Dølen (Christiania), 78n
Doyle, A. Conan, 215
Drama, Norway, 80, 81, 111, 176, 189, 206–208, 224; United States, 104, 105, 119n, 129n; France, 208; Germany, 208
Drammen Latin School, 11, 12
Dumas, Alexandre, 214
DuMaurier, George, 214
Dyer, Dr. Charles Volney, 22

Ebers, Georg, 153
Education, Boyesen's interest, 23, 41, 43, 88, 108, 122, 152, 168, 187, 188, 189, 197, 199, 200, 201, 210, 221
Eggleston, Edward, 116, 117, 156
Elder or Poetic Edda, 33n
Eliot, Charles W., 45, 46, 123
Eliot, George, 80, 82, 200, 213, 215, 224
"Elixir of Pain," serialized novel, 193
Elizabeth, queen of Romania, 204n
Ellis Island, 72n
Emerson, Ralph W., 87

Index

Emigrant agents, 14, 15
Emigration from Norway, 14, 15, 18, 64, 72, 130, 161. *See also* Immigration, Norwegian immigrants
England, literature, 119, 176, 177, 200, 210, 213, 215, 216; Boyesen's visit, 166
English language, use by Boyesen, 3, 22, 30, 31, 46, 56, 90, 99, 106, 151; use by immigrants, 58
English people, attacked by Boyesen, 85, 119, 159, 167, 169, 176; aped by Americans, 133, 134, 158, 197, 208
Episcopal Church, 114
Erickson, Leif, 32, 72
Essays on German Literature, 153, 176, 203–205, 211, 215
Essays on Scandinavian Literature, 154, 176, 208, 211, 224

Fairchild, Charles S., 181
Falconberg, novel, 47, 72–76, 109
Fearless Trio, juvenile fiction, 107
Fields, James T., 25n, 31n
Fields, Osgood, and Co., publishers, 31n
Fish, Hamilton, 109
Fiske, John, 109n
Fiske, Willard, 42, 53; friendship with Boyesen, 33, 36, 43, 45, 46, 52, 94, 96, 98, 101
Flaubert, Gustave, 82, 215
Frederic, Harold, 223
Fredriksværn (Norway), 5
Fremad (Milwaukee, Chicago), 21, 22, 73, 128
Freytag, Gustav, 34n, 51, 82, 83, 91, 153, 155
Fritiof's Saga, 16, 39, 79
Fuller, H. B., 223

Galaxy, 28n
Garfield, James, 120, 151
Garland, Hamlin, 214, 220
Gebhard Professorship, 98
German immigrants, 21
German language and literature, Boyesen's studies, 30, 33, 34, 41, 44, 46, 77, 81, 82–85, 91, 98, 99, 100, 111, 124, 153, 163, 168, 175, 176, 196, 203–206, 208, 221. *See also Essays on German Literature*
Germania, 205
Germany, Boyesen's visits, 30, 33, 35, 39, 50, 81, 167, 168; modern aspect, 82; education in, 88, 100, 168; Boyesen's popularity, 93, 94; militarism, 168, 205; position of women, 201. *See also* German language and literature
Gibson, Charles D., 188
Gilder, Jeanette, 94n, 113
Gilder, Joseph, 94n
Gilder, Richard W., 52n, 117, 119, 181; friendship with Boyesen, 38, 50, 94n; sketch, 39n; editor, 103, 124, 164
Gilder, Mrs. Richard W., 38, 40
Godkin, Edwin L., 116, 120n, 154
Goethe, Johann W. von, 134, 213; Boyesen's studies, 35, 39, 99, 100, 163, 181n, 204, 205, 206. *See also Goethe and Schiller: Their Lives and Works*
Goethe and Schiller: Their Lives and Works, 39, 45, 47, 49, 50, 51, 77, 84, 85, 168, 176, 203
Golden Calf, novel, 133, 189–191, 192, 222
Goldschmidt, Meïr Aron, 32
Grant, Robert, 103, 135n, 222
Grimm, Hermann, 205
Guernsey, Dr. Egbert, 96
Gunnar, novel, 23, 24, 26, 30, 36, 37, 54–59, 62, 89, 93, 94, 107, 146, 170, 202

Haggard, Henry Rider, 213, 215
Halbe, Max, 208
Hallock, Joseph N., 102n
Hardy, Thomas, 215, 220
Harte, Bret, 95, 104, 128, 129, 142
Hartleben, Otto E., 208
Harvard University, 24, 27, 45, 46, 123
Hauptmann, Gerhart, 208
Hawthorne, Nathaniel, 50, 60, 95, 128, 130, 137n, 141, 213
Hawthorne, Rose, 60
Hedge, Frederic H., 45
Hero in fiction, Boyesen's treatment, 75, 123, 128, 134, 137, 138, 142, 143n, 147, 158, 159, 160, 177
Heroine, 177, 200
Herrick, Robert, 223
Hertz, Henrik, 17
Hewett, W. H., 43
Heyse, Paul, 51, 153
Hicks, Granville, evaluation of Boyesen, 223, 225
Hjorth, Judge Georg Martin, 5, 6, 7, 8, 15, 35n; sketch, 4n; influence on Boyesen, 16, 19, 20, 64n, 142n
Hjorth, Mrs. Georg Martin (Christine So-

241

phie Smith Petersen), 4n, 6, 7, 10, 14, 16, 17, 35
Hoffmann, A. T., 84
Holland, J. G., 38, 40, 103, 192
Holme, Saxe, 129
Holmes, Oliver W., 113
Houghton, Mifflin, and Co., 31n, 117n
Hovind (Norway), Boyesen estate, 5
Howard, Bronson, 117
Howe, E. W., 214
Howells, Annie, 33n, 49
Howells, William D., 36, 49, 102, 104, 113, 181, 222; friendship with Boyesen, 10, 24–27, 30, 37, 40, 45, 46, 47, 48, 50, 54, 56, 57, 93, 95, 97, 103n, 124, 149, 162, 164, 165, 175, 192, 219, 220, 226; sketch, 24n; influence on Boyesen, 29, 34, 55, 90, 127, 210, 212, 217, 225; code of realism, 61, 89, 132, 172, 212; writings, 74, 125, 156, 157, 158, 159, 160, 163, 166n, 171, 172, 177, 213, 215, 216, 221
Howells, Mrs. William D., 67n
Hugo, Victor, 51, 52n, 87, 215, 216
Hutton, Laurence, 116, 119n
Hyde, George, 144

Ibsen, Henrik, 32n, 35, 81, 111, 176, 189, 224; Boyesen's studies, 206–208
Icelandic language, at Cornell University, 41
Idyls of Norway and Other Poems, 96, 150–152
Ilka on the Hill-Top and Other Stories, 95, 96, 146
Immigration, 225; Boyesen's attitude, 121, 152, 160, 170, 174. *See also* Emigration from Norway, Norwegian immigrants
International copyright, 93, 117–119, 152
"Iron Madonna," 126, 147, 156, 157, 177, 192, 198, 199, 202, 220
Ithaca (N.Y.), 185. *See also* Cornell University

Jackson, Helen Hunt, 42
James, Henry, Jr., 24, 25n, 94, 103, 104, 135n, 141, 147, 204; writings, 37, 60, 74, 86, 89, 102n, 156, 158, 159, 177, 198, 215, 216; influence on Boyesen, 95, 138, 140
James, Henry, Sr., 109n
Janson, Kristofer, 110, 154; sketch, 78n; writings, 82, 89
Janvier, Thomas, 166n, 175n

Kampen, Nils, 10
Karlsefne, Thorfinn, 72
Kazin, Alfred, evaluation of Boyesen, 225
Keen, Elizabeth, *see* Mrs. Hjalmar Hjorth Boyesen
Keen, William, 49
Keen, Mrs. William, 49
Keller, Gottfried, 51n
Kielland, Alexander, 111, 155, 210, 221
Kierkegaard, Søren, 32n
King, Clarence, 117
Knight, Grant C., 225
Kongsberg (Norway), national munitions works, 5
Kowaledsky, Waldemir, 112

Lærdalsøren (Norway), 13
Lake Chautauqua, *see* Chautauqua lectures
Landsmaal, 78n
Landstad, M. B., 24
Lang, Andrew, 166, 167, 175n, 178
Lapps, 168
Lathrop, George P., 50, 60
Lathrop, Mrs. George P., 60
Leipzig (Germany), university, 12, 30, 34, 35, 51, 81, 84
Lekanger (Norway), 169
Lessing, Gotthold E., 45
Lewis, C. T., 116
Lie, Jonas, 82, 83n, 89, 154
Light of Her Countenance, novel, 108, 147, 162, 198
Lincoln, Abraham, 22n
Lippincott's Magazine, 28n
Literary and Social Silhouettes, essays, 155, 177
Literature, American, 126, 157, 222. *See also* individual authors
Longfellow, Henry W., 24, 32n, 45, 46, 49, 72n
Lounsbury, T. R., 112
Lovell, John W., Co., 164, 165, 166
Low, Seth, 181
Lowell, James R., 24
Lowell Institute (Boston), 99, 101
Lutheran Church, Norway, 5, 6, 73, 193; schools, 21; in America, 72, 73, 109, 110, 114, 154; criticized by Boyesen, 73, 109, 110, 114

Mabie, Hamilton W., 117, 181
McClure, S. S., 175
McClure's Magazine, 175

Index

MacKoon, Bela, 53
Magazines, American, 126, 157
Mammon of Unrighteousness, novel, 41, 55, 124, 133, 162, 164, 165, 166, 171–173, 174, 184–187, 191, 192, 193, 213, 220, 222, 223, 225
Mansfield, Richard, 105
Matthews, Brander, 100, 117, 181, 221
Middle Sogn (Norway), 4, 9, 16
Modern Vikings: Stories of Life and Sport in the Norseland, juvenile fiction, 107
Müller, P. G., 21, 128
Munsey's Magazine, 163, 170, 171
Murger, Henri, 214

Nantucket (Mass.), 114, 221
Nation, 120
Naturalism, 52n, 132, 176, 208, 217, 222, 223. *See also* Realism
Negroes, 87
New Jerusalem Church, 5n
New Norse, 78
New York City, society life, 48, 49, 53, 68, 116, 130, 131, 132, 133, 135, 185, 192, 221
New York Staats Zeitung, 166
Newport (R.I.), 221
Newton, Isaac, 134
Nibelungenlied, 33
Nietzsche, Friedrich, 211, 223
Nineteenth Century Club, 221
Njals Saga, 33n
Norris, Frank, 132, 220, 224
Norseland Tales, juvenile fiction, 194
Norseman's Pilgrimage, novel, 37, 38, 59–63, 69, 141
North American Review, 28n, 81
Norway, 89; scenery, 4, 9, 23; political situation, 5, 65, 202; state church, 5, 6, 73; union with Sweden, 6, 155; class system, 6, 9, 11; folklore, 10, 16, 17, 24, 25n, 32, 58, 67, 72, 81, 95, 147, 151; nationalism, 11, 78, 106; economic conditions, 13, 14, 18; Boyesen's visits, 30, 31, 167, 168–170; peasant life, 55, 59, 65; literature, 77, 80–82, 89, 111, 154, 155, 174, 202, 210; history, 77n, 79, 101, 105–107
Norwegian immigrants, in Boyesen's writings, 8, 64–68, 69, 72–76, 111, 145, 193, 194, 202, 203; numbers, 30, 31n, 58; problems, 120, 122, 196. *See also* Americanization

Norwegian language, 22, 30, 58, 94; reforms, 78
Norwegian Synod, 73, 109, 110, 114, 154

Oehlenschlaeger, Adam, 208
Olmsted, Frederick L., 117
Osgood, James R., 30, 31, 36
Osgood and Co., 37, 45, 63, 85n

Page, Thomas N., 214
Page, Walter H., 154n
Palmer, Albert M., 119
Parrington, Vernon L., evaluation of Boyesen, 222, 225
Pattee, Fred L., evaluation of Boyesen, 222
Petersen, Erik L., 58
Phillips, David G., 224
Ploug, Carl, 32, 33n
Poe, Edgar A., 213
Politics, in Boyesen's writings, 73–75, 76, 120, 121, 147, 148, 186, 190, 191, 193
"Problematic Character," serialized novel, 138–141

Queen Titania, novelette, 95, 127, 129, 132

Ratner, Marc, study of Boyesen, 218, 226
Realism, Boyesen's efforts, 3, 16, 25n, 55, 59, 60, 62, 64, 66, 68, 69, 72, 74, 75, 82, 89, 90, 95, 120, 124, 126, 129, 130, 131, 132, 135, 146, 148, 152, 156, 158, 161, 162, 165, 171, 176, 177, 178, 184, 185, 186, 191, 196, 203, 208, 212–216, 218, 219–225; Russian, 60, 86, 90, 91; Norwegian, 81, 82, 83n, 111, 155, 207, 209, 210; German, 83, 91
"Realism of the commonplace," Howells' code, 61, 89, 132, 172, 212
Reform Club, 120, 135, 154, 221
Religion, *see* Episcopal Church, Lutheran Church, Swedenborgian Church of the New Jerusalem
Renan, Ernest, 51, 52n
Repplier, Agnes, 175n
Republican party, 73, 74, 76, 120, 147
Reuter, Fritz, 153
Rideing, W. H., 4n
Riley, James W., 119, 214
Roberts Brothers, publishers, 102, 103, 104, 132
Roe, Rev. E. P., 192
Romanticism, in Boyesen's writings, 3, 14, 55, 59, 60, 62, 69, 76, 84, 85, 89, 90, 91,

243

95, 106, 111, 124, 126, 129, 142, 194, 209, 212, 217, 220, 224; rejected by Boyesen, 55, 130, 146, 148, 152, 157, 161, 162, 167, 170, 172, 177, 178, 185, 201, 208, 212–216, 219; Norway, 81, 82, 89, 155; Germany, 83, 84, 203; England, 119
Rome, university, 88
Royal Fredrik University (Christiania, Norway), 12, 19, 41, 143
Runeberg, John Ludvig, 208
Russel, William C., 53
Russia, 202

Sagas, 16, 33n, 39, 72n, 78, 79, 80, 81, 82, 101, 200
St. Bartholomew's Church (New York), 181
Saintsbury, George, 167
Sarcey, Francisque, 175n
Sardou, Victorien, 208
Scandinavia, literature, 124, 175, 176, 196, 205, 208, 221, 225. See also *Essays on Scandinavian Literature*
Scandinavian immigrants, newspapers, 21, 22, 57, 73, 109, 110, 128; attitude toward Boyesen, 57, 111; numbers, 58, 110, 111n; politics, 73. See also various Scandinavian groups
Schiller, Johann Christoph Friedrich von, Boyesen's studies, 35, 99, 100, 204, 205. See also *Goethe and Schiller: Their Lives and Works*
Schmidt, Henry I., 98
Schmidt, Julian, 34, 83n, 86
Schurz, Carl, 120n, 154n, 181, 221
Scott, Walter, 176, 200, 210, 215, 216; influence, 83, 119, 133, 177, 220
Scribe, Augustin, 208
Scribner, Charles, 103
Scribner's, publishers, 38, 39, 40, 54, 63, 85n, 101, 102, 107, 114, 164, 192
Scribner's Monthly, 39n, 103
Scudder, Horace E., 102, 103, 117
Sewall, Anna, 195
Sewall, Frank, 28, 29, 71n
Shackford, Charles C., 43
Shaw, George Bernard, 208
Sheldon Co., publishers, 37
Skandinaven (Chicago), 57
Smith, C. S., 98
Smith, Munroe, 181
Social Darwinism, 154, 159, 218
Social life, Norway, 6, 8, 10, 13, 31; Urbana (Ohio), 23, 27; Cambridge (Mass.), 24; New York City, 48, 49, 53, 68, 116, 131, 132, 133, 135, 185, 192, 221
Social Strugglers, novel, 133, 192, 222
Sognefjord (Norway), 8, 9, 13, 168, 169
Southampton (N.Y.), Boyesen's summer residence, 125, 164, 174, 179, 180, 182, 192, 221
Spencer, Herbert, 101, 135, 158, 159, 168, 218
Spielhagen, Friedrich, 94, 137, 204, 221; writings, 51n, 82, 83n, 91, 153, 155
Spinoza, Baruch, 204
Stanton, Theodore, 42
Stedman, Edmund C., 45, 117, 119, 181, 221; sketches, 46n, 119n
Stevenson, Robert L., 176, 210, 213, 215, 216
Stockbridge (Mass.), 98, 111
Stockton, Frank R., 102n
Stoddard, R. L., 117
Storm, Theodor, 51n
Storting, Norwegian parliament, 6
Story of Norway, history, 101, 105, 106, 126
Stowe, Harriet B., 86, 213
Strindberg, August, 208
Sudermann, Hermann, 208
Suffragettes, 197, 199, 200, 201
Sweden, 106, 202; alliance with Norway, 6, 155; literature, 210
Swedenborg (Swedberg), Emanuel, 5n
Swedenborgian Church of the New Jerusalem, 5, 21, 22, 30
Swedish language, at Cornell University, 41
Sylva, Carmen, 204
Systrand (Sognefjord, Norway), Hjorth estate, 5, 6, 7, 8, 10, 11, 12, 13, 16, 169

Tales from Two Hemispheres, 38, 63–69, 93, 94, 107, 146
Taylor, Bayard, 53; friendship with Boyesen, 39, 40, 46, 50; death, 51
Tegnér, Esaias, author, 16, 39, 79, 208, 210
Tennyson, Alfred, 115, 224
Thackeray, William M., 84, 200, 213, 215
Thomas, Dr. Gaillard, 181
Tieck, Johann L., 84
Tolstoy, Leo, 213, 215, 216, 222, 223
Tourgée, Albion, 157
Transcendental Club, 46n
Trollope, Anthony, 215

Index

Turgenev, Ivan S., 213, 215; friendship with Boyesen, 25n, 34, 35, 36, 40, 51, 60, 87, 112, 167; influence on Boyesen's writings, 41, 54, 63, 69, 76, 81, 82, 85, 86, 90, 95, 108, 127, 130, 152, 212, 311
Twain, Mark, *see* Samuel Clemens

Unitarian Church, 45n, 110
United States Book Co., 165, 166
Urbana (Ohio), Swedenborgian center, 21, 22, 27, 55, 69, 71n, 185n
Urbana (Ohio) University, 21, 22, 26, 27, 29, 30, 71n, 185n, 221

Vagabond Tales, 102, 120, 141–146
Vanderbilt, Cornelius, 109
Vardø (Norway), 12, 13
Vinje, Aasmund O., 78
Von Arnim, Achim, 84

Wales, Salem H., 181
Walker, John B., 102n, 175, 181

Ward, Mrs. Humphry, 215
Warner, Charles D., 50, 117, 204, 205
Warner, John D., 154n, 181
Wendell, Barrett, 166
Westhampton (N.Y.), 112
Weyman, Stanley J., 163, 172n, 215
Wharton, Edith, 222
White, Andrew D., 30, 43, 53, 95n
Wildenbruch, Ernst von, 208
Wilder, Burt G., 43
Winter, William, 105, 208
Winther, Christian, 32, 33n
Woman's rights, 199
Women, Boyesen's attitude: 33, 49; American, 48, 66, 68, 119, 123, 130, 133, 135, 143, 147, 148, 156, 157, 158, 159, 170, 177, 178, 186, 187–189, 196–202, 220; European, 138–141, 196, 201, 204, 205

Zangwill, Israel, 175n
Zarnoke, Fr., 33, 35
Zola, Émile, 51, 52n, 155, 157, 208, 214, 223

NORMANDALE COMMUNITY COLLEGE
LIBRARY
9700 FRANCE AVENUE SOUTH
BLOOMINGTON MN 55431-4399